MW00679581

School Health
Policy and Practice

6th Edition

Author: American Academy of Pediatrics
Committee on School Health

American Academy of Pediatrics
141 Northwest Point Blvd
Elk Grove Village, IL 60007

Library of Congress Control Number: 2002107235

ISBN: 1-58110-094-9
MA0214

The recommendations in this publication do not indicate an exclusive course of treatment or serve as a standard of medical care. Variations, taking into account individual circumstances, may be appropriate.

Please note: Inclusion in this publication does not imply an endorsement by the American Academy of Pediatrics (AAP). The AAP is not responsible for the content of the resources mentioned. Addresses, phone numbers, and Web site addresses are as current as possible, but may change at any time.

AAP Committee on School Health

Howard L. Taras, MD
Chairperson 1999-2003
La Jolla, CA
E-mail: htaras@ucsd.edu

Barbara L. Frankowski, MD, MPH
Chairperson 2003-Present
Burlington, VT
E-mail: barbara.frankowski@
vtmednet.org

David A. Cimino, MD
Member 1995-2001
St. Petersburg, FL
E-mail: ciminod@allkids.org

Jane W. McGrath, MD
Member 1997-2003
Albuquerque, NM
E-mail: janemc@doh.state.nm.us

Cynthia Mears, DO
Member 2001-Present
Chicago, IL
E-mail:c-mears@northwestern.edu

Robert D. Murray, MD
Member 1999-Present
Columbus, OH
E-mail: rmurray@chi.osu.edu

Wayne A. Yankus, MD
Member 1995-2001
Midland Park, NJ
E-mail: wy@wydu.pcc.com

Thomas L. Young, MD
Member 1999-Present
Lexington, KY
E-mail: tlyoung@pol.net

Su Li, MPA
Primary Staff
E-mail: sli@aap.org

Contributors

Bradley J. Bradford, MD
Pittsburgh, PA

Paula Duncan, MD
Burlington, VT

Kristi Houser, MS, RD, LD
Columbus, OH

Paul Melinkovich, MD
Denver, CO

Marcia Rubin, PhD
Kent, OH

Martin Sklaire, MD
Madison, CT

Richard R. Verdugo, PhD
National Education Association

Mark Weist, PhD
Baltimore, MD

Robert Bidwell
Honolulu, HI

Deborah Helitzer, ScD
Albuquerque, NM

Alain Joffe, MD
Baltimore, MD

Jeffrey K. Okamoto, MD
Honolulu, HI

John Schlitt, MSW
Washington, DC

Mari Uehara, MD
Honolulu, HI

Mary Vernon, MD, MPH
Atlanta, GA

Lani S. M. Wheeler, MD
Annapolis, MD

The AAP Committee on School Health acknowledges the invaluable assistance provided by individuals who served as writers and reviewers in the preparation of *School Health: Policy and Practice,* 6th Edition. Their expertise, critical review, and cooperation were essential to the committee's development of recommendations on school health issues.

Every attempt has been made to recognize all those who contributed to *School Health: Policy and Practice,* 6th Edition. The committee regrets any omission that may have occurred.

The committee extends its gratitude to AAP staff members Jennifer Pane, Senior Medical Copy Editor; Claudia Appeldorn, Medical Copy Editor; Rebecca Marshall, Health Policy Analyst; Rachael Hagan, Division Coordinator; Bonnie Kozial, Department Assistant; Darlene Mattefs, Department Assistant; Chris Kwiat, Information Services Librarian; and Sandi King, Director, Division of Publishing/Production Services, for their assistance in the preparation of this publication.

Table of Contents

Chapter 1
An Overview of School Health

"We need to understand that health and education are closely intertwined and that school failure needs to be viewed as a health as well as an education crisis."[1]

The primary mission of schools is to educate students. At the same time, schools exercise a powerful role in shaping the health and well-being of young people in the United States. In fact, many of the factors that influence academic outcomes also affect health outcomes. Consequently, students who succeed in school are more likely to become healthy, productive adults than are students who experience academic failure. The power of school health programs lies in their improvement of the health status of students, which translates into increased educational potential.

The State of School Health Programs

School health programs involve multiple elements, including health and physical education, physical and mental health services, nutritional services, health promotion for staff, district policies, the physical and social environment, and linkages with families and community service providers. Ideally, these elements are linked and coordinated to provide a seamless system that supports the educational mission of schools and promotes the health and safety of students and staff. The reality, as reported in the School Health Policies and Programs Study by the Division of Adolescent and School Health, Centers for Disease Control and Prevention,[2] is that school health programs are implemented in an inconsistent and less-than-comprehensive manner in most states.

Progress in Some Areas but Deficits Remain

The School Health Policies and Programs Study 2000 found that districts were giving increased attention to some areas of health programming, including violence prevention, case management for students with chronic health conditions, and prevention of pregnancy and suicide. Compared with 1994 findings, school health services seem to be more available. The percentage of schools with a part-time or full-time school nurse increased from 65% to 74%, and the percentage of schools reporting a school nurse-to-student ratio consistent with the national standard of 1:750 increased from 28.2% to 52.8%. This is good news, but it remains sobering that 26% of schools still have no school nurse. Current estimates are that between 5 and 9 million low-income youth do not have medical insurance, underscoring the need for strong school health programs. One strategy for increasing access to care for uninsured students is the school-based health center. In response to a growing need, the number of school-based health centers grew substantially since 1992, with more than 1200 centers counted in a recent survey.

National concern about the growing epidemic of obesity in childhood and adolescence has had little impact on nutrition education, school food services, physical education, and activity programming in schools. Most schools continue to serve high-fat milk and offer students foods with high salt, sugar, and fat content in vending machines. Constrained by limited budgets, increasing numbers of school districts have entered into relationships with commercial businesses.[3] Approximately 20% of middle or junior and high schools offer brand-name fast foods from vendors such as McDonald's and Pizza Hut. Although most districts require some physical education (PE), the percentage that require continuing participation in PE throughout high school is reason for concern: 50% of districts require PE in the elementary grades, only 25% require PE through grade 8, and only 5% require PE through grade 12. Not surprisingly, the prevalence of overweight has doubled in recent years.

The landmark 1999 Surgeon General's Report on Mental Health[4] identified school-based mental health services as an important strategy for helping meet the mental health needs of American youth. Although more than 75% of districts have guidance counselors, only two thirds have school psychologists, and fewer than half have a school social worker. In many districts, these staff are available only on a part-time basis. The School Health Policies and Programs Study 2000 study concluded that, "although schools do have mental health and social services staff, increased fiscal and technical support from states and districts for these programs could improve the availability of services."[2(p311)]

Although drug use among youth has consistently decreased since the early 1990s, the use of alcohol, tobacco, and marijuana continues at an unacceptable level. According to the 1999 National Household Survey on Drug Abuse,[5] 10.9% of youths 12 to 17 years of age reported current use of illicit drugs. The percentage using tobacco increased with age, from 2.2% at 12 years of age to 43.5% at 20 years of age; an average of 15% reported current use of tobacco.

Schools are missing an important opportunity. There is a clear, inverse relationship between health instruction and health risk behaviors; as the number of schools requiring health education in grades 6 through 12 decreased, the number of students engaging in 2 or more health risks increased from 19% involvement in grades 7 and 8 to 36% in grades 11 and 12.[6] Clearly, schools will need help to meet the *Healthy People 2010* objectives.

The Pediatrician's Role in School Health Programs

Pediatricians traditionally have provided a range of health services to students in schools, although the role of medical advisor is no longer as common as it once was. Historically, the medical advisor, as an employee or a consultant, worked to improve health care by developing sound health policies, by training school health staff, and by offering advice on health related-problems and evolving issues. Today, physicians' involvement in schools often is limited to discussing the needs of a particular student who requires accommodations in school because of health problems. That is unfortunate, because today more than ever, physicians can have a critical role in schools. If physicians are to capitalize on the leadership vested in their profession, however, they must step out of the clinic and into the school environment. In schools, the culture and language are very different from the culture and language of a pediatric clinic or medical institution. To be effective, physicians need to work collaboratively with professionals from many other disciplines as well as with families, parent organizations, and other community service providers. In so doing, physicians can influence important school health policies that have direct effects on the health of students. Physicians also can increase awareness and understanding of scientific principles, epidemiology, data-based decision making, and the need for program evaluation and quality assurance. In some communities, certain elements of school health programs sometimes are associated with controversy. Physicians can provide balanced information and a voice of reason to help resolve what often are highly charged emotional issues.

In the current health care environment, many physicians do not believe they have the time and resources for involvement in their local school districts. They are urged, however, to find the time and resources. Investments made in providing health care to students benefit the entire community. The pediatrician also gains by getting an inside view of patients' lives and the many factors in schools that affect their health and day-to-day existence.

Residency Training Offers New Opportunities
Residency training has shifted toward community experience for all residents, and many now require school health training for graduation. Schools provide residents a different view of their patients' lives,

enabling them to see children and youth in their natural habitat. Students' health issues are closely entwined with their education and relationships to school. Examples of this linkage abound: students with chronic medical conditions who need treatments or medication during the school day; students with brain disorders or behavioral issues who disrupt their classroom; and students attempting to cope with stress by using drugs, engaging in premature sexual activities, or withdrawing into social isolation. Pediatricians who understand the nature of the school environment and how to navigate the bureaucratic structures and who have established a relationship with school staff can call on the many resources within the district and community to help address a particular student's problem. Pediatricians who are trained in a school setting are better able to meet the health needs of the children and adolescents they serve. And by meeting those needs more effectively, the long-term health of their patients, the community, and the nation is improved.

For practicing pediatricians who feel ill prepared to work in schools,[7] the American Academy of Pediatrics has a wealth of resources, such as the Section on School Health (http://www.schoolhealth.org) and the AAP Members Only Channel (http://www.aap.org). Appendix A provides examples of program models. Many state chapters have an active school health committee that can provide assistance and information. The state committee might meet periodically and provide continuing education programs. If there is no chapter school health committee, the local medical society might have a school health committee that offers networking opportunities.

National organizations such as the National Association of School Nurses, the American School Health Association, the National Assembly on School-Based Health Care, and the National Association of Pediatric Nurse Practitioners often have state chapters. They all have Web sites (see Appendix B), annual conferences, policy statements, and other helpful resources. Because hands-on experience is so valuable, serving on district health councils and meeting regularly with school staff can provide needed opportunities and insights for improving access to care, thereby improving the health of children and youth in the community.

School Health Councils

Many school districts have health councils or advisory committees that provide guidance and advice to school staff administering various aspects of the school health program. These advisory groups are required in districts receiving funding from the US Department of Education's Safe and Drug-Free Schools and Communities program. The council usually is made up of a broad cross-section of education, business, and community representatives, including health care professionals, representatives of the faith community, families, and school staff. In addition, there might be a similarly representative school health team at the school building level. By serving on a school health council, a pediatrician can help inform the decision-making process and serve as a liaison to other health professionals in the community.

School health councils assist in:

Program Planning:
- Assessing student health risk behaviors
- Identifying available district and community resources, including professionals willing to work with referred students
- Reviewing epidemiologic data on patterns of illness, disability, and disease
- Identifying gaps in prevention programming or narrowing priority areas in which to focus resources
- Developing program goals and objectives
- Suggesting strategies that maximize resources and are most effective
- Linking schools to community resources

Advocacy: building support for comprehensive, coordinated health programming, by advocating on behalf of the health program to the school board, school staff, and community

Fiscal Planning: identifying ways to increase fiscal resources or leverage current funding

Education: informing the public and the professional community about student health needs and offering guidance in the selection and implementation of instructional programs

Program Evaluation: ensuring that the school health program meets the needs of all students and their families, school health care professionals, and other school staff.

Funding for School Health Programs

When school districts experience budget problems, health programs often are the first eliminated or reduced, which is particularly troubling because innovative school health programs directly and indirectly enable academic success and effectively promote positive health habits, prevent risk behaviors, provide early intervention, and integrate health and mental health services. In addition, school health programs offer increased access to needed health care for students from low-income families or minority groups, who frequently are underserved and often faced with access barriers. However, as long as school health programs receive only marginal priority from the educational and medical establishments, their effectiveness will be limited.

Scattered and inconsistent funding patterns erect major barriers to coherent and comprehensive health programming. To influence the scope, characteristics, and effectiveness of health programming in schools, multiple funding sources must[8]:

- Focus on achieving shared goals and objectives;
- Be flexible in how dollars are spent to accomplish desired results;
- Support intra-agency, interagency, and intersystem planning and decision making;

- Protect vulnerable populations; and
- Reinvest dollars gained by increased efficiency and expenditures on prevention and early intervention.

Fortunately, multiple funding sources and potential partners in the community share similar concerns about and goals for the school health program. Physicians are ideally situated to facilitate collaboration among district representatives and personnel, families, and community service providers. In fact, a number of community partners, including public health departments and community-based youth-serving programs, have a long history of collaboration with schools and the medical community.

Public Health Departments

Public health departments have provided various health services to schools for more than 100 years. Beginning in the 19th century, public health nurses worked in schools to help combat outbreaks of infectious disease. Today, public health nurses continue to serve school districts by contract in many states. In a few states, public health departments provide primary care. For example, the Multnomah County Health Department funds school-based health centers in Portland, OR. Each health center is run by a public health nurse who coordinates services between school-based and community providers to meet the primary care, mental health, and health-promotion and disease-prevention needs of students. In New Mexico, as in many other states, the department of health provides technical assistance, training, and help with evaluation of school health programs.

Health departments are mandated by the US Public Health Service to monitor community health. To fulfill that responsibility, health departments collect data such as the prevalence of infectious diseases, immunization compliance, number of teen pregnancies, and prevalence of drug and alcohol abuse. The pediatrician can help school health councils and school health personnel use this information when attempting to justify the need for expanded school health programs. Public health departments remain a vital link in a coordinated and comprehensive school health program.

Community-Based Youth Development Programs

The National Longitudinal Study of Adolescent Health,[9] the largest, most comprehensive study of adolescents undertaken in the United States, involving 90 000 students in grades 7 through 12, found that students derive multiple benefits from linkages with the community. The youth development approach to adolescent health promotion and risk reduction first received national attention with the publication of 2 documents: *The Forgotten Half,* released in 1988 by the W. T. Grant Foundation's Commission on Work, Family, and Citizenship; and *Turning Points,* published in 1989 by the Carnegie Council on Adolescent Development. *The Forgotten Half* stated[9(p3)]:

> *Young people's experiences at home, at school, in the community, and at work are strongly interconnected, and our response to problems that arise in any of these domains must be equally well integrated… All young people need:*
> * *more constructive contact with adults who can help them guide their talents into useful and satisfying paths;*
> * *opportunities to participate in community activities that they and adults value, especially giving service to others;*
> * *special help with particularly difficult problems ranging from learning disabilities to substance addiction; and*
> * *initial jobs, no matter how modest, that offer a path to accomplishment and to career opportunity.*

Pediatricians Working With Schools

Working with schools in the most productive way is not always intuitive. Many pediatricians interact with schools as parents, not as professionals. The publication *How Schools Work and How to Work With*

Schools: A Primer for Professionals Who Serve Children and Youth,
published in 2003 by the National Association of State Boards of
Education, is available at http://www.nasbe.org.

The Future of School Health

As a nation, we look to schools to help solve many societal problems.
In the midst of educational reform, districts struggle under the heavy
burden of diverse expectations. Their primary mission is to produce
capable, literate, and adaptive youth who are ready and willing to enter
college or the job market. To fulfill this mission, however, schools also
must meet students' physical health, mental health, and social welfare
needs; teach English to immigrant students in a culturally competent
manner; combat substance abuse and sexual harassment; and educate
every student in the least restrictive educational setting. Staff turnover
is high, and salaries are low compared with jobs requiring similar levels of education in the private sector. In addition, state and federal regulations impose a broad range of obstacles. Pediatricians and other
health care professionals, community members, and business leaders
can make a critical difference in their local school districts. For those
of us who dedicate our professional lives to improving the health of
children and youth, working with schools simply makes sense.

References

1. Blum RW, Beuhring T, Rinehart PM. *Protecting Teens: Beyond Race,
   Income, and Family Structure.* Minneapolis, MN: University of Minnesota;
   2000. Available at: http://allaboutkids.umn.edu/kdwbvfc/beyondrace.pdf.
   Accessed July 28, 2003
2. School Health Policies and Programs Study (SHPPS) 2000: a summary
   report. *J Sch Health.* 2001;71:251-350
3. US General Accounting Office. *Public Education: Commercial Activities in
   Schools. Report to Congressional Requesters.* Washington, DC: US General
   Accounting Office; 2000

4. US Public Health Service, Department of Health and Human Services. *Mental Health: A Report of the Surgeon General.* Washington, DC: US Public Health Service; 1999. Available at: http://www.surgeongeneral.gov/library/mentalhealth/home.html. Accessed July 28, 2003

5. Substance Abuse and Mental Health Services Administration. *National Household Survey on Drug Abuse.* Rockville, MD: Substance Abuse and Mental Health Services Administration; 1999. Available at: http://www.samhsa.gov/oas/nhsda.htm. Accessed July 28, 2003

6. Lindberg LD, Bogges S, Porter L, Williams S. *Teen Risk Taking: A Statistical Portrait.* Washington, DC: Urban Institute; 2000

7. American Academy of Pediatrics, Division of Child Health Research. *Periodic Survey of Fellows #26: Pediatricians' Participation and Interest in School Health Programs.* Elk Grove Village, IL: American Academy of Pediatrics; 1999. Available at: http://www.aap.org/research/periodicsurvey/ps26ex1.htm. Accessed July 28, 2003

8. Ad Hoc Working Group on Integrated Services. *Integrated Service. Moving from Principles to Practice: A Resource Guide.* Washington, DC: American Academy of Pediatrics; 1996. Available at: http://www.aap.org/advocacy/washing/rguide.htm. Accessed July 28, 2003

9. *Protecting Adolescents from Risk.* Transcript of a Capitol Hill Briefing on New Findings from the National Longitudinal Study of Adolescent Health (Add Health). June 3, 1999. Washington, DC: The Institute for Youth Development; 1999. Available at: http://www.gumleafdesign.com/pdf/briefing.pdf. Accessed July 28, 2003

Chapter 2
Health Services

"Only when students are healthy will schools be able to fully meet their goals... If schools do not deal with children's health by design, they deal with it by default..."
Health is Academic 1998[1]

School health programs advance the well-being, academic success, and lifelong achievement of students. To that end, health services promote health and safety, intervene with actual and potential health problems, provide case management, and actively collaborate with the family and others in the district and community to ensure students' health problems do not interfere with learning.[2] A district's health services program should be flexible enough to meet the specific needs of all students and staff. It should collaborate with community resources and avoid duplicating services. Districts can provide a wide range of health services, but all schools must have the following basic minimum:

- State-mandated services that include health screening programs (such as vision and hearing), verification of immunization status, and infectious disease reporting;
- The capacity to make assessments of countless minor health complaints, administer medications, and care for students with special health care needs (approximately 10%-15% of the population); and
- The capability to handle emergencies and urgent situations. Some school districts with limited resources may benefit from the expertise and help of area health care professionals.

Districts that provide more comprehensive health services might administer immunizations, provide case management by school nurses, link students and families to community health professionals, and offer physical examinations such as for school entry and for sports. The most comprehensive array of health services generally is offered in school-based health centers, described in Chapter 6. Services districts can provide to students depend on the health resources available, the health needs of the community, and the degree to which the community believes health services support educational achievement. Some districts might provide only what is essential, whereas others provide comprehensive health services. Pediatricians who want to work with school districts or who have a patient with special health care needs should find out how health services are provided in their local school districts.

Responsibility for Health Care in Schools

School nurses are uniquely trained to provide communication linkages among the educational system, the health system, and the family.[3] They provide early recognition of and case management and referral for health problems. In addition, many school nurses counsel students individually about their health and health habits and educate their families. In some districts, school nurses also might teach in the classroom or work in a school-linked or school-based clinic.[4] Their ability to provide these services is directly related to the ratio of nurses to students and to the absence of clerical and other nonnursing duties assigned to them. *Healthy People 2010* recommends that districts employ 1 full-time school nurse for every 750 students.[5] In reality, many districts have nurse-to-student ratios that are far less optimal. Some schools do not have a nurse regularly on their campus for even 1 day a week.

Given that nurse-to-student ratios are often far less than optimal, districts compensate in various ways. Each state has a nurse practice act that outlines which nursing responsibilities can be delegated and how this can be done safely. In some states, school districts are exempt from the majority of stipulations in the nurse practice act, and they have some freedom to define the level of responsibility given to staff members who are not health care professionals. For example, in some districts, the nurse supervises health assistants or the nurse trains the principal or another staff member to perform some nursing functions. This arrangement can be helpful or a serious problem, depending on how this discretion is used.

Urgent and Emergency Care

When a student experiences an urgent or acute emergency situation, nurses or specially trained and designated individuals should follow established, written protocols.[6,7] These guidelines should be in compliance with the state's nurse practice act and should take into account local Good Samaritan laws. Emergency response information for individual students should be kept in a secure but accessible location. This information, generally, should include the following:

- Names, addresses, and telephone numbers (work and home) of parents or guardians;
- Other persons to contact in case of emergency;
- Parental consent forms; and
- Names, addresses, and telephone numbers of physicians, dentists, and insurance carriers.

For students with a chronic condition who are at risk of having an acute episode (eg, asthma, seizures, and diabetes), more detailed emergency response protocols should be part of the student's individual health care plan (IHCP).[8]

Each school also should have an up-to-date emergency plan that organizes staff and assigns responsibilities in case of an emergency involving a natural disaster, such as a flood, fire, or tornado; a man-made disaster, such as occurred on September 11, 2001; tragedies that affect the entire student body, such as a student suicide or the death of a favorite teacher; or crises that involve more than 1 student. Responsibility for coordinating medical care in each building should be assigned to a school nurse with training in emergency care. If no full-time, on-site nurse is available, school principals, teachers, or other school staff should have training in managing emergency situations. It is also helpful if districts coordinate with their local emergency medical services (eg, police, fire department, ambulance services) and arrange for these agencies to visit each building long before emergencies occur. This is particularly true if oxygen is stored or used in a building.

Medication Administration

Although it is preferable for students to take medications before or after school, accommodations must be made for students who need them during the school day. The American Academy of Pediatrics (AAP) policy statement "Guidelines for the Administration of Medication in School"[9] and the statement of the National Association of School Nurses[10] recommend that the administration of all medications in schools meet specific guidelines that include compliance with the state's nurse practice act and other applicable laws and policies. District policy should be clearly written and distinguish between over-the-counter and prescription medications. School policies should indicate the following:

- Who has access to medications and who can administer (designated, trained individuals);
- How medications are stored (all medications in original, labeled container; all parenteral medications and controlled substances appropriately secured);
- How medications will be administered; some procedures might need to vary on the basis of age (eg, older students might be able to administer their own medication or carry their own inhaler);

- How each administration should be documented in the record;
- Guidelines to avoid medication errors (eg, student given dose twice, wrong dose, missed doses, wrong student received medication);
- How to report errors in administration; and
- Frequency of policy reviews, error rate reviews, and revision.

Daily Prescription Medication

If feasible, the physician should consider medication regimens that do not involve dosing during the school day. Alternatively, if the home situation leads the doctor to suspect that compliance will be suboptimal, schools sometimes offer a more consistent system of medication administration. In such cases, the parent or guardian should provide a written request for school compliance with the physician's order. The physician should inform the school in writing of all prescribed medications, dosage, method of administration, and times to be administered. School staff should be alerted if a medication might cause a severe reaction even when administered properly. Any necessary emergency response should be outlined.

Self-Administration of Medication

Doctors should state in writing if they believe the student is qualified for self-administration of the medication. Students in middle school and higher grades are more likely to remember to take their medications, to report overuse, and to refrain from sharing or losing their medication than are students in lower grades. Districts should have policies that permit self-administration in some cases on the basis of a student's level of responsibility and the drug in question. Responsible students often can self-administer their own insulin and albuterol, for example. However, many districts will not permit students to take their own methylphenidate (Ritalin) and antibiotics because of their "street value" and their association with allergic reactions.

Over-the-Counter Medications

District policy should require parental permission for students to obtain and use over-the-counter medications at school. A physician's prescription should be required for regular long-term use of over-the-counter medications. The order should specify the type of medication, amount, timing, and reason for administration. Some schools permit "standing orders" for occasional headache or menstrual pain with written protocol for the dose, frequency, suggestions for handling possible adverse effects and contraindications, and guidelines for documenting each administration in the student's health records. In many states, a school physician needs to sign this protocol.

Medications on Field Trips

Students cannot be excluded from school-sponsored field trips because they require medication. The school nurse can place the required doses in individual pharmacy-labeled containers or an envelope with the student's name, the name of the medication, and the amount and timing of the dose. Emergency medications, such as epinephrine, albuterol inhalers, glucagon, and diazepam suppositories (for seizures), also should be marked clearly in red or another distinguishing color. The nurse must delegate and train 1 accompanying adult or more to administer the medications. Overnight trips require a physician's order for medications not usually taken during the school day.

Alternative Therapies

District medication policies also should address the use of homeopathic, herbal, and nutritional supplements used preventively and as remedies. These treatments are increasingly chosen by families and present a dilemma for the school nurse and the school medical advisor. In most cases, they are not approved by the US Food and Drug Administration for safety and efficacy. It is advisable that districts administer these products only when there is written permission from a state-licensed physician who is caring for the student. The logic behind this is that if the parent cannot find a physician who is comfortable taking responsibility for the student's receiving these products, then school staff cannot assume responsibility.

Legally Prescribed Alternative Medications

In some states, practitioners of folk medicine are recognized as licensed health professionals. School nurses in those states might be asked to administer these alternative therapies. Medical consultants to schools can be helpful in these situations by identifying practitioners who can educate and consult with the school nurse and by establishing appropriate and consistent standards for administering all medications, including alternative therapies. Often, medical consultants will need to support school nurses who express concern for administering therapies prescribed by a licensed practitioner of alternative medicine.

Students With Special Health Care Needs[11]
Laws Protecting the Rights of Students With Special Health Care Needs

Three major laws affect the provision of services to students with special health care needs. The first, passed in 1973, is Section 504 of the Rehabilitation Act. The second is the Americans with Disabilities Act (ADA), passed in 1990. The third, passed in 1975 as Public Law 94-142, was reauthorized as the Individuals With Disabilities Education Act (IDEA [Public Law 105-17]) in 1997.

Section 504 of the Rehabilitation Act

Section 504 prohibits discrimination on the basis of disability for any program or entity receiving federal funds, including public and private schools. As defined in Section 504, disability is a "mental or physical limitation that substantially limits one or more major life activities" including learning, walking, seeing, hearing, speaking, breathing, working, caring for oneself, and performing manual tasks. Section 504 covers students who require certain modifications to access education. For example, Section 504 might be helpful to students with a serious, prolonged illness or condition or students who are returning to school after a serious illness or injury. These modifications might require physical changes, such as providing a ramp for a wheelchair-bound student. Other modifications might include providing assistance to a student who must take insulin during the school day; without such assistance, the student could not attend school. Students do not need to be eligible for special education services under IDEA to receive accommodations under Section 504.

Section 504 requires that schools provide reasonable modifications and accommodations in the regular classroom setting. However, because there are no federal funds available and districts must fund services provided under Section 504, the meaning of "reasonable" is constantly challenged and evolving through litigation. In addition, there are no formal federal requirements for an eligibility assessment, although some districts use the same process as that required to determine eligibility for special education services under IDEA. Other districts review Section 504 requests separately; the process can vary widely.

Although Section 504 has been responsible for helping a great number of students succeed in school, it also has been misused and abused. For example, families of students who are struggling in school might petition the district under Section 504 to permit their child to spend more time taking standardized aptitude and knowledge examinations. Others request door-to-door transportation or air-conditioned classrooms for students with asthma when there is no underlying health rationale for either. Pediatricians often are asked to write letters supporting these requests. However, it is important that they take careful histories and consult with the school nurse or classroom teacher before complying with such requests.

SCHOOL HEALTH: POLICY AND PRACTICE
6TH EDITION

Examples of Health Services Provided Under Section 504

G. L., a 15-year-old with fibromyalgia, has had chronic pain for the past 2 years and requires more time to ambulate than other children. She is fatigued easily and cannot carry books to and from home without discomfort. G. L. was evaluated to determine eligibility for services under IDEA Part B. She did not meet the criteria because her disability does not limit her ability to learn in a regular education setting. Her parents and pediatrician requested accommodation under Section 504. Under Section 504 guidelines, G. L. had a physical condition that limited major life activities. A learning and health plan was written that provided 2 sets of books for G. L., 1 for school and 1 for home, to limit excess carrying. She was permitted a longer transition time between classes, and physical education classes were modified. The school nurse received a written plan for pain control for G. L. that was agreed on by G. L., her parents, and her pediatrician.

C. J. is a 6-year-old first grade student with diabetes requiring tight control. C. J. requires insulin during the school day but is too young to give her own insulin or to check her own blood glucose concentration. She also is not responsible enough to eat all her lunch. A nurse is present in the building only 1 day a week. In her state, the nurse practice act prohibits anyone other than a nurse from administering routine, nonemergency injections. C. J.'s parents requested a plan under Section 504. The school district arranged for a nurse to visit the school daily at 11:30 in the morning to assist C. J. with blood glucose testing and insulin administration. An aide was hired to observe and assist C. J. during her lunch and snacks. As part of their general orientation to various health conditions, all teachers were provided information about the signs of hypoglycemia.

21

Americans With Disabilities Act

This law clarifies that the public world is the domain of *all* people and guarantees civil rights to people with disabilities. The ADA requires reasonable accommodations unless there is undue burden on the district, the service provided by the institution is fundamentally altered, or the disabled person poses a threat to others. Most often, Section 504 and IDEA are used to attain necessary accommodations or modifications.

Individuals With Disabilities Education Act

This law addresses the needs of students with special education needs, many of whom also have special health care needs. Students are eligible for health services under this law if the degree of their health impairment is sufficient to affect their education. For example, a student with cancer whose participation in the typical educational program is precluded by adverse effects of medication and frequent absences can receive services and accommodation under IDEA. See Chapter 3, Special Education, for a more complete description.

The Individual Health Care Plan[12]

According to the Maternal and Child Health Bureau definition, children with special health care needs are those who have, or are at increased risk of, chronic physical, developmental, behavioral, or emotional conditions who require health and related services of a type or amount beyond that required by children generally.[13] These conditions are present for at least 3 months and might require hospitalization or in-home health services.

Each student with special health care needs should have a written IHCP. Districts have various names and formats for IHCPs. In many, if not most cases, the IHCP is a stand-alone document. However, in some cases, students receiving special education services might have their IHCP included in their individualized education program. Alternatively, the IHCP might be part of a Section 504 agreement.

One advantage of this format is that the plan is legally binding and follows the student from one school to another, even from state to state.

Parents, students (when appropriate), personal health care professionals (including medical specialists), and relevant community agencies can and should be involved in developing the IHCP. Each student's IHCP should be reviewed and updated on at least an annual basis. In all cases, an IHCP should include the following information:

- A description of health observations and services required during the school day;
- A plan to handle emergency situations that occur at school;
- Contact information for a local community primary care physician and any preferred emergency health care professionals;
- Requirements for the student engaging in physical activities or sports; and
- Procedures to ensure safety and care on field trips and school-sponsored after-school activities.

The school nurse is the most appropriate professional to coordinate the IHCP. To ensure student safety, a number of school staff might require information from the IHCP. In particular, classroom teachers, cafeteria staff, physical education instructors, coaches, and bus drivers might need certain information. Nevertheless, confidentiality must be respected, and information should be shared only on an as-needed basis.

Common Health Care Needs and Their Management
Allergies and Anaphylaxis

When a student with a known anaphylactic reaction to a substance has been or may have been exposed to the substance, the situation must be treated as an emergency. Food allergies and bee stings are potentially fatal. Some districts have standing orders for a school nurse to administer autoinjectable epinephrine if unanticipated anaphylaxis occurs.

All designated individuals, including adults accompanying students on field trips, should receive training in anaphylaxis response that includes individualized instructions for using an autoinject pen or other autoinjectable device. In addition, cafeteria staff, classroom teachers, playground monitors, bus drivers, and other students also might need training. Training should include how to help students with an actual or potential allergic reaction and how to help students avoid the allergen. A student's IHCP might include a stipulation about limiting or prohibiting the presence of garbage cans or certain flowering plants and other bee attractions in the student's outdoor play areas. The Food Allergy Network[14] often is a valuable resource. Responsibility needs to be assigned to ensure that the district's medical kits have fresh supplies of autoinjectable epinephrine, which must be replenished at least every 18 months.

Asthma

Asthma is a leading chronic health condition in children and youth. It is also one of the leading causes of school absence for illness. The following text box describes some basic steps that districts and schools can take.

Tips for Managing Asthma at School
- Identify all students diagnosed with asthma, and monitor their days absent.
- Maintain effective communication channels with physicians and families of students with symptoms who do not attend school regularly or who do not participate fully in activities.
- Obtain a written asthma management plan for students with asthma.[15]
- Ensure appropriate access to medications (including self-carry and self-administration options when appropriate for the individual student and approved by physician, parent, and school nurse).

- Establish policies promoting full participation in physical activity and physical education.
- Ensure that the school buildings and grounds are smoke free at all times.
- Reduce or eliminate indoor allergens and irritants (see the Indoor Air Quality Tools for Schools from the US Environmental Protection Agency).[16]
- Provide asthma awareness education programs for students and staff.[17]

Tips for Pediatricians
- Inquire about school history, including absenteeism, availability of a school nurse, and whether the student has declined to participate in school activities because of asthma.
- Complete an asthma action plan and asthma management plan (some districts have both on the same form), and be certain that the family and the school have copies.
- Obtain informed consent from parents to exchange information with school staff about asthma symptoms and management.
- Consider school nurses as partners in providing patient education, monitoring the method and frequency of inhaler use, monitoring peak flow, and other asthma-management strategies.
- Prescribe extra inhalers for school and, when appropriate, extra peak flow meters, spacers, and other needed devices. (Some insurance companies require that physicians complete waivers for the student to receive extra medication or equipment.)

Effective asthma management requires collaboration among the student, parent(s) or guardian(s), health care professional, and other school personnel, including the principal, bus driver, school nurse, classroom teacher, physical education instructor or coach, and guidance counselor. Many districts, states, and insurance companies have developed asthma action plan forms that can serve as IHCPs. The IHCP for students with asthma should include the following:

Severity:
(For example): Exercise induced only or moderately persistent

Known triggers:
Exercise, cold air, chalk, environmental conditions (humid rooms, such as bathrooms, laboratories, or art classes might harbor molds), animals in classrooms, and outdoor triggers during recess

Known early warning signs:
Encouragement of students to report early warning signs immediately and training of designated individuals to measure peak flows

Prescribed medications:
Controller and quick-relief medications, their mode of delivery, and whether students require assistance, observation, and reminders or can carry and administer their own medications (see sections about medications in this chapter for self-administration issues); instructions for documentation of overuse of medications and failure to take medication in the health record and reporting to parent and physician

Daily management plan:
Response to moderate and severe symptoms and whether a peak flow meter is available and should be used in school

Emergency plan of action:
Written for use by school personnel during an acute episode; plan should include transportation and emergency medical numbers

Parental permission:
Needed so physicians and school personnel can communicate about school-based symptoms, the school environment, and instructions and so school nurses can effectively assist with patient education or inhaled medication techniques

The American Lung Association's Open Airways program can help schools effectively teach children with asthma. More information is available in *Promoting Best Practice Guidelines for Management of Asthma in Children,* accessible online at http://www.aaaai.org or from the AAP Web site at http://www.schoolhealth.org. Tips for schools on how to create an asthma-friendly school, as defined by the National Institutes of Health, can be found at http://www.nhlbi.nih.gov/health/ public/lung/asthma/friendhi.htm.

Diabetes Mellitus (Hypoglycemia and Hyperglycemia)

The American Diabetes Association (1-800-ADA-ORDER) has a number of helpful publications for school staff and families. School staff can support the student with diabetes in several ways.[2] Foremost is regular and complete communication between the medical team and school personnel. Although meals should be scheduled in conjunction with peer meals to help preserve self-esteem and inclusion in usual school activities, teachers and aides monitoring the cafeteria should be trained to recognize the signs and symptoms of hypoglycemia, hyperglycemia, and ketoacidosis. For example, a student with diabetes who declines to eat is at risk of hypoglycemia. All districts should establish clear procedures for contacting school health care personnel about concerns about a particular student.

The IHCP for a student with diabetes should include the following:

- Daily schedule for meals, snacks, recess, and physical education;
- Schedule of routine blood glucose checks, where will they be performed, and who will help test and monitor the results;
- Clear guidelines for insulin administration (eg, standing orders for "sliding scale" administration or a notation that the nurse must check with parent or physician daily);
- Specific plan for when the student is feeling "low" (eg, provide snack, check blood glucose concentration, provide a "buddy" to accompany student to health office);

- Orders for rescue medication, such as glucose tablets or glucagon, and location of the medication;
- Personnel assignment for administering medication in the absence of the school nurse and how it should be given (eg, by injection if the child is combative, comatose, or having seizures);
- An emergency medical plan;
- A specific plan for when the student feels "high" (eg, bathroom access, checks for ketones); and
- A specific plan for any change in schedule (eg, field trips, sports, overnight trips).

Insulin pumps are becoming more common, even for younger students. The first time a school has a student with a pump, the school nurse might request an in-service program for up-to-date information about how the pump works and how it is maintained. The nurse needs to be able to respond correctly to a situation such as detachment of the catheter.

Seizure Disorders

Recurrent seizures and epilepsy usually are well controlled in school-aged children. The IHCP should describe seizure type, symptoms, and directions for safely positioning the student during a seizure. Medication type, dosage, and potential adverse effects should be identified. If rectal administration of diazepam (Valium [Roche Pharmaceuticals, Nutley, NJ]) is part of a student's IHCP, the nurse should be familiar with its therapeutic and adverse effects and be sure that someone qualified is designated to give it during the nurse's absence. Guidance for activities such as swimming, bicycling, and driving a motor vehicle should be provided. The Epilepsy Foundation of America is an excellent resource and advocacy organization (1-800-EFA-1000).

All school personnel should receive training about how to calmly, appropriately, and expediently provide safety for a student experienc-

ing a seizure. These actions might include moving sharp objects and
furniture out of the way and rolling the student onto his or her side
for proper drainage of secretions. Classmates of students with seizures
should have a general orientation to seizures and what to do if a class-
mate has a seizure. This is an opportunity for classmates to ask questions and for the person teaching the class to minimize potential
distress of the classmates.

Terminal Illness, Palliative Care, and Do-Not-Resuscitate Orders

Students with life-threatening problems are increasingly placed in
school, as the law states that they deserve an education and are entitled
to be in the classroom as long as it remains in their best interests. Students who receive palliative care and have do-not-resuscitate (DNR)
orders often request that school staff also withhold lifesaving intervention and therapies.[18]

> A student has muscular dystrophy and cardiac involvement. The
> risk of sudden death attributable to arrhythmia is considerable.
> Resuscitation is unlikely to be sufficiently successful for this student
> to return to an acceptable quality of life. Resuscitation might be
> frightening or painful for the child.

Many school districts do not honor DNR orders. The law and
recent court cases have not clearly delineated the best course of action
for schools. If a school district is to meet parent requests, the following
must be considered. It must be clear who is permitted to assess the
student's condition at school. The school must not consider the DNR
order as synonymous with abandonment of all medical treatment or
as rescinding the obligations of the school health care team to provide
quality care, such as suction, oxygen, and pain medications, when
these are prescribed. Rather, the DNR order is a dynamic part of the

management plan developed by the family, nursing personnel, teachers, administrators, emergency medical services personnel, and, when appropriate, the student.

An IHCP that includes honoring a DNR order must anticipate life-threatening situations. Response to circumstances that are not anticipated by the student's condition must be permitted and defined, such as choking on food or an injury that could happen to any student. The IHCP also should provide clear guidelines to distinguish easily reversible conditions, such as a mucous plug in a student with a tracheostomy, from critical life-threatening situations.

Students With Other Special Health Care Needs

Each school has a different array of students with special health care needs.[19,20] For each student, the school nurse should work with the appropriate people to coordinate the IHCP. Other examples of special health care needs that require physician participation in the plan are students with traumatic brain or spinal cord injuries, children with cancer (who return to school with adjustment needs), and children with arthritis, hemophilia, sickle cell anemia, or cystic fibrosis (often requiring chest physiotherapy). Recognition of the symptoms, the dangers of ignoring important symptoms, the timing of scheduled therapy, emotional issues related to health issues, and emergency plans also are important components of IHCPs.

Technology-Dependent Students

Technology-dependent students might have a wide range of disabilities, including cerebral palsy, spina bifida, and traumatic spinal cord injury. Many have special educational needs in addition to special medical needs. Almost all can attend school with proper support and planning. A few technology-dependent students are medically fragile (at high risk of sudden medical emergencies). The student's family, physicians, school educators and administrators, nurses, therapists, and other personnel should carefully weigh issues of socialization, stimulation, and education against any increased health risk of attending school.

Students who require assistive technology often require special nursing procedures, which require a physician's authorization and written protocols for school staff. These procedures generally are performed by a school nurse, but some are delegated to other school personnel under direct or indirect supervision. These procedures should be reauthorized yearly by the prescribing physician and the parent or guardian. Some examples of these follow.

Tracheostomy Management

Some states' nurse practice acts stipulate whether the school nurse can delegate the suctioning of clean secretions or small objects from the tube. Typically, this responsibility may not be delegated. The IHCP for a student with a tracheostomy should note that the student often is unable to express problems vocally and should be monitored closely.

The IHCP should specify protocols for accidental decannulation; describe all necessary equipment required by the student in school; specify whether oxygen therapy is required; and specify how and which irritants, such as smoke, chalk, dust, sand in sandboxes, sprays, ammonia, and chlorine, should be avoided. If a student requires a monitor or other electronic device, the IHCP should include plans for emergencies such as power outages. School staff should be informed of fire risks associated with oxygen use, and local emergency medical services and fire department personnel should be notified if oxygen is in use in the school building.

Clean Intermittent Catheterization

Students unable to achieve (or maintain) urinary continence because of a medical condition attend school. Self-catheterization every 2 to 4 hours is realistic for many students and can be learned by early school age. Learning self-catheterization is a reasonable educational goal for the student that the physician should consider adding to an

educational plan. Additional assistance for many years often is necessary for students with inadequate cognitive or physical abilities.

Ostomy Care

Physicians should provide specific information about ostomy care.[21]
Nurses need specific information about the particular devices used.
Most students can participate in most regular school activities (including swimming), and physicians should specify how to protect the
stoma. Any restrictions for contact sports should be noted. A helpful
resource is the International Ostomy Association (accessible online
at http://www.ostomyinternational.org).

Gastric Tube Feeding

This is a common procedure in many schools. The school nurse needs
information about the tube (size, type, balloon volume, button size,
and replacement schedule) and the feeding (bolus or continuous,
schedule, amount, water, flush). Often this low-risk task is delegated
to health aides or classroom teachers.

Indwelling Intravenous Lines

Maintaining intravenous lines is required and seldom is delegated
to anyone other than the school nurse or a contracted visiting nurse.
Physicians must be certain that the IHCP outlines associated risks and
signs of infection, such as the presence of fever. Any restriction on
physical activity (contact sports, for example), needs to be specified by
the physician on the written plan.

Lifting

There are many conditions in which students must be lifted. For older
and heavier students, written policies on 2-person lifts, lifting equipment, and other safe lifting procedures need to be outlined in school
policies to protect students and staff.

Public Health Requirements
Immunizations

Schools fulfill a public health role by routinely tracking immunizations and communicable diseases. Required immunizations are specific to each state; the annually recommended immunization schedules issued by the American Academy of Pediatrics, the Advisory Committee on Immunization Practices of the Centers for Disease Control and Prevention, and the American Academy of Family Physicians do not necessarily constitute state requirements. In most states, lists of required school entry immunizations are updated regularly. In particular, states vary in their requirements for hepatitis B, varicella, and pneumococcal vaccines. In addition to linking with the state department of health, districts must confer with the local public health department to determine reporting requirements. When a disease outbreak occurs or a new vaccine becomes available, collaboration between local public health departments and schools is essential.

Districts should establish a consistent method of documenting immunization status and reporting to students' primary care physicians and immunization registries. Refugees and recent immigrants should be admitted provisionally until immunization status can be verified, as long as they do not pose a health threat to other students and vice versa. Some districts with large numbers of immigrants offer immunization clinics in collaboration with the public health department or community health centers.

Communicable Disease Surveillance

Large numbers of young people and adults are brought together in schools, creating ideal circumstances for transmission of a variety of communicable diseases. The school nurse or a designated individual should have written guidelines for required reporting to the local health department. Factors that contribute to the spread of communicable disease in schools are limited hand hygiene facilities and supplies, improper handling or selection of classroom pets, failure to segregate sick individuals from others, and close contact with large numbers of young children.

Exclusion Policies for Acute Health Problems

Schools need clear policies or guidelines for excluding students from school. Exclusion is necessary when a student's illness requires a greater degree of observation or care than school staff can safely provide, poses a threat to the health or safety of others, or precludes any benefit of attending class because of inability to focus and learn. Relatively few illnesses mandate exclusion from school. Students with upper respiratory infections, stomachaches, or headaches are too often excluded because of the wishes of parents or school staff.

School Exclusion Criteria
- Temperature above 101°F, unless there is a known noninfectious cause of fever and the physician and family want the student to remain in school
- Undiagnosed rash (concomitant with fever or behavior changes) suggestive of contagious disease
- Repeated episodes of vomiting or diarrhea
- Headache accompanied by fever or vomiting
- Irritability, lethargy, persistent crying, difficulty breathing, or other signs

---

Head Lice

Pediculosis (head lice) is common in elementary schools, triggering emotional overreactions and causing many unnecessary days of absenteeism.[22] Transmission in most cases occurs by direct contact with the head of another infested individual. Indirect spread through contact with combs, brushes, or hats is unproven and unlikely, because lice that fall from the head are generally damaged and unable to infest another person. Pediculosis does not cause any disease except, rarely, impetigo from scratching and breaking the skin.

Screening for nits alone is not beneficial, because few nits-only cases convert to active infestation. In addition, screening for live lice does not significantly affect the incidence of head lice over time. Because of the lack of evidence of efficacy and cost-effectiveness, classroom and schoolwide screening should be discouraged strongly.

Educating families and lay school staff is the most important strategy for managing head lice in the school setting. Districts should provide clearly written, accurate information to all families about the diagnosis, treatment, and prevention of head lice. Information sheets in different languages and visual aids for families with limited language skills should be available.

Although students with live head lice are asked not to return to school the next day unless they are treated, it is AAP policy to recommend that schools never exclude a student because of nits.[22]

Screening and Health Assessments

Screening detects previously unrecognized conditions or preclinical illnesses and offers an opportunity for early intervention to limit disability and negative effects on learning. The scope and nature of a screening program should be based on the documented health needs of a student population, state law, availability of a reliable and valid screening tool, and effective referral mechanisms. If districts have no resources for follow-up, screening should not be implemented.

Vision and hearing screenings are usually mandated in every state. Many schools also include screenings related to scoliosis, blood pressure, height and weight, dental caries, and lead. Screenings at school for certain infectious diseases, physical disabilities, obesity, and certain chronic health conditions, such as a high cholesterol concentration, are more rare. Screenings sometimes are available for mental illness, depression, suicide risk, learning disabilities, and athletic eligibility. Assessment for pregnancy, alcohol and other substance abuse (urine testing, for example), eating disorders, and other nutritional deficits also has been performed at school. Many of these screenings do not meet public health criteria as described in the preceding section ("Exclusion Policies for Acute Health Problems") and, therefore, should not be considered as reasonable school activities. It is often the physician's role to discourage such screenings. The reasons for inappropriate or irrelevant screenings should be sought and discussed; for example, certain screenings performed for historic reasons may no longer be necessary.

Vision and Hearing Screening

Most states mandate vision and hearing screenings. If conducted by a primary care pediatrician, parental permission should be obtained to send a summary of the results to the school. Following up with students who have failed vision or hearing screenings can be a time-consuming task for school nurses.

Early and Periodic Screening, Diagnosis, and Treatment Examinations

Unfortunately, considerable numbers of youth do not have medical insurance. Some schools establish formal linkages with volunteer community service providers to meet these students' health needs. Some schools offer on-site Early and Periodic Screening, Diagnosis, and Treatment (EPSDT) examinations for students eligible for Medicaid or State Children's Health Insurance Program (SCHIP) benefits.[23] At a minimum, schools should establish a process whereby students who do not have insurance or a primary care physician are identified and assisted with finding a medical home and enrolling in private or public health insurance programs. Further information can be obtained from the AAP Web site at http://www.aap.org/advocacy/staccess.htm.

Mass Physical Examinations

Although not recommended or supported by the AAP, some schools still perform mass physical examinations, primarily to determine eligibility for sports. The rationale most often offered is that the school board, the state education department, or the district athletic department requires eligibility physicals and mass screenings are an inexpensive way to provide them.

However, there are several disadvantages to mass screenings:

- Lack of history: a medical history for each student is seldom available, the parent generally is not present to provide further detail, and there is little time to explore numerous issues directly with students.

- Lack of thoroughness: the examination should assess the heart, lungs, reproductive status, extremities, and neurologic status, but 1 health care professional often examines as many as 40 students per hour. As a result, mass examinations are seldom as thorough as they should be. In addition, if the examination is not performed by a physician knowledgeable about the growth and development of children and youth, the quality of the examination is compromised. Moreover, an ideal opportunity for youth to voice subtle or intimate concerns is lost.

- Breach of privacy: when districts lack adequate facilities to provide private offices for interviews with students, parents, or staff members about individually identifiable health information, alternatives that protect privacy should be arranged. Otherwise, confidentiality might be compromised or the examination might be construed as invasive.

- Lack of follow-up: examination results often are not communicated to families in a timely manner and might not be communicated at all. If an examination requires follow-up, it can be weeks until a specialist is seen.

For these reasons, the AAP recommends that mass physical examinations be eliminated and that students be referred to a medical home in which examinations can be performed in a careful, detailed manner by a qualified health care professional.[24,25]

Oral Health Screening and Dental Sealants

Working in partnership with school-based health centers, local dental societies, or health departments, some districts offer screening for dental disease. A few offer programs that apply dental sealants, usually after 6-year-old molars are in or around 9 years of age (third grade), or fluoride varnishes.[26] Students without a dental home should be referred to cooperating dentists in the community for follow-up. The oral exam includes examination for dental caries, developmental anomalies, malocclusion, pathologic conditions, trauma, and identification of risk factors, such as tobacco use.

Criteria for Successful Screening

- Disease: undetected cases of the disease must be common (high prevalence), or new cases must occur frequently (high incidence). The disease must be associated with adverse consequences (morbidity), either physical or psychological.
- Treatment: treatment must be available that will effectively prevent or reduce the morbidity from the disease. There must be some benefit from this treatment before the disease would have become obvious without screening; that is, there must be an early intervention benefit.
- Screening test: the ideal test detects all subjects who have the disease (high sensitivity) and correctly identifies all who do not (high specificity). A good test is simple, brief, and acceptable to the person being screened. The test must be reliable; that is, repeated testing will yield the same results.
- Screener: the screener must be well trained.
- Target population: to reduce inefficiency, the screening should be focused on groups in which the undetected disease is most prevalent or in which early intervention will be most beneficial. Not all screening is appropriate for all school settings.

- Referral and treatment: all students with a positive screening result must receive a more definitive evaluation and, if indicated, appropriate treatment. School nurses who provide screening should have the necessary community links for referral in place.
- Cost-benefit ratio: cost includes all expenses of screening, referral, and treatment, including administrative costs and the cost and anxiety that result from false-positive results. The benefit is the reduction in morbidity from early intervention among students with true-positive results who are in need of treatment. This benefit is difficult to quantify in dollars and can vary among communities. Greater efficiency at any level will improve this ratio.
- School as the screening site: not all proven, cost-effective screenings are appropriate in school or cost-effective if performed in school. School-based screenings require signed parental permission and interaction with the parent when the screening result is positive or negative. Compared with a physician's office, where most children are accompanied by a parent, schools have difficulty reaching parents in person in any cost-effective way. Telephone and mail contact with parents are only slightly better, particularly with older students and working parents and when English is only one of multiple languages understood at home. Some conditions (eg, high cholesterol concentration, obesity, signs of type 2 diabetes mellitus) are confounded with emotional issues, making telephone or mailed information inappropriate.
- Program maintenance: the need for improvements in program efficiency is determined by periodic review of research on the value of each screening program and an assessment of program effectiveness within a community. Local review also permits community leaders to make reasonable decisions about the allocation of limited resources for screening. School screenings that are no longer necessary in a community should be discontinued.

Case Management, Health Counseling, Promotion, and Education and Referrals

School health care professionals offer counseling and anticipatory guidance for students regarding physical fitness, nutrition, cardiovascular risk reduction, injury and violence prevention, sexual development and sexual issues, stress management, alcohol and other drug abuse, and tobacco use. The importance of "casual consultations," particularly for adolescents, about these topics should never be underestimated. The school nurse might be the first adult aware of an eating disorder or a substance abuse problem. School nurses are, thus, in a position to link students back to their medical home or another community health care professional. They can act as case manager for students with special health care needs. School health care professionals also can serve as resources for faculty and staff and can help develop staff wellness programs. Depending on time commitments and other priorities, the school nurse might also teach in the classroom.

The primary mission of schools is to educate students, and health care is a secondary issue. Nurses often may feel isolated from health care colleagues and from readily available professional resources. Physicians can offer support by encouraging districts to offer staff development opportunities through which nurses can update their skills and knowledge. Networking within the local community also is extremely important. Informing local health care professionals about the school health program is essential. For students in schools that have well-developed referral patterns, the advantages are enormous. In communities with nearby universities, the school of nursing can provide consultation, placement of nursing students in the school setting, and opportunities for school nurses to collaborate in nursing research in school health.

Health Information: Accountability and Documentation

With increasing numbers of students requiring health and mental health services and adaptive educational plans to attend and succeed in school, documentation standards and systems that enhance coordination while protecting confidentiality are more critical than ever before.[27] Although most school districts have policies and procedures for educational records based on the Family Educational Rights and Privacy Act of 1974 (FERPA ["Sharing Information and Protecting Confidentiality"]), IDEA,[28] and state education laws, generally they do not provide sufficient guidance, detail, or protection for the types and levels of sensitive health and mental health data that are obtained, used, and maintained by school health care personnel. School physicians can assist districts in developing specific policies and procedures related to obtaining, maintaining, storing, transferring, and destroying personally identifiable student health information.[29]

The Health Insurance Portability and Accountability Act of 1996 (HIPAA)[30] and its Privacy Rule[31] can be used as a framework for developing sound school district policies and procedures for student health records. Other useful resources for policy and procedure development include the following:

- American Medical Association performance measures for ethics[32]
- *Guidelines for Protecting Confidential Student Health Information*[33]
- *Legal Issues in School Health Services* (chapters 7-10)[34]
- *Protecting the Privacy of Student Education Records*[35]

Sharing Information and Protecting Confidentiality

Student records in schools, including student health records, are subject to FERPA, also known as the Buckley Amendment. This law protects the privacy of students and their families by restricting outside access to, and guaranteeing the confidentiality of, personally identifiable information about students in education records. Education records include "any form of information directly related to a child which is collected, maintained or used by the school,"[36] whether in oral, written, electronic, or other form. School districts can classify various types of school records and establish administrative regulations regarding who may directly access each type or class of record.

Specifically, FERPA provides that, internally, education records may be accessed without parental consent by school officials who have a "legitimate educational interest" in the records. School officials include employees of the school district and those contracted by the district to provide educational services or consultation, for example, the school medical advisor. Protections and requirements of FERPA apply to health records that are made or maintained by a school physician, school nurse, school psychologist, or other recognized health care professional or paraprofessional. Guidelines from the National Task Force on Confidentiality of Student Health Information recommend that student health records be classified separately from other educational records and that only persons with a legitimate health interest, as defined by the district, can access such records directly. The health care professional who is the maker or keeper of the record then decides what information from the record should be communicated internally to others. Records of a school-based health center that is operated independently in a school setting (not operated by the school district) are not subject to FERPA; rather, they are subject to HIPAA.

Standards of practice for privacy and confidentiality are fundamental principles incorporated into the professional preparation and training of health care professionals. However, teachers, administrators, and other school staff may have little background in these issues. Paraprofessionals and community volunteers working in schools frequently receive no instruction in the principles of privacy and confidentiality. In poorly understood or socially charged situations (such as adolescent pregnancy, human immunodeficiency virus infection, or mental illness), inappropriate disclosure, unnecessary withholding of information, or a breach of confidentiality can result in serious negative effects. School physicians can assist by participating in staff development programs for teachers, other school staff, contractors, and volunteers involved in health-related practices. Regular periodic training on protecting student privacy and confidentiality should be included as part of this training. Staff should be familiar with relevant federal and state laws, district policies, and the disciplinary measures and sanctions for violating district confidentiality policies.

Communicating Confidential Health Information Within the School

At no time should confidential student health information be shared with school staff members who do not have a need to know to serve the student. On the other hand, sharing information that is necessary to benefit the student is critical. Only under limited circumstances is it necessary to disclose a student's medical diagnosis to other school officials, and it is considered a violation of privacy to have a student's name and medical diagnosis on a "health problems list" circulated to all teachers. An emerging practice in schools is not to reveal medical or psychiatric diagnoses to non-health care professionals without specific consent, except as required in special circumstances, for example, when determining eligibility for and planning services under Section 504 or special education. If the health care professional determines that release of a medical or psychiatric diagnosis is relevant to providing appropriate health or educational services, clear and easily understood confidentiality policies and informed consent procedures help allay parental concerns about providing consent. In turn, timely response from parents ensures adequate continuity of care for students.

A fundamental principle of FERPA is that student information is shared within the school district on the basis of legitimate educational interest or "need to know." Teachers and others working with a particular student might need to have confidential, relevant health information about that student to provide appropriate services. When such information is needed, the health care professional can discuss the functional implications of the medical condition within the classroom and during other school activities, procedures necessary for health interventions, problem recognition, and emergency plans. A description of the functional implications of a medical or psychiatric condition, including strengths, limitations, and needs, constitutes the most important and useful information to share with other school officials who have a legitimate educational interest to serve the student.

Communicating Confidential Health Information Outside the School

School health care professionals generally establish and maintain relationships with a variety of community-based professionals who provide specific services to supplement what the district is able to provide or who can offer a medical or dental home to students. District staff should be informed of the HIPAA guidelines affecting community health professionals (see Chapter 6, School-Based Health Centers). Districts should establish written policies and procedures for obtaining and transferring confidential information about students to community-based professionals.

Occasionally, school physicians or other school health care professionals need advice or a professional opinion from a health care professional outside the school. Consultation about a particular student without parental consent generally is considered acceptable as long as the identity of the student and family is fully protected. It should not be necessary to release personal information about the student to fulfill the purpose of the consultation. When information about a particular student is required from private health care professionals, hospitals, clinics, psychiatrists, or psychologists, it can be obtained only with the written informed consent of the parent, legal guardian, or the student (depending on the age of the student and the nature of the information).

Emerging Issues

Many school districts are starting to obtain information about student health insurance status so they can assist eligible families in obtaining insurance from Medicaid and SCHIP. Congress enacted SCHIP in 1997 to reduce the number of low-income, uninsured children in families with incomes too high to qualify for Medicaid. The appropriation for 10 years (1998-2007) was $40 billion, with funding distributed according to the number of low-income children in a state. SCHIP generally targets children in families with incomes up to 200% of the poverty level ($35 000 for a family of 4 in 2001), but 13 state programs cover children in families above that income level. Although enrollment in SCHIP program was initially low, it has been growing rapidly and reached 2.7 million in December 2000.

Many states have taken advantage of the rule change by the US Department of Agriculture that permits schools to share the application for US Department of Agriculture-sponsored free and reduced-price school breakfast and lunch programs with other programs serving individuals in poverty. In most states, but not all, the level of poverty required for eligibility for SCHIP and Medicaid programs falls within the range required by the meals program (for additional information, see the Center on Budget and Policy Priorities Web site, available at http://www.cbpp.org). In states with expedited Medicaid eligibility, the school nurse, health assistant, or other school employee might be trained to provide on-site enrollment. School-based Medicaid enrollment initiatives help remove barriers to health care for low-income families.

Recommendations for Pediatricians

- Introduce yourself to the district's health coordinator, school nurses, principals, and/or superintendent and express interest in the school health program.
- Determine what health services are provided in your community's schools.

- Meet with the key school health personnel and offer your help and support. If your school has a school health council or a healthy school team, ask to be invited to the next meeting.
- Assess which community health resources might augment the district's health services.
- Volunteer to assist the district health coordinator or school nurse in linking schools with community professionals and agencies interested in working with schools.
- Work with the school health coordinator, school nurse, and school health council to review, update, and develop new district health policies.
- Acquaint the school health coordinator, school nurse, and school health council members with AAP school health policies and other helpful resources.

References

1. Marx E, Wooley SF, eds. *Health is Academic.* New York, NY: Teachers College Press; 1998
2. Duncan P, Igoe JB. School health services. In: *Health is Academic.* New York, NY: Teachers College Press; 1998:169-194
3. National Association of School Nurses. *Position Statement: The Professional School Nurse Roles and Responsibilities: Education, Certification, and Licensure.* Scarborough, ME: National Association of School Nurses; 1996
4. American Academy of Pediatrics, Committee on School Health. The role of the school nurse in providing school health services. *Pediatrics.* 2001;108:1231-1232
5. US Department of Health and Human Services. *Healthy People 2010: Understanding and Improving Health Objectives for Improving Health.* 2nd ed. Washington, DC: US Government Printing Office; 2000
6. American Academy of Pediatrics, Committee on School Health. Guidelines for emergency medical care in schools. *Pediatrics.* 2001;107:435-436

7. American Academy of Pediatrics, Ohio Chapter. *Emergency Guidelines for Schools.* Columbus, OH: Ohio Chapter, American Academy of Pediatrics; 2001. Available at:http://www.schoolhealth.org/EmergencyGuidelines forSchools.pdf. Accessed July 28, 2003

8. American Academy of Pediatrics, Committee on Pediatric Emergency Medicine. Emergency preparedness for children with special health care needs. *Pediatrics.* 1999;104(4):e53. Available at: http://www.pediatrics.org/ cgi/content/full/104/4/e53

9. American Academy of Pediatrics, Committee on School Health. Guidelines for the administration of medication in school. *Pediatrics.* 2003;112:697–699

10. National Association of School Nurses. *Medication Administration in the School Setting.* Scarborough, ME: National Association of School Nurses; 2003

11. American Academy of Pediatrics, Committee on Children With Disabilities. Provision of educationally-related services for children and adolescents with chronic diseases and disabling conditions. *Pediatrics.* 2000;105:448–451

12. American Academy of Pediatrics, Committee on Children With Disabilities. The pediatrician's role in development and implementation of an individual educational plan (IEP) and/or an individual family service plan (IFSP). *Pediatrics.* 1999;104:124-127

13. National Policy Center for Children with Special Health Care Needs. *Definition and Identification of Children With Special Health Care Needs.* Baltimore, MD: Johns Hopkins School of Public Health. Available at: http://www.jhsph.edu/centers/cshcn/quality_3.html. Accessed July 28, 2003

14. National Institutes of Health, National Heart, Lung, and Blood Institute. *Students With Chronic Illnesses: Guidance for Families, Schools, and Students.* Bethesda, MD: National Heart, Lung, and Blood Institute. Available at: http://www.nhlbi.nih.gov/health/public/lung/asthma/guidfam.htm. Accessed July 28, 2003

15. Schering Corporation. Asthma Action Plan. Available at: http://www.schoolasthmaallergy.com/2002-2003/sections/toolkit/library/ ActionPlan.pdf. Accessed July 28, 2003

16. American Lung Association. Indoor Air Quality (IAQ) Tools for Schools Action Kit. Available at: http://www.lungusa.org/air/air00_iaq.html. Accessed July 28, 2003

17. American Lung Association. Open Airways for Schools (OAS). Available at: http://www.lungusa.org/school/oas.html. Accessed July 28, 2003

18. American Academy of Pediatrics, Committee on School Health and Committee on Bioethics. Do not resuscitate orders in schools. *Pediatrics.* 2000;105:878–879

19. Jackson PL, Vessey JA. *Primary Care of the Child with a Chronic Condition.* 3rd ed. St Louis, MO: Mosby; 2000

20. American Academy of Pediatrics, Committee on Children With Disabilities. Care coordination: integrating health and related systems of care for children with special health care needs. *Pediatrics.* 1999;104:978–981

21. Borkowski S. Pediatric stomas, tubes, and appliances. *Pediatr Clin North Am.* 1998;45:1419–1435

22. American Academy of Pediatrics, Committee on School Health. Head lice. *Pediatrics.* 2002;110:638–643

23. American Academy of Pediatrics, Committee on School Health. School health assessments. *Pediatrics.* 2000;105:875–877

24. American Academy of Pediatrics, Committee on Sports Medicine and Fitness. Medical conditions affecting sports participation. *Pediatrics.* 2001;107:1205–1209

25. Hergenroeder AC. The participation sports examination. *Pediatr Clin North Am.* 1997;44:1525–1540

26. Marinho VC, Higgins JP, Sheiham A, Logan S. Fluoride toothpastes for preventing dental caries in children and adolescents. *Cochrane Database Syst Rev.* 2003;(1):CD002278

27. Gelfman MHB. School health records and documentation. In: Schwab NC, Gelfman MHB, eds. *Legal Issues in School Health Services: A Resource for School Administrators, School Attorneys, and School Nurses.* North Branch, MN: Sunrise River Press; 2001:297–316

28. Individuals With Disabilities Education Act. 20 USC §1400 et seq; Regulations at 34 CFR §300 (June 4, 1997)

29. Schwab N, Gelfman MHB. School health records: nursing practice and the law. *J Sch Nurs.* 1991;7:26–34

30. Health Insurance Portability and Accountability Act. 26 USC §294, 42 USC §§201, 1395b–5 (1996)

31. Final Rule – Individually Identifiable Health Information; Privacy Standards. *Federal Register.* 2000;65:82461–82829. Available at: http://www.access.gpo.gov/su_docs/fedreg/a001228c.html. Accessed July 28, 2003. Proposed modifications. *Federal Register.* 2002;67:14776–14815. Available at: http://www.hhs.gov/ocr/hipaa/propmods.pdf. Accessed July 28, 2003

32. American Medical Association. *The Ethical Force Program: Creating Performance Measures for Ethics in Health Care—The Domain of Health Care Information Privacy.* Chicago, IL: American Medical Association; 2000. Available at: http://www.ama-assn.org/ama/upload/mm/369/ ef_privacy_rpt.pdf. Accessed July 28, 2003

33. National Task Force on Confidential Student Health Information. *Guidelines for Protecting Confidential Student Health Information.* Kent, OH: American School Health Association; 2000

34. Schwab NC, Gelfman MHB, eds. *Legal Issues in School Health Services: A Resource for School Administrators, School Attorneys, and School Nurses.* North Branch, MN: Sunrise River Press; 2001

35. Cheung O, Clements B, Pechman E. *Protecting the Privacy of Student Education Records: Guidelines for Education Agencies.* Washington, DC: National Center for Education Statistics, US Department of Education; 1996

36. Boomer LW, Hartshorne TS, Robertshaw CS. Confidentiality and student records: a hypothetical case. *Preventing School Failure.* 1995;39:15, 21

Chapter 3
Special Education

...to ensure that all children with disabilities have available to them a free appropriate public education that emphasizes special education and related services designed to meet their unique needs and prepare them for employment and independent living.
Individuals With Disabilities Education Act, 1997

Special services for students with disabilities is the largest categorical program in public schools, serving nearly 5 million students, or 11% of all students.[1] Students receiving special education services include those with chronic medical conditions such as cerebral palsy, those with learning disabilities such as dyslexia, and those with pervasive and chronic maladaptive behaviors. This chapter reviews the various categories of students served in special education programs with special emphasis on students requiring special health considerations.

The Individuals With Disabilities Education Act
The Individuals With Disabilities Education Act[2] (IDEA), originally passed in 1975 as Public Law 94-142, was reauthorized as Public Law 105-17 in 1997. The IDEA provides special education and related services for children with disabilities, including students with mental retardation, hearing impairments (including deafness), speech and language impairments, visual impairments (including blindness), serious emotional disturbances, orthopedic impairments, autism, traumatic brain injury, other health impairments, or specific learning disabilities (IDEA, 3Ai).[2] In general, the term "specific learning disability" means a disorder in 1 or more of the basic psychological processes involved in understanding or in using language, spoken or written, that may manifest in impaired ability to listen, think, speak, read,

write, spell, or do mathematical calculations. Conditions such as perceptual disabilities, brain injury, minimal brain dysfunction, dyslexia, and developmental aphasia are included (IDEA, 26 AB).[2]

Related services include transportation and developmental, corrective, and other supportive services (including speech-language pathology and audiology services; assistive technology; psychological services; physical and occupational therapy; recreation, including therapeutic recreation; social work services; counseling services, including rehabilitation counseling; orientation and mobility services; and medical services, except that such medical services shall be for diagnostic and evaluation purposes only) as may be required to assist a child with a disability to benefit from special education. These services include the early identification and assessment of disabling conditions in children (IDEA, 22).[2]

Students receiving services must have an individualized education program (IEP [see "Individualized Education Programs"]) developed by a multidisciplinary team that must include the family and may include a physician.[3] This is an ideal opportunity for the pediatrician attending to students with special needs to collaborate closely with the family and school staff.

Evaluation to Determine Eligibility

By using the federal guidelines, each state determines the specific eligibility requirements and classifies the types of disabilities considered. There is significant state-to-state variability. In conducting the evaluation, districts use a variety of assessment tools and strategies to obtain relevant functional and developmental information. Assessment instruments gauge the relative contribution of cognitive and behavioral factors, in addition to physical or developmental factors. Parents provide additional information that might assist in determining whether the student has a disability, including information related to the student's ability to participate and progress in the general curriculum.

If after a review of existing evaluation data, including classroom-based assessments and observations by teachers and related services providers, it is determined that the student needs special education and related services, the team will develop an IEP for the student.

The Office for Civil Rights in the United States Department of Education protects the educational rights of students in programs or activities receiving federal support. If a student or parent believes services have been denied because of age, disability, sex, national origin, race, or color, an appeal may be filed. The first step in dispute resolution is negotiation, followed by mediation with a hearing officer.

Early Intervention (Birth to Age 3)/IDEA Part C

To determine who administers the state's early intervention program, physicians should contact the state department of public health or the National Information Center for Children and Youth With Disabilities (1-800-695-0285). In some states, the public schools are responsible for screening all referred children, not just those of school age, to determine eligibility for services. Physicians can refer at-risk infants or toddlers younger than 3 years who would be at risk of experiencing a substantial developmental delay, as defined by each state,[3] if early intervention services were not provided. Premature infants and others who require neonatal intensive care, exhibit growth retardation, or have known risk factors might be eligible for services. These services permit children who might have delayed development to receive help as soon as possible, and the services assist the family through difficult times. Early intervention services are provided under public supervision at no cost unless state law provides for a system of payments by families, including a schedule of sliding fees. These related services are designed to meet physical, cognitive, communication, social, emotional, and adaptive developmental needs. Additional help is available for families through the Parent Training and Information (PTI) program in each state.

In general, physicians should refer children younger than 3 years if they are developmentally delayed, are at risk of developmental delay, or have a disability. Parents and caregivers can provide relevant information about their child's developmental milestones during well-child and acute care visits. If reported information suggests children are not developing normally, there are several prescreening questionnaires and screenings that can be completed in the waiting room or returned on subsequent office visits. (See the American Academy of Pediatrics [AAP] Committee on Children With Disabilities policy statement "Developmental Surveillance and Screening of Infants and Young Children."[4]) Such measures might not screen every child appropriately; more thorough and sensitive testing can be beneficial. Referral ensures that the child will receive more comprehensive and specific testing.

Screening Questionnaires
- Ages and Stages
- Minnesota Child Development Inventory
- Infant Child Monitoring Questionnaire
- Language Development Survey
- Denver Prescreening Development Questionnaire (Revised)

Screening Tests
- Battelle Developmental Inventory
- Early Screening Inventory
- Denver II
- Early Language Milestones

Early Intervention Services
Under Section 636, for each infant or toddler with a disability, the family receives an individual family service plan (IFSP) that is formulated after a multidisciplinary assessment of the unique strengths and

needs of the child and the identification of services appropriate to meet those needs. The team formulating the individual family service plan must consider reports and recommendations made by outside professionals, although the team is not bound to follow such recommendations, even when they are made by a major medical center. Early intervention services include the following:

- Family training, counseling, and home visits
- Special instruction
- Speech-language pathology services
- Audiology services
- Occupational and physical therapy
- Psychological services
- Service coordination
- Medical services for diagnostic or evaluation purposes only
- Vision services
- Assistive technology devices and services
- Social work services
- Transportation
- Early identification, screening, and assessment services
- Health services necessary to enable the infant or toddler to benefit from the other early intervention services

Individualized Education Programs

States are required to develop policies and procedures that ensure a smooth transition to preschool or other appropriate services for toddlers receiving early intervention services. Once it is determined that a student is qualified to receive special education services, a multidisciplinary team that must include the family develops an IEP. Students who can participate in the process should be encouraged to do so and supported in their efforts. Family members often are the experts on their child's condition, strengths, and needs and can lead or be active participants in helping to coordinate the student's educational, medical, and home services.[5] Families want their children treated as individuals rather than as patients. When the IEP team incorporates the principles of family-centered care, the resulting IEP is more likely to benefit the student optimally.

Principles of Family-Centered Care

- Recognize that the family is the constant in a child's life. Schools, service systems, and support personnel within schools and service systems fluctuate. Policies and practices must serve the family first.
- Facilitate family and professional collaboration at all levels of school, hospital, home, and community care.
- Provide families with complete and unbiased information in a supportive manner at all times.
- Recognize and respect cultural diversity, strengths, and individuality within and across all families.
- Recognize and respect the various ways families cope.
- Encourage and facilitate family-to-family support and networking.
- Ensure flexible, accessible, and comprehensive support systems in schools, hospitals, the home, and the community for children who need specialized health and developmental care.
- Appreciate families as families and children as children, recognizing that they possess a wide range of strengths, concerns, emotions, and aspirations beyond their need for specialized health and developmental services and support.[6]

The IEP identifies the district's general educational goals and objectives for all students and states specific educational goals for each student with special needs. It outlines teaching strategies related to academic content and pacing that are consistent with the student's level of functioning. A detailed behavior management plan often is included. Necessary supports and services to meet the individualized goals are listed, and methods and benchmarks to evaluate progress are included.

The IEP is intended to maximize students' learning potential in the least restrictive environment. Whenever possible, it is preferable to modify the regular classroom to accommodate and include students with special needs rather than teach them in a separate special education classroom. Although the IEP must accommodate limitations resulting from chronic conditions, at the same time it should enable all students to participate to the greatest extent in the full educational environment, including the broader range of school activities such as clubs, student government, and athletics. Other considerations include the following:

- Each teacher and service provider who will be responsible for some aspect of implementing the IEP should have access to the student's IEP. These individuals must be informed of the specific accommodations, modifications, and supports listed in the IEP.
- The IEP team must consider a number of special factors when developing the IEP, including:
  - Positive intervention strategies for behavior that interferes with learning
  - Limited English proficiency
  - Assistive technology needs
  - Communication needs, including communication in the preferred methods, that is, those appropriate for deaf or hearing impaired and blind or visually impaired students
  - How parents will be informed of their child's progress (reports must be made at least as often as those to other parents who do not have children with disabilities)

Students with disabilities must participate, with appropriate accommodations and modifications, in general statewide and district-wide assessments. Assessments must be done in the language used by the student in the home or learning environment, unless it is clearly not feasible to do so.

Example of How IDEA Supports Health Services

B. W. is an 8-year-old with blindness and moderate cerebral palsy. He has above-average intelligence and no other significant medical problems other than gastroesophageal reflux disease. The IEP team met, including B. W.'s parents, and determined that he meets criteria for services provided by IDEA Part B because he has a visual disability and also has long-term orthopedic impairments. The IEP team established that B. W. needs accommodation for his blindness, including access to educational materials in Braille, after-school tutoring to keep up in his classes, and computer access for daily homework assignments. He needs physical therapy consultation and equipment to ambulate in school, as well as provisions to prevent reflux. B. W. can stay in a regular classroom setting with these services, as this is the least restrictive environment possible.

Physician Involvement in Placement and Services

Pediatricians too often make the error of recommending placement or the level of service before consultation with other members of the IEP team. A recommendation for a nurse-to-student ratio of 1:1 or home schooling might seem appropriate, but when other members of the team are consulted, other equally safe, less restrictive options might be developed.

A pediatrician managing a student with special needs, in addition to a school physician, may serve on the IEP team and can contribute in significant ways. The AAP Committee on Children With Disabilities outlined and elaborated on the multiple roles that exist for the pediatrician to support any child with a disability, a serious chronic illness, or a special health need.[3] If a pediatrician's schedule does not permit attendance at IEP meetings, the pediatrician's input is still possible and important. The pediatrician should telephone or write the IEP coordinator, the school nurse, or the principal and emphasize the student's functional needs during the school day, not who should meet the needs or where the needs should be met. The pediatrician is the expert on a student's medical needs, but the school staff members have expertise on how the school can best meet educational needs. To determine whether the placement and personnel adequately meet the student's needs, the pediatrician should review the preliminary plan devised by the IEP team. Collaboration on the IEP best serves the student. Teachers, aides, and administrators want to support chronically ill and disabled students. Nevertheless, students with chronic illnesses and disabilities can arouse strong emotions in school staff, including anxiety, resentment, fear, and other attitudes that can block constructive approaches to solving educational and social problems. Helping teachers understand the nature of chronic illnesses and the specific health care requirements of students in their classes and providing added resources for added responsibilities helps alleviate these problems.

Disability Categories (3 to 18 Years of Age)
Mental Retardation
Of students in special education, 11% have cognitive disabilities ranging in severity from mild (IQ 50-70) to profound (IQ <25), although the majority (75%) fall into the mild category, with deficits in adaptive behavior. Some students with a single diagnosis, such as Down syndrome, can range along this continuum, so it is best to use a functional diagnosis to determine needed services. Most districts have some experience working with students who have Down syndrome. Students with severe mental retardation are more likely to have other complications, such as cerebral palsy, epilepsy, visual or hearing impairment, and other

structural, chromosomal, or metabolic birth defects affecting the nervous system. These students will require more extensive supportive services throughout their lives.

Genetic Syndromes

An explosion in genetic research has led to many more children being diagnosed with genetic syndromes, conditions, or anomalies than in the past. Although this group is growing as a whole, the conditions remain rare, often fewer than 1 in 1000 in the population. Pediatricians can help districts that may be unfamiliar with many genetic conditions. Students with genetic syndromes often have cognitive, behavioral, or social impairments that prevent them from realizing their academic and physical potential.[7]

Several genetic disorders have a characteristic behavioral profile (phenotype). Prominent syndromes include Prader-Willi, Williams, Rett, Klinefelter, fragile X, and Lesch-Nyhan. The behaviors range from hyperactivity, food hoarding, stealing, and verbal inhibition to depression, self-mutilation, and self-injury. With parental permission, pediatricians can share information with school health care staff about potential problems and about past and present behaviors of students with a particular disorder.

Pediatricians also can link families and school staff to local and national support organizations. Some support groups are formed by families with members who have a particular genetic condition or a group of related conditions. Larger organizations tend to have more sophisticated and professional resources, including conferences, meetings, Web sites, and literature written for the lay population. The Alliance of Genetic Support Groups (1-800-336-GENE), the National Organization for Rare Disorders (1-800-999-NORD), and Exceptional Parent (1-201-634-6550) are some of the reputable national organizations.

Cerebral Palsy

Although some people with cerebral palsy have several cognitive and learning disabilities, assessment of intelligence and cognitive skills is critical. Students with cerebral palsy can have gross and fine motor difficulties that make eating and walking difficult or that require bracing and technologic support, including ventilators. Despite these motor difficulties, many students with cerebral palsy have above-average intelligence and can learn and achieve with appropriate supports.[8]

Hearing and Visual Impairment

Hearing Impairment

Students with hearing impairments are a heterogeneous group ranging from profoundly deaf students, often born to deaf parents, who identify with the deaf culture, to students with mild hearing loss, often resulting from ear infections. A few students have deafness and blindness; among students with both conditions, there is a range of severity for each condition. Some students with hearing impairment have other disabilities, including epilepsy, cerebral palsy, mental retardation, and specific learning disabilities.

"Total communication" has emerged as a dominant approach in education for deaf students, containing elements of oral and manual expression as well as speech reading. Some students are candidates for restored hearing and speaking; for others, particularly students with total or more profound deafness, learning sign language remains an important skill. Pediatricians can provide families with information about the many kinds of programs and supports available to students with hearing and vision disabilities. Families also should be informed of the many types of hearing aids and technologic supports available, including telecommunication devices and cochlear implants.

Speech and Language Impairment

Of the students eligible for special education services, 22% have speech or language disorders.[9] Nearly half of these have difficulties with articulation that can be improved or resolved with speech therapy, although it might require months or years. Language impairments most often result from mental retardation, hearing impairment, central nervous system disorders, or environmental factors, such as lack of stimulation.[10] Language impairments can result in substantial learning difficulties because the student has difficulty with language comprehension, expression, word finding, speech discrimination, or a combination of these problems.

Visual Impairment

Serious visual impairment or blindness usually is identified early. More subtle but identifiable problems such as strabismus, myopia, hyperopia, and astigmatism might be missed. The pediatrician can provide district staff with signs and symptoms that signal a need for referral.

Serious Emotional Disturbances

Students with emotional disabilities who also require special education services are served under IDEA according to the student's needs. Students with mental health problems who must remain at home, who are assigned to day treatment programs, or who require long-term inpatient treatment and do not require special education are eligible for regular educational services. Students with mental health problems who are hospitalized should be offered the same services as students who have medical problems who are hospitalized. That is, they must receive educational services directly or indirectly from their district. Many inpatient mental health facilities and day treatment programs have permanent in-house teaching staff designated as the educators for patients during long-term inpatient stays. Some are school district employees stationed at medical sites. These teachers set up curricula for students, often in conjunction with the home teacher. When hospitals do not have these in-house educators or when a student must remain at home, the district is responsible for sending a teacher to the student to provide instruction for a few hours each week, according to a set curriculum.

For short-term hospital stays, the classroom teacher can arrange to have homework and reading assignments brought to the hospital by parents, assuming the student is capable of learning during the stay and no acute problem precludes completing the homework. As with short-term medical problems, school districts are not legally required to provide special services but often make these casual arrangements with parents' assistance so that students do not fall behind academically.

Orthopedic Impairments

For students with orthopedic impairments to move from one class to another, schools might need to make stairs, door handles, and rest rooms more user friendly and accessible. Several relatively common orthopedic conditions affect school-aged children.

Arthritis and Osteogenesis Imperfecta

Students with arthritis have pain and joint difficulties arising from a multitude of conditions, and students with osteogenesis imperfecta are susceptible to frequent fractures. In both cases, students experience discomfort and fatigue, and schools must accommodate on an as-needed basis. Facial expression, manner of walking, and other behaviors can signal joint swelling or hairline fractures that are not seen. School staff should know that medications used to treat arthritic conditions can produce adverse effects including puffiness, obesity, or other problems that make it uncomfortable for the student to participate in school activities. Students might need to adjust body position or move around rather than sit in a particular position for a prolonged time. Occupational and physical therapy in schools is of great benefit to these students. Adaptive physical education teachers can also modify physical education and sports activities to enable students with arthritis to participate. For both of these conditions, the Arthritis

Foundation (1-800-282-7800) provides checklists for assessing common movements and activities before starting the school year to delineate areas of potential difficulty, such as preparing for school, activities related to getting to school, and activities at school.

Spina Bifida

Students with spina bifida can have multiple orthopedic problems resulting from the failure of the spine to close completely.[11,12] Although surgery can reduce the risk of infection and neurologic damage, most individuals require adaptive equipment. School personnel should be informed about such devices, how they function, how they should fit, the risk of skin irritation, and appropriate adjustments. Emergency and transportation plans are important and should be in place. The student should be monitored for signs of fractures: swelling, deformity, local heat or redness of extremity, or fever.[13] Other problems might include the following:

- Hydrocephalus: enlargement of the ventricles resulting from an imbalance of cerebrospinal fluid production and absorption. It usually is controlled by a surgical procedure (shunt). The student needs monitoring for the signs of shunt malfunction: headache, vomiting, lethargy, swelling along the shunt, seizures, and changes in personality, sensory or motor functions, or school performance.
- Incontinence: for urination, see the "Clean Intermittent Catheterization" section in Chapter 2, Health Services. The goal of bowel management is twofold: first, to maintain soft-formed stool, and second, to establish a consistent schedule of evacuation every 1 or 2 days on a toilet. Meeting these goals will reduce the chances of constipation and soiling. Stool consistency should be monitored, as should rectal bleeding and the skin condition around the anus.
- Latex allergy: avoiding contact with latex is highly recommended.[14-16] Common sources of latex in the school environment include art supplies, pencil erasers, balloons, rubber bands, gym mats or floors, and gloves used for medical procedures.

For further information, consult the Spina Bifida Association of America at http://www.sbaa.org.

Autism

Autistic spectrum disorders include autism, Asperger syndrome, pervasive developmental disorder, Rett syndrome, and childhood disintegrative disorder.[17] Additional information is available in the AAP policy statement "The Pediatrician's Role in the Diagnosis and Management of Autistic Spectrum Disorder in Children."[18]

Students with these disorders require a combination of services, including behavioral programs and speech and language services. Although school environments provide an important social milieu, controversy remains whether "normal" school environments are helpful. A more intensive, repetitive, behaviorally reinforced special education model might be better for some students with autistic spectrum disorders.[19] Common goals include social interaction, effective communication, and family support. Some students with autistic spectrum disorders require medication for targeted symptoms, such as aggressive, hyperactive, anxious, or stereotypic behaviors. The primary support group for children with autism and their families is the Autism Society of America (1-800-3-AUTISM or 1-800-328-8476).

Traumatic Brain Injury

Although brain injury is one of the more common causes of death and disability in children in the United States, many children experience mild head injuries, with full recovery in most cases. However, some children have more severe injuries that have serious repercussions in home and school functioning. Recovery tends to be greatest during the first year after injury. Academic and cognitive problems can persist even after intensive rehabilitation.

Districts need to monitor the cognitive and behavioral functioning of students who have experienced traumatic brain injury. Impaired social perception, social awareness, and self-control are frequent problems. Hyperactivity, personality problems, depression, and psychosis can be problems for some students after head injury. Sometimes, preexisting problems might worsen. Self-esteem issues are prominent as classmates and peers try to reconcile the student's present functioning with that before the injury.

The educational team needs to work with neurology and psychiatry staff. Rehabilitative personnel, such as occupational, physical, and speech and language therapists, all have important roles in schools in helping to increase the student's functioning and coping abilities. Fatigue can have a major role in preventing a student from progressing. Regular reevaluations are needed, because the functioning of students after traumatic brain injury can improve with the proper supports. The National Head Injury Foundation (1-800-444-NHIF) is an important resource for schools and families.

> Reduce the proportion of children and adolescents with disabilities who are reported to be sad, unhappy, or depressed (*Healthy People 2010*, Objective 6-2)

Other Health Impairments
This category includes attention-deficit/hyperactivity disorder (ADHD) and other chronic medical conditions, such as severe cardiac disease, cancer, or severe persistent asthma, that require adaptions for the student to succeed in school.

Attention-Deficit/Hyperactivity Disorder
The most common neurobehavioral disorder of childhood, ADHD, is estimated to affect 2.5 million young people. The majority of these students (85%-90%) take stimulant medication, often methylphenidate (eg, Ritalin [Novartis Pharmaceuticals, East Hanover, NJ]), to control their behavior. Although students with ADHD should have an individual health care plan listing potential adverse effects of the medication and the frequency of medication administration, not all students with

ADHD need special education services under IDEA. With parental permission, teachers or others closely observing the student can complete standardized behavioral rating scales that can provide clinicians with helpful information and observations for adjusting behavioral and medication management plans.[20]

There is considerable concern that many students are given the diagnosis of ADHD incorrectly. There is no simple test for ADHD; rather, observation of the student in several environments and interviews are necessary for a comprehensive evaluation. In general, the diagnosis depends on long-standing and habitual behaviors that begin before 7 years of age, interfere with normal social and academic progress, and are inconsistent with the student's age.

Some students with ADHD are exceptionally inattentive, impulsive, and/or hyperactive,[17] disrupting classrooms with their hyperactivity and impulsivity and often affecting other students. Other students with ADHD seldom are disruptive or bother others but are inattentive and do not make satisfactory achievements in school. In these students, ADHD might go undetected. Regardless of symptoms, students with ADHD require prompt and expert identification, management, and support. Pediatricians can inform school staff of the signs and symptoms requiring referral. Compared with parents, teachers and counselors have a broader context in which to identify a wide range of problems and often are the first to recognize a need for assessment. They can readily identify students at the extremes of activity and behavior. If a teacher or school staff member thinks a student might have ADHD, a multidisciplinary team meeting should be held. In addition to the classroom teacher and the counselor, the special education teacher or resource specialist, school nurse, and family should participate to determine other causes that might explain the student's symptoms or identify conditions in addition to ADHD. This information should be reported to the student's physician and can be critical during the first assessment.

Students thought to have ADHD might have a variety of conditions or problems masquerading as ADHD, including hearing and vision problems, home and other psychosocial problems, learning disabilities, sleep disorders, and adverse effects of medication. A collaborating relationship with mental health professionals can be invaluable, because students with ADHD often have coexisting conditions, such as oppositional defiant disorder, conduct disorder, learning disabilities, anxiety disorder, and mood disorders.

A variety of services are available in the health care system and from community social service agencies, but they are seldom part of a coordinated program in the schools. The pediatrician can help schools and families optimally integrate their behavioral, health, and educational services. Treatment for ADHD uses a combination of behavioral, educational, and medication supports. In schools, suggested educational interventions include the following:

- Structuring classroom environments to minimize distractibility: avoiding open classroom arrangements, if possible; assigning the student to the front seating row; encouraging the student to use an enclosed study carrel when doing seat work or homework;
- Including strategies to improve organizational skills, such as calendars and assignment books;
- Using instructional techniques that increase the probability of success, thereby improving self-image and sense of efficacy;
- Multiple reinforcements and incentives for appropriate behavior while offering diminished attention to inappropriate or provocative behavior;
- Increased assistance by teaching aides or tutors, if possible;
- Establishing predictable, daily routines in the classroom;
- Providing written and oral assignments, given 1 task at a time, with monitoring to ensure completion before moving to the next task; and
- Ensuring frequent opportunities for gross motor activity to help energy release.[20]

Some students with ADHD do not want others to know of their condition. This right should be respected while ensuring that students and their families understand that teachers, counselors, social workers, and health aides can help manage and monitor the student's progress. See publications from the Agency for Health Care Policy and Research[21,22] and the AAP Subcommittee on Attention-Deficit/ Hyperactivity Disorder[23,24] for additional guidance.

Learning Disabilities

The majority (51%)[25] of students served under IDEA have learning disabilities. This is a broad category, defined differently in different states and most commonly diagnosed on the basis of a substantial discrepancy between the student's academic achievement and the ability to learn, as measured by IQ. The American Psychiatric Association defines "substantial" as a discrepancy of 2 standard deviations or 1 standard deviation plus other factors such as motor, sensory, or language differences. Learning disabilities frequently are found in association with medical conditions such as lead poisoning, fetal alcohol syndrome, or fragile X syndrome.[17]

Some students with a learning disability have difficulty learning despite average intelligence and normal hearing and vision. Students with a learning disability also can be gifted or talented, often called "twice exceptional," or students with dual exceptionalities. These students do not have problems in all areas of learning and can have substantial strengths in certain areas. However, they might have difficulty depending on the area of learning involved, particularly if language (speech, reading, or writing) is affected. For example, students with excellent math skills can have problems if a reading disability prohibits their solving math problems written in words.

Disciplinary Actions Involving Students With Special Needs

When students with disabilities are involved in violence or misbehaviors, pediatricians might be asked to consult during a formal review, called a manifestation determination review, to determine whether a causal relationship exists between the misconduct and the disability. If it is established that the misconduct is a function of the disability, a school cannot impose a long-term suspension (more than 10 days) or expel the student. The school can, however, review and revise the student's IEP. In the case of a disabled student bringing a weapon or drugs to school, a 45-calendar-day referral to an alternative education environment can be made. If it is determined that the student's misbehavior is not related specifically to the learning disability, the student is subject to the same disciplinary procedures as a general education student. During the period of expulsion from the regular educational setting, school administrators must comply with the student's IEP and in the alternative education setting.

Emerging Issues
Prescribing Rehabilitative Services

Physicians should take great care in making rehabilitative therapy recommendations unless they have expertise in determining the appropriate duration and frequency of these therapies. Schools often receive prescriptions or letters from physicians demanding rehabilitative therapy services or door-to-door transportation for a child with a particular medical condition. Before recommending such services, pediatricians should meet with the student's family and school staff to discuss the relevance of such services to academic success.

Some students clearly could not attend school unless some accommodations were made. For example, it might be difficult for a family member to prepare a student for school if the preparations required lifting an older student with profound mental retardation or a student with severe contractures because of cerebral palsy. Such students might require door-to-door transportation. Another student receiving services under IDEA (for example, an intelligent student with ADHD) might not require the same services. The pediatrician should facilitate thoughtful discussions with school staff and families that best meet the medical and educational needs of the individual student.

Recommendations for Pediatricians

The AAP Committee on Children With Disabilities addresses the multiple ways the pediatrician can collaborate with the school system in supporting any child with a disability, serious chronic illness, or special health need:

- Ensure that every child has a medical home.
- Provide screening, surveillance, and diagnosis.
- Learn about state and local mandates and services for disabled students.
- Refer children and their families to needed services.
- Evaluate and determine eligibility.
- Participate as a member of the multidisciplinary IEP team.
- Counsel and advise.
- Coordinate medical services.
- Advocate on behalf of children with disabilities and their families.

Frequently Asked Questions

Q. *How many services do districts have to provide? Aren't there some limits?*

The only limits are the needs of the students to benefit from their education. Although lower courts initially stated that districts were not expected to provide continuous skilled nursing services,[25-27] on March 3, 1999, the United States Supreme Court required "a public school district to fund continuous, one-on-one nursing care for disabled children." The case of *Cedar Rapids Community School District v Garrett F.* (No. 96-1793)[28] involved a boy who was paralyzed from the neck down at 4 years of age. He required urinary catheterization, suctioning of his tracheostomy, assistance with eating and drinking, repositioning in his wheelchair, monitoring of his blood pressure, and an aide familiar with the various alarms on his ventilator. District officials argued that his needs were not covered under IDEA. The Supreme Court disagreed. If the IEP team agrees that a student needs particular services to attend school and benefit from education, the district must ensure the provision of the service at no cost to the family. The district is not required to pay for the service if it can be covered by pubic health insurance, such as medical assistance.

Q. *How can medical assistance help pay for school health services?*

Medical assistance can pay directly for 1:1 services (such as a private duty nurse) or by reimbursing the school for specific health services provided to medical assistance-eligible students in accordance with state guidelines. These guidelines often require that the service be listed on the student's IEP or Section 504 Plan (of the Rehabilitation Act of 1973). The Technical Assistance Guide on Medicaid and School Health is available online at http://cms.hhs.gov/medicaid/schools/scbintro.asp.

Q. *Why are districts not required to follow orders for physical therapy (or other therapies, such as vision training or sensory integration therapy) in schools?*

The IEP team, not a physician, optometrist, or therapist, decides the services that are required by the student. Schools must provide an appropriate program, not everything the family may want for the child. Disagreements are especially common when families are advised to request a specific brand name program or an unproven therapy. School teams must consider recommendation from outside experts but are not bound by them. School teams should attempt to mediate a solution that serves the student's needs.

Q. *What can I do if my patient's school states, "We don't have enough nurses (or other professionals such as therapists or audiologists) to provide that service"?*

Assist families with pursuing the appeals process. All schools must provide parents with information on how to file an appeal. Mediation or a hearing will be scheduled. Provide specific information on the patient's needs in school to support the parents' request for service. When nursing services are in dispute, learn about your state nurse practice act and any school health laws. Advocate for adequate school health staff for all students.

Q. *What if a child is extremely cognitively limited? Is the school still required to provide services?*

Yes. All children are entitled to a free and appropriate education. The student's IEP should include objectives that are appropriate for that individual student.

References

1. Parrish TB, Chambers JG. Financing special education. *Future Child.* 1996;6:121–138
2. Individuals With Disabilities Education Act. Pub L No. 101–476 (1990)
3. American Academy of Pediatrics, Committee on Children With Disabilities. The pediatrician's role in development and implementation of an Individual Education Plan (IEP) and/or an Individual Family Service Plan (IFSP). *Pediatrics.* 1999;104:124–127
4. American Academy of Pediatrics, Committee on Children With Disabilities. Developmental surveillance and screening of infants and young children. *Pediatrics.* 2001;108:192–196
5. Hostler SL, ed. *Family-Centered Care: An Approach to Implementation.* Charlottesville, VA: University of Virginia; 1994
6. Shelton TL, Jeppson ES, Johnson BH. *Family-Centered Care for Children with Special Health Care Needs.* 2nd ed. Washington, DC: Association for the Care of Children's Health; 1987
7. Levine MD, Carey WB, Crocker AC. *Developmental Behavioral Pediatrics.* 3rd ed. Philadelphia, PA: WB Saunders Co; 1999
8. Miller F, Bachrach SJ. *Cerebral Palsy: A Complete Guide for Caregiving.* Baltimore, MD: John Hopkins Press Health Book; 1995
9. Terman DL, Larner MB, Stevenson CS, Behrman RE. Special education for students with disabilities: analysis and recommendations. *Future Child.* 1996;6:4–24
10. Oyer HJ, Hall BJ, Haas WH. *Speech, Language, and Hearing Disorders: A Guide for the Teacher.* 2nd ed. Boston, MA: Allyn and Bacon; 1994
11. Dias MS, Li V. Pediatric neurosurgical disease. *Pediatr Clin North Am.* 1998;45:1539–1578, x
12. Hall DMB, Hill PD. Neural tube defects and other motor disorders. *The Child with a Disability.* London, England: Blackwell Science; 1996:277–305
13. McLone DG, Ito J. *An Introduction to Spina Bifida.* Chicago, IL: Children's Memorial Hospital Bifida Team; 1998
14. Niggemann B, Buck D, Michael T, Wahn U. Latex provocation tests in patients with spina bifida: who is at risk of becoming symptomatic? *J Allergy Clin Immunol.* 1998;102:665–670
15. Landwehr LP, Boguniewicz M. Current perspectives on latex allergy. *J Pediatr.* 1996;128:305–312
16. Kumar S, Williams K. Latex allergy. *Pediatr Rev.* 1999;20:35
17. American Psychiatric Association. *Diagnostic and Statistical Manual of Mental Disorders, Fourth Edition.* Washington, DC: American Psychiatric Association; 1994

18. American Academy of Pediatrics, Committee on Children With Disabilities. The pediatrician's role in the diagnosis and management of autistic spectrum disorder. *Pediatrics.* 2001;107:1221–1226

19. Siegel B. *The World of the Autistic Child: Understanding and Treating Autistic Spectrum Disorders.* New York, NY: Oxford University Press; 1996

20. Diagnosis and treatment of attention deficit hyperactivity disorder. *NIH Consens Statement.* 1998;16:1–37

21. Agency for Health Care Policy and Research. Diagnosis of Attention-Deficit/Hyperactivity Disorder. Summary, Technical Review: Number 3. Rockville, MD: Agency for Health Care Policy and Research; 1999. Available at: http://www.ahrq.gov/clinic/epcsums/adhdsutr.htm. Accessed July 28, 2003

22. Agency for Health Care Policy and Research. Treatment of Attention-Deficit/Hyperactivity Disorder. Summary, Evidence Report/Technology Assessment: Number 11. Rockville, MD: Agency for Health Care Policy and Research; 1999. AHCPR Publication No. 99-E017Available at: http://www.ahrq.gov/clinic/epcsums/adhdsum.htm.Accessed July 28, 2003

23. American Academy of Pediatrics, Committee on Quality Improvement, Subcommittee on Attention-Deficit/Hyperactivity Disorder. Clinical practice guideline: diagnosis and evaluation of the child with attention-deficit/hyperactivity disorder. *Pediatrics.* 2000;105:1158–1170

24. American Academy of Pediatrics, Subcommittee on Attention-Deficit/Hyperactivity Disorder, Committee on Quality Improvement. Clinical practice guideline: treatment of the school-aged child with attention-deficit/hyperactivity disorder. *Pediatrics.* 2001;108:1033–1044

25. Eighteenth Annual Report to Congress on the Implementation of the Individuals With Disabilities Education Act. Washington, DC: US Department of Education; 1996. Available at: http://www.ed.gov/pubs/OSEP96AnlRpt/. Accessed July 28, 2003

26. *Irving Independent School District v Tatro E.T.* 468 US 883; 104S Ct 3371; 1984

27. *Cedar Rapids Community School District v Garrett F.* 526 US 66, 119 S Ct 992; 1999

28. Schwab NC, Gelfman MHB, eds. *Legal Issues in School Health Services.* North Branch, MN: Sunrise River Press; 2001

Chapter 4
Populations With Unique Needs

Within every school district and community, there are small subgroups of students who require special care and services. The pediatrician or school health care professional working with these groups might need to link with other health care and mental health professionals or receive additional training to serve these groups effectively. This chapter discusses 6 of these subgroups: pregnant and parenting adolescents; gay, lesbian, bisexual, transgendered, and questioning youth; neglected or abused youth; students infected with human immunodeficiency virus (HIV); recent immigrant youth; and homeless youth.

Pregnant and Parenting Adolescents

Despite a steady decline since 1992, the birth rate among adolescents in the United States remains higher than it was in 1980 and still exceeds the rate in other industrialized nations.[1] Approximately 4 in 10 American females 15 to 19 years of age become pregnant.[2-5] Although the overall downward trend is encouraging, it is disturbing that the birth rate among adolescents younger than 15 years remains stable. Although most young adolescents are in better physical condition, have fewer chronic diseases, and engage in fewer risky health behaviors than adult women from similar socioeconomic backgrounds, they are nearly twice as likely to give birth to low birth weight and preterm infants who require expensive care and are more likely to die during the first year of life.[3-5] Babies born to adolescent mothers are at risk of developmental delays, school failure, intentional and unintentional trauma, and delinquency and are more likely to become adolescent parents themselves.[3-5]

Compared with other groups of adolescents, teenagers who become pregnant are more likely to:

- Be poor;
- Be a member of an ethnic minority;
- Come from single-parent or dysfunctional families;
- Report past physical, sexual, or emotional abuse;
- Mature early and begin sexual activity earlier than their peers;
- Have legal and other behavioral problems;
- Experiment with alcohol and other drugs;
- Have older boyfriends who discourage contraceptive use and encourage conception;
- Perceive adolescent childbearing to be the norm because they have numerous friends and relatives who are or were adolescent parents; and
- Have trouble in school and fail to graduate from high school.[3-5]

In addition, they are less likely to become financially independent adults. Adolescent pregnancies are costly in human and financial terms.[3-5] It is estimated that the annual direct and indirect costs of adolescent pregnancies total nearly $6 billion in social support payments, medical and food subsidies, foster care, and prison expenditures.[3]

Healthy People 2010 identifies several objectives related to reducing adolescent sexual activity, adolescent pregnancy, sexually transmitted diseases (STDs), and cervical cancer. Although some parents, teachers, and school administrators are concerned that sexuality education might convey the impression that adolescent sexual activity and parenthood is acceptable, public schools are increasingly involved in prevention efforts. In part, this is because of a growing consensus that schools can offer effective programs that can prevent adolescent pregnancy.[6] Some of the multifaceted programs being implemented are comprehensive and targeted educational programs beginning in elementary school, prompt medical and psychosocial referrals, and programs to prevent school failure and dropout, substance abuse, juvenile crime and delinquency, unemployment and underemployment, and welfare dependency.

> Reduce pregnancies among adolescent females (*Healthy People 2010*, Objective 8-8).

Primary Prevention

Adolescents become pregnant for a variety of complex reasons, including early sexual intercourse, poor contraceptive use, partner attitudes, and lack of "connectedness" to schools, families, and community.[7-11] Because the reasons for pregnancy are so varied, no single approach is sufficient. Abstinence-only programs target all adolescents with interventions designed to delay the onset of sexual activity. Other programs, sometimes called *abstinence plus* programs, *abstinence first* programs, or comprehensive programs, include information on contraception or safer sex practices. A few programs provide improved access to condoms and other contraceptives or offer multicomponent, communitywide initiatives. To date, there has been little rigorous evaluation of abstinence-only programs compared with programs that include a broader approach to pregnancy prevention.[8]

> Increase the proportion of young adults who have received formal instruction before turning age 18 years on reproductive health issues, including all of the following topics: birth control methods, safer sex techniques to prevent HIV, prevention of sexually transmitted diseases, and abstinence (*Healthy People 2010*, Objective 9-11).

Among comprehensive sexuality and HIV education programs, several have been shown to delay sexual intercourse or increase condom or other contraceptive use without increasing sexual behaviors.

Curriculum-based programs that have successfully changed adolescent behaviors share 10 necessary characteristics.[9] These programs:

- Focus on reducing 1 or more sexual risk-taking behaviors that can lead to unintended pregnancy, HIV infection, or infection with an STD;
- Contain goals and teaching methods appropriate to the age, sexual experience, and culture of the students;
- Incorporate theoretic models that go beyond cognitive information approaches to include social influences, group norms, and building social skills;
- Provide at least 14 hours of instruction or at least a sufficient length of time to complete important activities;
- Use a variety of teaching methods that actively involve students and help them personalize the message;
- Provide basic, accurate information about risks of unprotected intercourse and methods to avoid unprotected intercourse;
- Address social pressures on sexual behaviors;
- Reinforce clear, consistent messages about abstaining from sexual activity or unprotected intercourse;
- Provide modeling and practice in communication, negotiation, and refusal skills; and
- Select teachers or peer leaders who believe in the program and offer adequate training before implementing the program.

> Increase the proportion of sexually active, unmarried adolescents aged 15 to 17 who use contraception that both effectively prevents pregnancy and provides barrier protection against disease (*Healthy People 2010*, Objective 9-10).

One strategy to prevent adverse medical and psychosocial outcomes of adolescent childbearing is to delay the onset of sexual activity. If that fails, sexually active adolescents need information about and access to

contraceptive services. Many parents and school personnel fear that
the availability of contraceptives on campus will be misinterpreted as
approval of sexual behavior; consequently, most schools refer students
to community-based health care professionals.

Although studies suggest that establishing direct linkages between
the classroom and school-based health clinics eliminates traditional
access barriers and increases the usefulness of sexuality education,
only a few school-based clinics provide students with a full range of
reproductive health services.[10] This is unfortunate, because there is
now clear evidence that particular clinic protocols can be effective
in delaying sexual behaviors and preventing risky sexual behaviors
without increasing sexual activity.[11] Similar to curriculum-based
programs, clinic programs for adolescents:

- Provide youth with educational materials and information about
  abstinence, condoms, and contraception;
- Engage youth in one-on-one discussions about their sexual
  behaviors;
- Reinforce clear and consistent messages about abstaining from
  sexual intercourse or using condoms and contraception; and
- Provide condoms or contraceptives.

Secondary Prevention

Secondary prevention programs encourage early recognition of
pregnancy to maximize management options and ensure optimal
outcomes. One-on-one discussions can help adolescents weigh the
advantages and disadvantages of pregnancy options and ensure that
they do not unnecessarily delay action on their decision. When possible, the pregnant adolescent's family and partner should be included
in the discussions.

Caring for Pregnant Adolescents

Title IX of the 1972 Education Amendments established certain legal
requirements of all federally funded schools on behalf of pregnant

and parenting adolescents.[12] This law prohibits schools from expelling pregnant and parenting students and encourages districts to develop programs that encourage pregnant and parenting adolescents to finish high school and delay subsequent pregnancies. Two types of programs have evolved to meet these needs: (1) freestanding, alternative programs that offer enrollees a general educational curriculum and course work relevant to childbearing and parenting apart from mainstream classes and (2) supplemental programs that provide extra for-credit courses relevant to adolescent parents along with the mainstream curriculum. Either type of program can provide additional services such as child care, counseling, and medical care for adolescent parents and their children.[13]

Freestanding Alternative Programs

Because many adolescents who become pregnant have had problems in traditional school settings, these students often are best served in freestanding programs. These programs offer increased opportunities for individual help and remedial education. In addition, students who are self-conscious about their pregnancy or find it difficult to meet the time demands of a regular school program might be happier and less apt to drop out of a freestanding program.[13] These programs provide critical training in parenting and offer support for young parents. Many are strengthened by the addition of mental health and substance abuse services.

The main disadvantage of freestanding programs is that students often transfer into them relatively late in gestation. In addition, after receiving additional support and assistance during pregnancy, many students find the transition back into the mainstream education system difficult after delivery. Overwhelmed by the complexity of dealing with academic course work, personal health concerns, and child care arrangements, many give up and drop out. Although high school graduation is an important goal for parenting adolescents, overly aggressive programs for motivating postpartum school return can be counterproductive.[14]

Supplemental Programs

Supplemental programs that are integrated into the regular school day might be most appropriate for students who have done well in school and have career goals other than motherhood. Freestanding programs seldom offer the variety of classes typically available in regular schools. Additional advantages of supplemental programs include the opportunity to maintain friendships with nonpregnant peers, ease of enrollment, and greater possibilities for involving partners and adolescent fathers. Because transfers are unnecessary, pregnant students can take advantage of special support services immediately. After delivery, students can remain in the supplemental program, and the support staff can help smooth their transition back into the mainstream educational system.[15]

Regardless of the type of program a school district offers, the consensus is that most of the associated medical complications of adolescent pregnancy are minimized by early, consistent, adolescent-oriented care that focuses on reducing risk.[5,13] This care involves patient education, evaluation for physical and social conditions requiring special treatment, and serial assessment of maternal and fetal well-being in addition to genuine and sincere "caring." Caring is a critical component for positive outcomes, because although most adolescent mothers are physically healthy, they are psychosocially stressed.[5,13]

Medical Services for Pregnant Adolescents
Prenatal Care

Making medical services available within the school setting greatly reduces problems related to access and increases compliance with care.[13] If such services are unavailable at the school, however, school staff still can encourage compliance with prenatal appointments; provide information to dispel common myths and fears about the adverse effects of exercise, work, and regular school attendance on fetal growth; and encourage adolescent fathers to take an active role during the pregnancy. School nurses can monitor blood pressure, weight gain, and dietary practices and screen for other medical problems such as anemia, urinary tract infections, and STDs. All adults in schools can offer support and caring. In addition, educators, counselors, and health care professionals must work cooperatively to help pregnant and parenting adolescents overcome their natural tendency to deny the existence of stress-related problems.

Postpartum Care

Postpartum programs for adolescent mothers are designed to provide well-baby care in addition to well-adolescent care. Ongoing primary health care addresses a wide variety of common adolescent concerns, such as weight loss and acne; and psychosocial concerns, such as school attendance, future career plans, and symptoms of stress and depression.[13,15-17] Gynecologic and contraceptive concerns constitute only a small part of a young mother's total health care needs after delivery. Most programs enable young mothers to obtain contraceptives from their child's primary care physician.[13,15-17] In addition, some programs offer incentives designed to provide immediate, tangible rewards for behaviors that limit the possibility of a second pregnancy.[16]

Recommendations for Pediatricians

For additional information, see the American Academy of Pediatrics (AAP) policy statement "Care of Adolescent Parents and Their Children."[18]

1. Provide continuity of care and a medical home for adolescent parents and for their children. Specific attention to anticipatory guidance, early childhood education, and the teaching of basic caregiving skills should include the infant's father, when possible.

2. Provide care for parenting adolescents that is culturally competent, multidisciplinary, and comprehensive, and use community resources, such as social services and the Special Supplemental Nutrition Program for Women, Infants, and Children (WIC). Early and Periodic Screening, Diagnosis, and Treatment (EPSDT) examinations and Title XXI (State Children's Health Insurance Program [SCHIP]) provide developmental and medical services to low-income adolescent parents and their children. Facilitate coordination of these services.

3. Promote breastfeeding among non–HIV-infected mothers. Be the advocate for the breastfeeding adolescent in the school setting.

4. Initiate contraceptive counseling during and after pregnancy with an emphasis on long-acting methods coupled with condom use.

5. Emphasize the importance of completing high school.

6. Encourage healthy lifestyles during pregnancy. Information on the effect of maternal substance use and cigarette smoking on infant and child health and development should be provided at mother and infant visits.

7. Assess for risk of domestic violence during and after pregnancy.

8. Stress the importance of having the adolescent parent care for her own child even if other adults are involved in the caregiving (eg, grandmothers and great-grandmothers). These other caregivers need support and education to encourage optimal infant development while helping the adolescent to achieve her own developmental milestones.

9. Adapt counseling to the culture and developmental level of the adolescent, using office-based and school-based interventions that incorporate intensive instruction on infant care and development, discipline, and the stress associated with parenting. Use of support groups in the office, clinic, or school setting; home visits; and creative use of videos and media can improve the skills of adolescent parents.

10. Attend to the development of both the infant and the adolescent parent. Refer patients to community resources for services, such as home visits, sensitive and effective preterm and infant classes, child care programs, and well-managed programs supported by Head Start and the Individuals with Disabilities Education Act, Part C (for children 0 to 3 years of age with disabilities or who are at risk), when available and appropriate.

11. Provide positive reinforcement for success, including praising adolescents who are successful (eg, graduating from high school or college; abstaining from use of drugs, alcohol, and nicotine; continuing breastfeeding; keeping the child's immunizations current; and attending all well-child visits).

12. Recommend universal HIV screening for pregnant adolescents.

Condom Distribution

Distributing condoms in schools often is controversial, yet more than 400 high schools in the United States supplement their educational programs with condom availability. Districts use a number of strategies, including assigning a school nurse or a faculty member to distribute them, making condoms available during a visit to the school-based health center, or simply having condoms in vending machines, baskets, and drawers for students to take as needed.

Gay, Lesbian, Bisexual, Transgendered, and Questioning Youth

Gay, Lesbian, and Bisexual Youth

The origins of sexual orientation and gender identity are uncertain, but the medical community now recognizes that sexual orientation is established by early childhood and is not chosen. A gay, lesbian, or bisexual orientation is considered part of the spectrum of normal human sexuality. Nevertheless, because there are few healthy outlets for the exploration of their emerging sexuality, some gay, lesbian, or bisexual youth engage in high-risk behaviors, such as substance use, running away, and acting out, that result in poor school performance and alienation from family and peers. Some seek risky, anonymous sexual encounters in parks or bars or through the Internet. A significant number find escape through suicide.[19]

Transgendered Youth

Transgendered identity still appears in the *Diagnostic and Statistical Manual of Mental Disorders, Fourth Edition (DSM-IV)*[20] under the term "Gender Identity Disorder," although this classification is increasingly questioned.[21] Transgendered youth, a small part of the group of gay, lesbian, bisexual, transgendered, or questioning youth, perceive themselves as "trapped" in the body of the opposite sex. They often cross-dress and are at particular risk of being victims of violence and harassment. Pediatricians, psychiatrists, and psychologists can work with school districts to devise guidelines that respect transgendered students' self-identification and ensure their safety on campus. This might mean that teachers address transgendered students by their preferred first name or that transgendered students have access to private rest rooms or to unisex staff rest rooms. Wherever possible, school districts should accommodate transgendered students in physical education classes, in yearbooks, and in graduation ceremonies.

Questioning Youth

Students questioning their sexual identity might seek care in the health office or visit the counselor's office with seemingly unrelated issues: anger, depression, substance use, or academic problems. Only through gentle but direct questioning, with appropriate assurances of confidentiality, will the underlying issues of sexual orientation or gender identity emerge. A few questioning youth might identify themselves as such and seek supportive counseling on their own, but some will be referred to counseling by concerned teachers, peers, or families.

Issues for Sexual Minorities

Three themes emerge from research on the experience of growing up in one of the sexual minority groups in American society:

- *Isolation.* Most gay, lesbian, bisexual, transgendered, and questioning youth believe they are the only ones experiencing their feelings. In fact, they have few opportunities to meet other adolescents like themselves. Positive role models are seldom visible, and the mass media seldom transmit positive messages about what it means to be gay, lesbian, or bisexual. They seldom have access to accurate information about the spectrum of human sexuality and often question their normalcy but are afraid to seek supportive counseling.
- *Fear.* Most youth in sexual minority groups perceive an environment hostile to their sexual identity. They live with the daily fear that their secret will be discovered, and if it is, they fear ridicule, rejection, and harassment by families, friends, and teachers. In fact, many of these youth are thrown out of their homes and often resort to street life and prostitution for survival.
- *Violence.* Their fears are not unfounded. Many youth who are or are perceived to be gay, lesbian, bisexual, transgendered, or questioning are victims of verbal and physical harassment and violence from both peers and school staff at times.[21]

How Districts Can Help

A first step is for the school community to acknowledge that youth in sexual minority groups exist in every school and that their educational needs must be met. Many resources are available that school districts can use to effectively meet the needs of all sexual minority youth.[22] Two goals are critical: (1) to ensure the safety of all students; and (2) to reduce the sense of isolation of youth in sexual minority groups. School health care professionals and pediatricians can advocate for a district-wide commitment to support and protect all students. Student handbooks, posters, and pamphlets should inform all students that the counselor's office or health office is a safe place to discuss personal issues when they are ready to do so. To reduce isolation, some districts include discussions of diversity, sexual orientation, and gender identity in their health curricula; others include supportive books and other materials in the school library media center. Other districts offer support groups for sexual minority students through their counseling programs. If that is not feasible, school health care staff can refer students to supportive community resources. However, referral of youth for "reparative therapy" that is designed to change sexual orientation is unethical and dangerous.[23]

Recommendations for Pediatricians

1. Provide health care and supportive counseling for youth in sexual minority groups.[23] Although the medical care of these youth is identical to that of the general adolescent population, youth sexual minority groups also need accurate information on sexual orientation and gender identity as well as anticipatory guidance to minimize risk behaviors.

2. Advocate for and inform school staff about the issues of sexual minority groups, and participate in staff development programs to increase staff comfort related to sexual orientation and gender-identity issues. Emphasizing the physical and emotional dangers that stem from isolation, fear, and violence is critical.

3. While acknowledging the various religious and cultural views about sexual identity, encourage and support the development of nondiscrimination policies that explicitly protect all students, including sexual minorities, from harassment or violence. Experience has shown that unless youth in sexual minority groups are explicitly included in such policies, schools often will not intervene when harassment is based on sexual identity.

4. Understand that families of youth in sexual minority groups often need support and guidance. Correct mistaken beliefs and link these families with similar families. Inform students and their families

unequivocally that they have a right to a safe school environment and can seek legal recourse if their safety is threatened.

5. Work together with schools to foster environments that respect diversity and ensure the safety and educational success of all students. A school district's choice to recognize or to ignore the needs of students in sexual minority groups can have a profound effect on these youths' transition to a healthy adulthood. For some students in sexual minority groups, school may be the only setting where they are accepted without judgment or threat of violence.

Neglected and Abused Students

In 1999, nearly 830 000 confirmed cases of child maltreatment were reported by the United States Department of Health and Human Services.[24] The definition of child neglect and abuse established by the Child Abuse Prevention and Treatment Act in 1974[25] and amended in 1996[26] is "the physical or mental injury, sexual abuse, negligent treatment, or maltreatment of a child under the age of eighteen by a person who is responsible for the child's welfare under circumstances which indicate that the child's health or welfare is harmed or threatened." All individuals in regular contact with children and youth, including school staff, are mandated to report suspicions of abuse, neglect, or imminent danger of abuse.

Corporal Punishment

The Society for Adolescent Medicine estimates that between 10 000 and 20 000 school-aged children each year require medical evaluation or treatment as a result of corporal punishment used as a method of discipline.[27] Wissow[28] stated that "punishments that result in injury, that is, leave marks, break the skin or bones, or involve real or perceived threats to life or health, are generally regarded as abusive." Numerous organizations, including the AAP, have voiced strong opposition to corporal punishment in general, and the AAP Committee on School Health has recommended that corporal punishment be abolished in schools.[29]

Expectations, behaviors, and discipline of children vary from one ethnic group to another and often within the same ethnic group separated geographically. Although cultural differences must be considered when addressing this issue, punishment that involves visible and deliberate injury or neglect is considered abusive and must be reported, irrespective of the ethnic background of the abusive person or victim.

Neglect

Neglect accounts for most maltreatment cases and is defined broadly as the failure of a parent or caregiver either willingly or unwillingly to meet the basic needs of their child or children.[30] General categories of neglect include physical neglect, emotional neglect, educational neglect, and medical neglect.

- *Physical neglect* includes lack of safety, adequate nutrition, housing, hygiene, and clothing.
- *Emotional neglect* implies lack of emotional support and encouragement necessary for normal development.
- *Educational neglect* is characterized by failing to enroll a child in school or permitting or causing excessive absences and truancy.
- *Medical neglect* is a spectrum of failure to meet medical needs, such as well-child care, immunizations, or care for acute or chronic medical conditions, resulting in increased mortality and morbidity. Medical neglect sometimes is motivated by religious beliefs.[31]

Signs and Symptoms of Physical Abuse

Multiple factors contribute to abusive behaviors. Pediatricians need to take an ecological approach that encompasses individual, family, and community risk factors. Signs and symptoms of abuse include the following:

- *Contusions* (bruises, ecchymoses, hematomas, petechiae). (Avoid attempting to determine the age of contusions by their color or by visual inspection.[32,33] The time it takes for a bruise to appear, the length of time to resolve, and the color changes [if any] are so variable as to make aging bruises, at best, purely subjective. Even broad category assignment of "old" and "new" contusions is not supported by the literature.[32])

- *Abrasions and lacerations* (scratches and scrapes, splitting of the skin from blunt trauma)
- *Incisions* (sharp trauma)
- *Thermal and chemical burns* (scalds, direct heat, caustic injuries)
- *Internal injuries* (fractures resulting in compromised functioning with or without obvious deformity)

It also is helpful to evaluate all injuries systematically using 4 criteria:

- *Age and developmental capabilities of the child.* Children in certain special education and side-by-side programs might not be able to relate the circumstances leading to their injuries.
- *Explanation for how the injury occurred.* Most school-aged youth usually can explain how they were injured; however, they might hesitate if the injuries were inflicted. The explanation given by parents, caregivers, or the child might be the first indication that the injury is other than unintentional. Inconsistent or noncredible explanations are grounds for reporting.
- *Type of injury.* Patterned injuries should be considered suggestive of abusive trauma, especially if the explanation is not consistent with the injury.
- *Location of the injury.* Certain sites indicate a higher or lower probability of intentional trauma.

Common Sites of Unintentional Injury

- Forehead
- Chin
- Spinal prominences
- Hips and iliac crests

- Elbows
- Distal arms
- Knees
- Shins

Common Sites of Intentional Injury
- Ears and sides of the face
- Neck
- Trunk
- Upper arms
- Thighs
- Buttocks
- Genitalia

By themselves, none of these sites are mutually exclusive for determination of intentional or unintentional injury. When the 3 other criteria are considered, however, location can help determine whether physical abuse is a concern.

Sexual Abuse

Sexual abuse is sexual contact or interaction for sexual stimulation or gratification of an adult or older child who is a parent or caregiver and is responsible for the child's care.[34] Although it is difficult to ascertain the true incidence of sexual abuse, it is estimated that 1 in 4 girls and 1 in 6 boys are sexually victimized by 18 years of age.[34] In 1 study, 97% of sexually abusive persons were male, 50% to 80% were known to the victim, and 30% to 50% were parents and other relatives.[35] When no overt signs of abuse are present, stress-related conditions, such as sleep disturbances and related somatic complaints might be noted. Other indicative behaviors include excessive eating, aggression, depressed activity level, poor school performance, and increased or inappropriate fears. Alternatively, regressive behaviors or sexual acting out might be observed, although not all sexualized behavior indicates sexual abuse. However, developmentally inappropriate sexual knowledge

or experiences warrant further evaluation and investigation. These
behaviors might include[35]:

- Diminished personal boundaries, including sexualized behavior;
- Seductive behavior;
- Sexual curiosity not appropriate for developmental level;
- Negative reactions to bathing or toileting;
- Extreme fear of the opposite sex;
- Bulimia or gross weight gain;
- Running away and truancy; and
- Borderline personality characteristics.

Making a Report of Suspected Neglect or Abuse
All individuals working with children and youth should be familiar
with their state's laws and reporting procedures for suspected neglect
or abuse. School districts should have written guidelines about how
to report and refer cases of suspected neglect and abuse. Training all
staff to detect and respond appropriately to suspicions of child abuse
or neglect is key. Teachers often are the first to note evidence of neglect
or abuse. The school nurse can examine the student and evaluate and
document any physical evidence. The school counselor can assess and
substantiate the student's explanation. However, it is not required that
these assessments be performed, and such assessments should not sway
the mandated reporter from making a report if there is a suspicion of
neglect or abuse.

The reporting individual is not expected to "prove" the allegations.
Law enforcement personnel, protective services, and the judicial system
will investigate and confer to make a determination of intentional or
unintentional injury. In addition, if a report is made from school, a
confidential protective services interview with the student can be performed at school; this is especially important when the potential abusive person is a parent. During this process, a critical concern will be

to determine whether the student is in imminent danger of further abuse in the home and whether immediate action is warranted.

District officials and health care professionals often are concerned about where to keep the record of the report, which identifies the student and the reporter, and whether parents have access to the report. The Family Policy Compliance Office of the US Department of Education, which has responsibility for regulations under the Family Education Rights and Privacy Act of 1974 (FERPA),[36] has determined that parents have a right to examine the report of suspected abuse but that school administrators may copy the record and delete the name of the reporter from the copy.[37] Regardless of such safeguards, reporting suspected neglect or abuse can be stressful for staff. It is not uncommon for parents to react angrily and to act belligerently toward staff. For this reason, it is helpful if school administrators are notified when a report is made in case an angry parent enters the school and police are needed. Because school staff members are required to report "suspected" neglect or abuse, it is essential that all information concerning the situation be treated confidentially.

Child protective service agencies in many communities are understaffed. As a result, reports of suspected abuse are not always handled in a timely manner. For this reason, school staff members sometimes are reluctant to make a formal report. They often argue that making the report without immediate follow-up will not improve the situation and ultimately might make it worse if it antagonizes the parent and disrupts an established therapeutic relationship with the student. However, in the case of suspected neglect or abuse, a report is required by law, and the referral builds a case that eventually can lead to appropriate intervention, if necessary.

Recommendations for Pediatricians

1. Volunteer to provide training to school staff, teachers, and nurses on recognizing signs and symptoms of child abuse and neglect.
2. Offer to review school protocols on how to respond to a suspected case of child abuse or neglect. If the school does not have a protocol, work with the school nurse and others to develop one.

HIV-Infected Students
Education Programs

Adolescents who are sexually active or using alcohol or illicit drugs are at risk of HIV infection. Information should be provided on abstinence from sexual activity and use of safer sexual practices to reduce the risk of unplanned pregnancy and STDs, including HIV. All sexually active adolescents should be counseled about the correct and consistent use of latex condoms to reduce risk of infection. Guidance about prevention should include helping adolescents understand the responsibilities of becoming sexually active.

The school district should offer effective education to prevent HIV infection within the context of a quality comprehensive health program from kindergarten through grade 12. As part of its Programs That Work initiative, the Division of Adolescent and School Health at the Centers for Disease Control and Prevention reviewed findings from published research studies of curricula intended to reduce risk behaviors related to HIV infection. Effectiveness was defined as reducing the proportion of students who engaged in sexual intercourse or increasing the consistent and correct use of condoms among sexually active youth. Effective curricula share several characteristics. For example, each provides:

- Information about risk behaviors and their consequences;
- Lessons that help students realize their personal vulnerability to the negative consequences of unprotected sexual behaviors; and

- Opportunities to practice skills for avoiding risky behaviors.
  More information about these programs can be found at
  http://www.cdc.gov/nccdphp/dash/rtc.

HIV Testing

HIV testing should be discussed with all adolescents and encouraged
for students who are sexually active or substance users. A negative HIV
test result can allay anxiety resulting from a high-risk event or high-
risk behaviors and is a good opportunity to counsel on reducing high-
risk behaviors to reduce future risk. Although parental involvement
in adolescent health care is a desirable goal, consent of an adolescent
alone should be sufficient to provide evaluation and treatment for
suspected or confirmed HIV infection. Adolescents with a positive
HIV test result should be informed of their serostatus. It is important
to provide support, address medical and psychosocial needs, and
arrange linkages to appropriate care.

Best Practice Guidelines

Best practice guidelines for supporting these students address their
educational programs, the need for educating school staff, and school
safety issues.[38,39] Districts should establish safeguards to protect the
privacy and confidentiality of all students' health information. Informed consent for testing or release of information about serostatus
is necessary.[40]

Only authorized school health personnel should have access to
records containing confidential health information. Only the student's
parents, other guardians, and physician have an absolute need to know
that the student is infected with HIV. The number of personnel aware
of the student's condition should be kept to the minimum needed to
ensure proper care. The family has the right, but is not obligated, to
inform the school. Persons involved in the care and education of an
infected student must respect the student's right to privacy.[41]

Information about HIV infection and acquired immunodeficiency syndrome and the availability of HIV testing should be regarded as an essential component of anticipatory guidance provided by pediatricians and school health professionals to all adolescent patients. This guidance should include information about HIV prevention and transmission and implications of infection. Particular efforts should be made to provide access for adolescents who may not have a regular primary care physician.

School Attendance

In the absence of blood exposure, HIV infection is not acquired through the types of contact that usually occur in a school setting, including contact with saliva or tears. Hence, students with HIV infection should not be excluded from school for the protection of other students or personnel, and disclosure of infection should not be required. Specific recommendations about school attendance of children and adolescents with HIV infection include the following[41]:

- Most children and all adolescents infected with HIV should be permitted to attend school without restrictions, provided the student's physician gives approval.
- Children infected with HIV might be at increased risk of experiencing severe complications from infections such as varicella, tuberculosis, measles, cytomegalovirus, and herpes simplex virus. Districts should notify all parents of communicable diseases such as varicella or measles.
- Routine screening of students for HIV infection is not recommended, although all pregnant students should be tested.

Recommendations for Pediatricians

1. Review district protocols for universal precautions.
2. Offer to educate all district staff about HIV, transmission, and prevention.

3. Offer to educate school nurses and other health care personnel about medication protocols.

Immigrant Populations

The United States is home to a growing foreign-born population that currently exceeds 28 million people and accounts for 10% of the total population.[42] In 1999, 20% of school-aged children had at least 1 foreign-born parent, and 5% of students were foreign born.[42] More than half were born in Latin America, a quarter were born in Asia, approximately 15% were from Europe, and the remainder were from other regions. Households with a foreign-born person tend to be larger than those of natives and are more likely to be below the poverty level.[43] School can be stressful for all students, but immigrant students, especially refugees, face additional challenges, including school entry requirements, unrecognized medical problems, post-traumatic stress, and cultural differences.

School Entry Requirements

Meeting school entry requirements is sometimes difficult for immigrant children, because they often lack immunizations because of lack of vaccines in their home country, lack of adequate documentation of immunizations received, or a combination of these factors.

Unrecognized Medical Problems

Immigrant children often have diseases with which pediatricians in the United States might be less familiar, including malaria, amebiasis, schistosomiasis, and other helminthic infections.[44] Immigrant children also have a higher risk of developing tuberculosis because of the higher prevalence of tuberculosis in many countries, particularly in southeast Asia, Mexico, and Central America. Symptoms might be observed in parents as well as children.[44] The chapter on internationally adopted children in the current edition of the *Red Book*,[45] the CDC Web site (www.cdc.org,) and the World Health Organization Web site (http://www.who.int) are good resources to determine screening needs in particular children on the basis of their country of origin.

Post-traumatic Stress Disorder

Immigrant families often are separated from their support systems—extended families, friends, and other people with similar cultural or religious beliefs. This separation can exacerbate anxiety and depressive symptoms. In some cases, refugees experience post-traumatic stress disorder after loss of a family member or another loved one or after witnessing war or experiencing persecution. These students are at higher risk of poor school performance[46] and should receive appropriate referrals to mental health and social services.

Cultural Issues

Compared with their classmates, immigrant children often dress differently, speak differently, and eat different foods. These cultural differences can cause anxiety and affect school performance. Pediatricians can provide support and help students adapt to their new environment. Pediatricians might be the immigrant family's first and only contact with any form of health care or social service in the United States. They can educate school staff about the student's culture and advocate for flexibility so district rules can accommodate different cultural beliefs.

Culturally Competent Practice

Immigrant children and youth often have values, attitudes, assumptions, and behaviors that are different from those of the pediatrician. To offer effective health care to immigrant children, pediatricians must understand their culturally based assumptions and those on which US medicine is based and distinguish the potential impact of these assumptions on individuals who do not share them. For example, Western medicine assumes that life is governed by a series of physical and biochemical processes that can be studied and manipulated.

Western medical practice is based on certain assumptions. The following are examples of some of these assumptions:

- *Time.* The physician's time is important; patients must make an appointment.
- *Privacy and confidentiality.* Discussing a patient's care with non-professionals is not acceptable.
- *Distancing.* Personal involvement with patients is not professional.
- *Technology.* Because technology is essential for treatment, its use often comes before human needs.
- *Efficiency.* Efficiency is best accomplished through centralization of health services.
- *Rational.* Understanding science is necessary for effective treatment.
- *Compliance.* The physician knows best, and patients should follow orders.

These values and assumptions often conflict with those of people from non-Western cultures and can impede the provision of effective health care. In particular, they can result in limited data collection by restricting the definition of what is considered "relevant" to the condition. For example, in many cultures, it is appropriate for family members to give information about the patient. In other instances, the patient is less willing to trust and accept the physician's guidance because the Western practitioner failed to inquire about the patient's expectations and goals for treatment, resulting in decreased likelihood of collaboration and cooperation.[47,48] To overcome these limitations, pediatricians must examine their beliefs and endeavor to understand those of the children and families served. In particular, it is important to elicit information about the following:

- Family structure, roles, and relations;
- Health beliefs, particularly related to the cause, prevention, diagnosis, and treatment of illness and disability;
- Religious beliefs and their interrelationship with health beliefs;
- Sexual attitudes and practices;

- Dietary practices and the role of different foods in health, religion, and social activities;
- Drug use patterns; and,
- Styles of communication, particularly those that affect education.[48,49]

Working with different cultural groups or in culturally diverse communities is challenging. It requires sufficient time and openness to new ideas but can be extremely rewarding.

Recommendations for Pediatricians

1. Teach the school nurse and other school health care personnel about the medical and psychosocial needs of immigrant students and families.
2. Advocate for flexibility so that district rules and policies can accommodate the different cultural beliefs of immigrant families.

Runaway and Homeless Students

Homelessness, particularly for adolescents, is on the rise. It is estimated that 1.3 million youth have run away or are homeless on the streets of America.[47] In a representative sample of 6496 households with adolescents 12 to 17 years of age across a broad spectrum of geographic and sociodemographic factors, researchers found that 7.6% of the adolescents had spent at least 1 night in a youth or adult shelter, 3.3% had stayed in a public place, 2.2% had slept outdoors, 2.2% had hidden in an abandoned building, 1% had gone underground, and 0.4% had stayed with a stranger. Boys were more likely to have experienced a homeless episode than were girls.[48]

Homelessness is caused by many factors, but the absence of a supportive functional family is the most common factor cited. Death, divorce, loss of a parent's job, and parents who were alcoholics, drug abusers, or convicted criminals are all causes.[49,50] Adolescents who have problems at home or in school, are gay or lesbian, are pregnant or parenting, are in unsatisfactory foster care settings, or have mental illness are at greater risk of becoming homeless.

The McKinney-Vento Homeless Education Act (January 2002)
Provisions in the act include:

- Homeless children and youth must be afforded the same free and appropriate public education as all youth.
- Homelessness alone is not sufficient to separate students from the mainstream school environment.
- No state shall segregate homeless students in a separate school or in a separate program within a school because of homeless status. Counties that have exceptions:
  - San Joaquin County, CA
  - Orange County, CA
  - San Diego County, CA
  - Maricopa County, AZ
- If there is dispute as to where a student should be admitted, the child will be admitted to the school where enrollment is sought pending resolution of the dispute.

School Enrollment

A school cannot deny enrollment to any student because the student lives in a shelter, lacks a permanent address, or is homeless. Many schools can enroll homeless students without having health and school records. Homeless students have the right to enroll in:

- The school they attended when they were permanently housed;
- The school in which they were last enrolled; or
- Any school within the attendance area in which they reside.

They can remain in their selected school as long as they remain homeless or until the end of the academic year if a new permanent home is identified. Urban districts are more likely to provide transportation.

Medical Needs of Homeless Youth

Homeless students have multiple needs and require referrals to a variety of service providers. Many states require districts to identify free or reduced-cost medical services for homeless students. In addition, referrals for dental and mental health should be established. Some districts have a homeless student liaison who can facilitate referrals. Many homeless youth do not receive health or mental health services despite high levels of need. Half of street youth and 36% of youth living in shelters do not have a regular source of health care but rely on drop-in centers and shelters.[51] Health care professionals need to be aware that homelessness often precedes or contributes to physical or sexual abuse, increased rates of unprotected sex, drug and alcohol abuse, and more sexual partners.[52] Five thousand adolescents per year are buried in unmarked graves because they are unidentified or their bodies are unclaimed.[53] They die of assault, illness, and suicide.[53,54]

Recommendations for Pediatricians

1. Review district policies and regulations concerning homeless students.
2. Help determine how best to meet the medical and mental health needs of homeless students.
3. Find out what resources are available for homeless youth in your community (eg, shelters, medical care, and mental health resources). Additional resources on homeless youth include the following:

- National Association for the Education of Homeless Children and Youth (http://www.naehcy.org)
- National Center for Homeless Education at SERVE (http://www.serve.org/nche)
- National Law Center on Homelessness and Poverty (http://www.nlchp.org)
- Opening Doors—an Illinois State Board of Education grant-funded project under the Stewart B. McKinney Homeless Children and Youth Program (http://www.homelessed.net)

References

1. American Academy of Pediatrics, Committee on Adolescence. Adolescent pregnancy—current trends and issues. *Pediatrics.* 1999;103:516-520
2. American Academy of Pediatrics, Committee on Adolescence. Contraception in adolescents. *Pediatrics.* 1999;104:1161-1166
3. Maynard RA. *Kids Having Kids: a Robin Hood Foundation Special Report on the Costs of Adolescent Childbearing.* New York, NY: Robin Hood Foundation; 1996
4. Luker K. *Dubious Conceptions: The Politics of Teenage Pregnancy.* Cambridge, MA: Harvard University Press; 1997
5. Stevens-Simon C, White MM. Adolescent pregnancy. *Pediatr Ann.* 1991;20:322-331
6. American Academy of Pediatrics, Committee on Psychosocial Aspects of Child and Family Health and Committee on Adolescence. Sexuality education for children and adolescents. *Pediatrics.* 2001;108:498–502
7. Blum RW, McNeely CA, Rinehart PM. *Improving the Odds: The Untapped Power of Schools to Improve the Health of Teens.* Minneapolis, MN: Center for Adolescent Health, University of Minnesota; 2002. Available at: http://allaboutkids.umn.edu/kdwbvfc/publications.htm. Accessed July 28, 2003
8. Kirby D. *No Easy Answers: Research Findings on Programs to Reduce Teen Pregnancy.* Washington, DC: The National Campaign To Prevent Teen Pregnancy; 1997
9. Frost JJ, Forrest JD. Understanding the impact of effective teenage pregnancy prevention programs. *Fam Plann Perspect.* 1995;27:188–195
10. Schlitt JJ. *Creating Access to Care for Children and Youth: School-Based Health Center Census 1998–1999.* Washington, DC: National Assembly on School-Based Health Care; 2000
11. Stevens-Simon C. Providing effective reproductive health care and prescribing contraceptives for adolescents. *Pediatr Rev.* 1998;19:409–417
12. Title IX of the Education Amendments of 1972, 34 CFR § 106
13. Stevens-Simon C, Beach RK. School-based prenatal and postpartum care: strategies for meeting the medical and educational needs of pregnant and parenting students. *J Sch Health.* 1992;62:304–309
14. Quint J, Bos JM, Polit DF. *New Chance: Final Report on a Comprehensive Program for Young Mothers in Poverty and their Children.* New York, NY: Manpower Demonstration Research Corporation; 1997
15. Stevens-Simon C, Fullar SA, McAnarney ER. Teenage pregnancy. Caring for adolescent mothers with their infants in pediatric settings. *Clin Pediatr (Phila).* 1989;28:282–283

16. Stevens-Simon C, Dolgan JI, Kelly L, Singer D. The effect of monetary incentives and peer support groups on repeat adolescent pregnancies. A randomized trial of the Dollar-A-Day Program. *JAMA.* 1997;277:977–982

17. Stevens-Simon C, Kelly L, Kulick R. A village would be nice but…it takes a long-acting contraceptive to prevent repeat adolescent pregnancies. *Am J Prev Med.* 2001;21:60–65

18. American Academy of Pediatrics, Committee on Adolescence and Committee on Early Childhood, Adoption, and Dependent Care. Care of adolescent parents and their children. *Pediatrics.* 2001;107:429–434

19. Rotheram-Borus MJ, Murphy DA, Kennedy M, Stanton A, Kuklinski M. Health and risk behaviors over time among youth living with HIV. *J Adolesc.* 2001;24:791–802

20. American Psychiatric Association. *Diagnostic and Statistical Manual of Mental Disorders, Fourth Edition (DSM-IV).* Washington, DC: American Psychiatric Association; 1994:535–538

21. Ryan C, Futterman D. Lesbian and gay youth: care and counseling. *Adolesc Med.* 1997;8:207–374

22. Remafedi G, Resnick M, Blum R, Harris L. Demography of sexual orientation in adolescents. *Pediatrics.* 1992;89:714–721

23. American Academy of Pediatrics, Committee on Adolescence. Homosexuality and adolescence. *Pediatrics.* 1993;92:631–634

24. US Department of Health and Human Services. HHS reports new child abuse and neglect statistics [press release]. Washington, DC: US Department of Health and Human Services. Available at: http://www.acf.dhhs.gov/news/press/2001/abuse.htm. Accessed July 28, 2003

25. Child Abuse Prevention and Treatment Act. Pub L No. 93–247 (1974)

26. Child Abuse Prevention and Treatment Act. Pub L No. 104–235 (1996)

27. Corporal punishment in schools. A position paper of the Society for Adolescent Medicine. *J Adolesc Health.* 1992;13:240–246

28. Munkel WI. Neglect and abandonment. In: Monteleone JA, Brodeur AE, eds. *Child Maltreatment: A Clinical Guide and Reference.* 2nd ed. St Louis, MO: GW Medical Publishing Inc; 1998:339–356

29. American Academy of Pediatrics, Committee on School Health. Corporal punishment in schools. *Pediatrics.* 2000;106:343

30. Wissow LS. Child maltreatment. In: Oski FA, DeAngelis CD, Feigin RD, Warshaw JB, eds. *Principles and Practice of Pediatrics.* Philadelphia, PA: JB Lippincott Company; 1990:589–605

31. Asser SM, Swan R. Child fatalities from religion-motivated medical neglect. *Pediatrics.* 1998;101:625–629

32. Schwartz AJ, Ricci LR. How accurately can bruises be aged in abused children? Literature review and synthesis. *Pediatrics.* 1996:97:254–257

33. Dailey JC, Bowers CM. Aging of bitemarks: a literature review. *J Forensic Sci.* 1997:42:792–795

34. Monteleone JA, Glaze S, Bly KM. Sexual abuse: an overview. In: Monteleone JA, Brodeur AE, eds. *Child Maltreatment: A Clinical Guide and Reference.* 2nd ed. St Louis, MO: GW Medical Publishing Inc; 1998:129–150

35. McNeese V. Sexual abuse: the interview. In: Monteleone JA, Brodeur AE, eds. *Child Maltreatment: A Clinical Guide and Reference.* 2nd ed. St Louis, MO: GW Medical Publishing, Inc; 1998:185–212

36. Family Educational Rights and Privacy Act, 20 USC § 1232g. Regulations at 34 CFR

37. American School Health Association. Responsibility to disclose some types of information. In: *Guidelines for Protecting Confidential Student Health Information: National Task Force on Confidential Student Health Information.* Kent, OH: American School Health Association; 2000:16–18

38. American Academy of Pediatrics, Committee on Pediatric AIDS and Committee on Adolescence. Adolescents and human immunodeficiency virus infection: the role of the pediatrician in prevention and intervention. *Pediatrics.* 2001;107:188–190

39. Crocker AC, Cohen HJ, Kastner TA. *HIV Infection and Developmental Disabilities: A Resource for Service Providers.* Baltimore, MD: Paul H. Brookes Publishing Co; 1992

40. American School Health Association. *Guidelines for Protecting Confidential Student Health Information.* Kent, OH: American School Health Association; 2000

41. American Academy of Pediatrics, Committee on Pediatric AIDS and Committee on Infectious Diseases. Issues related to human immunodeficiency virus transmission in schools, child care, medical settings, the home, and community. *Pediatrics.* 1999;104:318–324

42. Lollock L. *The Foreign-Born Population in the United States: March 2000. Current Population Reports P20-534.* Washington, DC: US Census Bureau; 2001. Available at: http://www.census.gov/population/www/socdemo/foreign/reports.html. Accessed July 28, 2003

43. Jamieson A, Curry A, Martinez G. *School Enrollment in the United States—Social and Economic Characteristics of Students: October 1999, Current Population Reports P20-533.* Washington, DC: US Census Bureau; 2001. Available at: http://www.census.gov/prod/www/abs/school.html. Accessed July 28, 2003

44. American Academy of Pediatrics, Committee on Community Health Services. Health care for children of immigrant families. *Pediatrics.* 1997;100:153–156

45. American Academy of Pediatrics. Medical evaluation of internationally adopted children for infectious diseases. In: Pickering LK, ed. *Red Book: 2003 Report of the Committee on Infectious Diseases.* 26th ed. Elk Grove Village, IL: American Academy of Pediatrics; 2003;173–180

46. McCloskey LA, Southwick K. Psychosocial problems in refugee children exposed to war. *Pediatrics.* 1996;97:394–397

47. Ka'Opua L. *Training for Cultural Competence in the HIV Epidemic* [videotape]. Honolulu, HI: Wandering Star Productions; 1992

48. Randall-David E. *Strategies for Working with Culturally Diverse Communities and Clients.* Washington, DC: Association for the Care of Children's Health; 1989

49. Gonzalez VM. *Health Promotion in Diverse Cultural Communities.* Palo Alto, CA: Health Promotion Resource Center, Stanford Center for Research in Disease Prevention; 1991

50. Sherman DJ. The neglected health care needs of street youth. *Public Health Rep.* 1992;107:433–440

51. Klein JD, Woods AH, Wilson KM, Prospero M, Greene J, Ringwalt C. Homeless and runaway youths' access to health care. *J Adolesc Health.* 2000;27:331–339

52. Rotherman-Borus MJ, Parra M, Cantwell C, Gwadz M, Murphy D. Runaway and homeless youths. In: DiClemente RJ, Hansen WB, Ponton LE, eds. *Handbook of Adolescent Health Risk Behavior.* New York, NY: Plenum Press; 1996:369–392

53. DeRosa CJ, Montgomery SB, Kipke MD, Iverson E, Ma JL, Unger JB. Service utilization among homeless and runaway youth in Los Angeles, California: rates and reasons. *J Adolesc Health.* 1999;24:449–458

54. Rotherman-Borus MJ, Mahler KA, Koopman C, Langabeer K. Sexual abuse history and associated multiple risk behavior in adolescent runaways. *Am J Orthopsychiatry.* 1996;66:390–400

Chapter 5
Mental Health

In the United States today, 1 in 10 children and adolescents has a mental illness severe enough to result in significant functional impairment. Children and adolescents with mental disorders are at much greater risk for dropping out of school and having long-term impairments.... These childhood mental disorders impose enormous burdens and can have intergenerational consequences. They reduce the quality of children's lives and diminish their productivity later in life. No other illnesses damage so many children so seriously.[1]

American youth have significant mental health needs. An estimated 12% to 22% of children and adolescents have emotional or behavioral issues warranting a mental health diagnosis, and many more would benefit from counseling related to conditions of risk or stress in their lives.[2,3] Although there is increased awareness of children's mental health needs as exemplified by the US Surgeon General's Report on Mental Health in 1999, fewer than a third of youth with clearly identified mental health problems receive any care.[4] Schools provide some mental health services—in some communities, the only services—but the needs of students have far outstripped the ability of most schools to address them. In addition, stigma continues to be a problem. Mental illness is not accorded the same level of credibility as other health problems, resulting in neglect, bias, and prejudice. Families often feel helpless and have real concerns about privacy, labeling, and fair treatment. Nevertheless, a few districts recognize the gap between students' mental health needs and available services, and progress is being made. These districts are creating multifaceted programs that include curriculum-based programs to promote social and emotional health, targeted interventions to prevent risky behaviors resulting from unmet mental health needs, early identification of students with problems, and referral of at-risk students for assessment, treatment, and case management.

Curriculum-Based Programs That Promote Social and Emotional Health

There is mounting evidence that schools can have a critical role in the promotion of social and emotional health and in the primary prevention of risky behaviors that, in some students, might have links to emotional disturbances.[5] Examples of these risky behaviors include acting out, early sexual behavior, and substance abuse. Most districts implement a variety of strategies, including curriculum-based programs and after-school youth development programs, to prevent or reduce these risky behaviors. A major challenge is integrating these curriculum-based prevention programs with health and mental health services. To be effective, such programs require considerable resources and a sustained effort. Given schools' limited resources for addressing students' health and mental health needs, it is critical that administrators and school health professionals identify the programs that clearly have been shown to be effective rather than squander resources on programs that are popular with various constituencies in the community or with funders but do not demonstrate effectiveness in preventing or treating social and emotional disorders.

Screening and Assessment

Increase the number of persons seen in primary health care who receive mental health screening and assessment (*Healthy People 2010*, Objective 18-6) and increase the proportion of children with mental health problems who receive treatment (*Healthy People 2010*, Objective 18-7).

There is a broad range of mental health assessment services for schools, often depending on the staff available. They may include broad screening of groups of students to identify those in need of assistance, focused assessments of individual students, and intensive individual assessments for students with identified needs. Screening for mental illness differs significantly from early identification of mental illness. A screening program, for example, might evaluate all students in a ninth-grade class for mental illness, whereas an early identification program would educate staff to recognize early signs and symptoms of illness. Many mental health screening tools have been shown to be effective when used in physicians' offices and in school-based health centers, but there is not yet scientific evidence to support performing school-based mental health screening programs using these tools. Any screening program would require parent consent and availability of a comprehensive and prompt assessment (as well as subsequent treatment for those who require it) that is ensured for each student with a positive screening result, regardless of their language, health insurance status, or geographic location.

Broad screening measures can be used by school physicians, nurse practitioners, or school nurses to assess certain psychosocial issues when mental health professionals are unavailable. These include the *Guidelines for Adolescent Prevention Services (GAPS)* of the American Medical Association.[6] The GAPS questionnaire includes items on depression, suicidal thoughts, drug and alcohol use, and concerns about body image. It is available for both middle school and high school students and is available in Spanish. Suicide ideation also can be identified by the Columbia TeenScreen suicide screen.[7] The Pediatric Symptom Checklist[8] screens for psychosocial dysfunction. A youth self-report form, the PSC-Y, has been well received by students in school-based health centers.[9] The CRAFFT[10] clinical screening instrument is a mnemonic tool that is useful for identifying adolescents at risk of substance abuse. It is composed of the following 6 questions:

- Have you ever ridden in a Car driven by somebody (including yourself) who was high or had been using alcohol or drugs?
- Do you ever use alcohol or drugs to Relax, feel better about yourself, or fit in?
- Do you ever use alcohol or drugs while you are Alone?
- Do you ever Forget things that you did while using alcohol or drugs?
- Do your Family or Friends ever tell you that you should cut down on your drinking or drug use?
- Have you ever gotten into Trouble while you were using alcohol or drugs?

There are a variety of individual, family, school, peer, and community factors that can contribute to substance abuse, and these should be explored during a full history with the student. Additional information might be obtained from the family and school staff.

Focused assessments help determine whether students need targeted interventions such as skill training or mentoring; individual, group, family, or combination therapy offered at school; or referral to a community agency or private health care professional for a full psychological evaluation or for medication. Because schools seldom provide care for substance-related problems, assessment for these problems usually is limited, as are treatment options.

Intensive individual assessments usually are performed by psychiatrists, social workers, psychologists, or licensed professional counselors in 1 or 2 sessions and include the following:

- Past and current life stressors;
- Individual strengths and protective factors, such as reading for pleasure or current involvement in meaningful activities;

- Environmental strengths and protective factors within the student's family and neighborhood, such as supportive adults and recreational opportunities;
- Emotional and behavioral problems or mental status and diagnostic assessment; and
- Social skills related to school, peers, and family relationships.

School districts and health care professionals have an ethical responsibility to provide access to care for students assessed and identified with mental health needs. If the community is unable to respond to identified needs, screening should not be performed. In these cases, health care professionals must advocate for increased services or resist continued screening.

Diagnosis of Mental Health Problems in Children and Adolescents

Diagnosis of mental health problems affecting children and adolescents requires appropriate processes and use of the *Diagnostic and Statistical Manual of Mental Disorders, Fourth Edition (DSM-IV)*[11] or, more appropriately, the *Diagnostic and Statistical Manual for Primary Care (DSM-PC), Child and Adolescent Version.*[12] In general, disorders are grouped into 2 categories: externalizing disorders that typically involve some level of acting out, and internalizing, or less observable, disorders. There probably are more office visits in schools for disruptive behavior disorders than for other conditions because of the need for students to get along in schools. The following are some of the commonly seen problems.

Externalizing Disorders
Attention-Deficit/Hyperactivity Disorder
Students with attention-deficit/hyperactivity disorder (ADHD) often have difficulty paying attention in class (inattention), calling out or not waiting their turn (impulsivity), and restlessness (hyperactivity).[13]

(A more extensive description of this disorder can be found in Chapter 3, Special Education.)

Oppositional Defiant Disorder

Oppositional defiant disorder consists of an enduring pattern of uncooperative, defiant, and hostile behavior toward authority figures that does not involve major antisocial violations, is not accounted for by the child's developmental stage, and results in significant functional impairment.[11] Affected students have problems controlling their tempers; often seem to be angry, mean, and easily annoyed; and frequently are perceived as bullies. Students should be referred for assessment when their behaviors are more frequent and more intense than those of same-age peers or when they cause problems in social, academic, or work-related situations.

Conduct Disorder

Conduct disorder describes a persistent pattern of behavior that is not socially acceptable and often violates the rights of others. Among younger students, these might be more extreme acts of disobedience, defiance, bullying, and aggression or cruelty to animals. Older students might lie repeatedly, steal, destroy property, abuse chemical substances, or engage in precocious sexual behaviors. Many students exhibit some of these symptoms at certain times, but the behavior does not persist. These behaviors might range from mild, occasional acting out to severe, chronic aggression.

Disruptive behavior disorders often occur with other problems, such as anxiety disorders, obsessive-compulsive disorder, major depressive disorder, and communication disorders. Accurate assessment requires at least 2 qualitatively different measures. For example, parents' ratings of their child's behavior can be compared with interview data, direct observation, or teachers' ratings of behavior. The American Academy of Pediatrics recommends multimethod assessment with multiple informants.[14] Early recognition and assessment are critical, because a significant number of students who exhibit these problems as children exhibit these same behaviors as adolescents, highlighting the importance of early intervention and treatment.

Internalizing Disorders
Anxiety Disorders

Although various fears and worries can be developmentally appropriate and most individuals experience anxiety at one time or another, students with anxiety disorders generally have excessive worries, nervousness, irritability, and concentration problems. For example, it is normal for a toddler to experience separation anxiety. However, if a 6-year-old refuses to go to school, cannot sleep, and experiences restlessness, muscle tension, hyperventilation, and sweating, intervention might be necessary. Many students experience generalized anxiety disorders, such as fear of performing poorly in school or fear of failure, imperfection, or judgment. Students with social phobias often are labeled as shy, timid, or fearful. They tend to avoid situations that produce anxieties rather than dealing with them, and as a result they fail to develop adaptive and coping skills. When these students are referred for diagnosis, it is critical to involve family members, because anxiety disorders in children often are linked to parental psychopathology, substance abuse, and impaired family functioning. The American Academy of Child and Adolescent Psychiatry[15] suggests the following components for a thorough assessment:

- Parent and child interviews;
- Caregiver and child report measures;
- Physical examination to rule out somatic conditions or medication reactions that can mimic anxiety; and
- Screening for comorbid conditions.

Depressive Disorders

The US Surgeon General estimates that approximately 5% of the adolescent population in the United States experiences some form of depression.[16] There are variations in the types and number of symptoms, severity, and persistence. The 3 most prevalent types of depressive disorders in adolescents are dysthymic disorder, major depressive disorder, and bipolar disorder.

Dysthymic Disorder
This is a form of depression characterized by chronic, long-term symptoms that are not disabling but cause functional impairments. Symptoms include the following:

- Depressed or irritable mood for more days than not, for at least 1 year;
- Appetite or sleep changes;
- Low energy or fatigue;
- Poor concentration; and
- Hopelessness.

Ten percent of young people with dysthymic disorder eventually develop a major depressive disorder.

Major Depressive Disorder
This is more serious than dysthymic disorder and is characterized by the following symptoms, which occur most of the day, nearly every day for at least 2 weeks:

- Depressed or irritable mood;
- Diminished interest or pleasure in almost all activities;
- Significant changes in weight, appetite, or sleep;
- Agitation;
- Fatigue or loss of energy;
- Diminished ability to think or indecisiveness; and
- Recurrent thoughts of death or suicide.

Bipolar Disorder
This is a serious, lifelong mental illness that affects perceptions, thoughts, moods, and behavior. Approximately 20% of all people

with bipolar disorder have their first episode during adolescence, with the peak age of onset between 15 and 19 years. Adolescents with bipolar disorder experience uncharacteristically intense mood swings ranging from depression to elation. The extreme, disruptive moods during the elated phase are characterized by impulsive or reckless behavior, feelings of grandiosity, elevated and expansive mood, agitation, and frenzied activity. An adolescent experiencing a manic phase might:

- Talk constantly;
- Act angry, suspicious, or irritable;
- Have difficulty staying on one subject or idea;
- Be easily distracted;
- Sleep very little for days at a time; or
- Experience psychotic symptoms.

There is a strong relationship between depression and substance abuse in adolescents. National data indicate that 20% to 40% of adolescents with substance abuse problems also have comorbid depressive disorders.[17] In addition, psychiatric symptomatology in adolescents predicts substance use severity in young adulthood.

Suicidal Ideation and Behavior

Thoughts and attempts at self-harm often are associated with depression. An estimated 19% of adolescents seriously consider suicide, with almost 9% making one or more suicide attempt in the last 12 months.[18] Females are more likely to attempt suicide, usually by drug overdose, and males tend to use more lethal methods, such as firearms or hanging. Completed suicides are relatively rare, with a rate of 12.9 per 100 000 youth between 15 and 19 years of age dying.[19] Nevertheless, the prevalence of adolescent suicide is increasing. More than 90% of adolescent suicides are associated with depressive disorders, and 70% to 80% of adolescents who died of suicide had alcohol in their systems. More adolescents and young adults die of suicide than of cancer, heart disease, acquired immunodeficiency syndrome, birth defects, stroke, pneumonia and influenza, and chronic lung disease combined.[20]

Most completed suicides occur shortly after a youth experiences an acute stress, such as getting into trouble with the law or at school, breaking up with a partner, or being humiliated by peers. Highest-risk adolescents are those with a family history of suicide attempt or completion in close relatives. Adolescents with a history of mental illness or who have made a previous attempt are also at great risk. Adolescents confused about their sexual identity and those dealing with depression, substance abuse, and bipolar disorders constitute the rest of the at-risk population.

> Reduce the proportion of children and adolescents with disabilities who are reported to be sad, unhappy, or depressed (*Healthy People 2010*, Objective 6-2).

> Reduce the suicide rate (Healthy People 2010, Objective 18-1) and reduce the rate of suicide attempts by adolescents (*Healthy People 2010*, Objective 18-2).

Eating Disorders

Eating disorders affect males and females and are characterized by abnormal eating habits, extreme weight management techniques, and distorted body image. These behaviors can appear as early as elementary school and can be life threatening.[21] Given the pervasive media messages and cultural norms equating body size and shape with physical attractiveness, all adolescents are at risk of developing eating disorders, and approximately 3% of young women and 1% of young men are estimated to have some form of eating disorder.[22] These obsessive behaviors indicate serious emotional problems, and individuals displaying symptoms (see the following sections, "Anorexia" and "Bulimia") should be referred as quickly as possible for assessment and treatment. Unfortunately, eating disorders in many adolescents are not recognized until starvation or binging and purging are far advanced, leading to other symptoms that necessitate a health office visit.

Anorexia

Anorexia is characterized by an irrational fear of body fat and weight gain.[5] Individuals are obsessively preoccupied with food and eating but display rigid self-control of eating and exercise on the basis of a distorted perception of body image. Symptoms include refusal to maintain recommended weight for height, intense fear of weight gain, and a fixation on body weight and shape. Weight loss is accomplished through restricted caloric intake (decreased amounts of food, skipped meals, or change to low-fat, low-calorie foods), increased exercise, binging and purging, or a combination of these measures. Although less common than bulimia nervosa, anorexia often is identified earlier because of the dramatic changes in eating and exercise patterns and resultant weight loss. Students with anorexia nervosa can enter into a state of starvation with predictable physical and psychological consequences, including cachexia, fatigue, weakness, abdominal pain, chest pain, palpitations, light-headedness, menstrual changes, irritability, and depression. When purging is involved through self-induced vomiting or laxative, emetic, or diuretic use, the combination of dehydration, electrolyte imbalance, and starvation is particularly dangerous.[23] It is unusual for students with anorexia nervosa to identify themselves as having the disorder and to seek help on their own. Students experiencing anorexia nervosa often come to the attention of school staff when concerned teachers, counselors, nurses, or fellow students report their worries about the student's excessive weight loss. These concerns are justified, because the leading cause of death among individuals with eating disorders is suicide and the second is cardiac dysfunction.[24]

Bulimia

Bulimia is characterized by repeated episodes of binge eating often accompanied by purging (self-induced vomiting or excessive use of laxatives or diuretics), excessive exercise, or caloric restriction. Bulimic behavior often goes undetected because the binging and purging usually take place in private and because the signs and symptoms are subtler than the dramatic weight loss associated with anorexia nervosa. Students with bulimic behaviors are more likely to ask for help, recognizing their behaviors as abnormal and out of control.

Treatment of Mental Health Problems in Youth

Given the time and resources, school mental health professionals can offer a range of treatment services, including individual, group, and family therapies. For some conditions, such as mood, anxiety, and eating disorders, a number of empirically supported treatments are effective. Unfortunately, staffing shortages frequently result in caseloads of 40 or more and daily schedules often exceeding 15 students.[25] These demands, coupled with case management responsibilities and the unanticipated crises that occur in schools on a daily basis, mitigate against effective treatments. Substance-related problems present even more challenges. Drug abuse treatment requires skilled substance abuse specialists who are seldom available in schools. In most school districts, students with substance abuse problems are referred to community agencies for treatment. Unfortunately, in the referral process, many students "fall through the cracks" because of the significant barriers of transportation, motivation, confidentiality, and cost. Effective outside referral of students with substance abuse problems requires effective case management at the school to overcome these barriers and ensure that treatment plans are monitored.

Unless a school is linked to a clinic or community health care professional, it is difficult for schools to meet the standards of care required for appropriate, effective treatment, particularly for students with severe problems. This is especially troubling when the problems involve conditions of significant risk, such as depression with suicidal ideation. Ideally, linkages should be established so that when youth have more serious problems, they can be referred and evaluated in a timely manner in a collaborating community mental health center, substance abuse treatment center, or private office. Such linkages enable youth to receive a range of more intensive services, including emergency coverage. Without such linkages, the problems, for the student and the school, are likely to escalate.

Externalizing Disorders

Other than for the treatment of ADHD, pharmacologic interventions have not been researched sufficiently to demonstrate effectiveness with oppositional defiant disorder and conduct disorder.[26] Behavioral interventions, on the other hand, have demonstrated long-term success in dealing with externalizing disorders. Successful programs are characterized by their breadth and their intensity; most require significant contact with students, often more than 20 sessions. Effective interventions are based on cognitive-behavioral therapies and teach students specific skills to manage behaviors. These programs often are combined with skill development programs for families to maximize treatment gains. Important skills for parents (and teachers) include how to:

• Observe and accurately define their child's behavior;
• Use reinforcement to encourage appropriate behaviors;
• Use practice, modeling, role playing, corrective feedback, and social and token reinforcement to teach new behaviors;
• Use negotiating and behavioral contracting;
• Use "time out" to discourage inappropriate behavior; and
• Reduce or eliminate use of verbal reprimands.[15]

The most difficult problem in helping teachers and families deal with disruptive behaviors is helping them adhere to the treatment recommendations. Some adults get into a coercive cycle; their behavior produces equally reactive behavior on the student's part, which in turn leads to further coercive behavior on the adults' part. Once a student is in treatment, whether adults attempt to discipline or ignore the behavior, whatever they do can result in increased oppositional behavior. Understandably, this results in frustration if the adults are not forewarned of a likely increase and prepared to persevere with treatment protocols. Families and teachers coping with students with an externalizing disorder need ongoing support and reassurance to sustain the motivation and behavioral changes needed for long-term success.

Internalizing Disorders

Although pharmacologic interventions are routinely prescribed, there is insufficient documentation of their efficacy and safety in students with anxiety disorders.[27] There are, however, efficacious cognitive-behavioral therapies.[28] Interventions focus on identifying elements in the environment that trigger anxiety, identifying how the student internalizes that information, and providing information and skills to cope more effectively. In one of the most successful programs,[28] students are taught the acronym FEAR (feelings, expectations, actions, and reward) to help recall the steps for coping successfully. Modeling, role playing, positive reinforcement, and relaxation techniques are used throughout the program. Younger students, but not older students, also benefit from programs that involve their families in learning new skills.[29,30]

Appropriate referral from the school, home, or primary care physician to a mental health professional will help to prevent adolescent suicide. Emergency psychiatric consultation should be available at all schools. Recognition and appropriate treatment of mental and substance abuse disorders hold great suicide prevention value. Improving the recognition and treatment of depression in medical settings is a promising way to prevent suicide in adolescents.

Once the possibility of an eating disorder is recognized, the student should be approached in a sensitive but candid manner to obtain further history and facilitate further evaluation if appropriate. Health staff should be concerned even if a student does not meet all the *DSM-IV* criteria for an eating disorder or denies feeling fat or wanting to lose weight. Significant weight loss should be considered a probable eating disorder until ruled out by a comprehensive health evaluation. Because eating disorders are potentially life threatening, parents must be informed of the school's concerns.

Once students have been identified as possibly having an eating disorder, they should be referred to their primary care physician, who will be responsible for the overall treatment plan and coordination of care. The plan should include specific strategies to monitor levels of physical activity, eating, and other aspects of treatment, including accommodation for possible periodic school absences because of hospitalization. Many communities have eating disorder teams consisting of a pediatrician, dietitian, and psychiatrist or psychologist.

The school physician or nurse also has an important role in collaboration with school mental health professionals in monitoring students with eating disorders. Health office personnel can monitor vital signs, weight, eating behaviors, physical activity, and possible danger signs, such as syncope, dehydration, or excessive fatigue. They can provide timely feedback on compliance or relapse to the primary care physician. They can meet with other school personnel to develop ways to ensure that both staff and students refrain from insensitive comments related to weight. Finally, health care staff, teachers, and counselors can provide supportive counseling as the student deals with the difficult requirements of treatment. Some schools have found that on-campus support groups for students with eating disorders are useful.

Many adolescents experiencing eating disorders, particularly anorexia nervosa, might strongly resist treatment aimed at normalizing eating, exercise patterns, and weight gain. Because of profound physical consequences of eating disorders, including death, the pediatrician is in the best position to confront initial patient or family denial that there is a problem. It is also the pediatrician or psychiatrist who will determine whether outpatient treatment is possible or whether medical or psychiatric hospitalization is in order. Early intervention is critical, and services should include the following:

- Triage assessment and assisting youth and families in rapidly connecting to appropriate resources in the school or community;
- Brief, problem-focused therapies for 1 to 3 sessions;
- Skills training for small groups of 4 to 8 students on coping with stress, avoiding and coping with violence, and anger management; and
- Interactive classroom discussions with students to better inform them about stress, protective factors, specific emotional and behavioral problems associated with various stages of development, and effective coping and help-seeking strategies.

Pediatricians can collaborate with school mental health professionals, school nutritionists, physical education teachers, and coaches to ensure that students receive accurate and appropriate information on how to maintain appropriate weight to compete in athletics or perform in dance. Girls involved in ballet, modeling, gymnastics, or cheerleading and boys in wrestling can be at higher risk of eating disorders. Health care and counseling staff can explore these issues and help students set reasonable expectations. All school personnel (school physician, nurse, health aides, teachers, counselors, coaches, and administrators) should recognize the major signs and symptoms of eating disorders. Staff development should emphasize the importance of early identification and intervention. Overheard conversations or concerned friends' reports to school staff about a student's possible eating disorder should be taken seriously and addressed. Any student exhibiting even modest but rapid weight loss, altered eating patterns, and increased exercise habits or physical symptoms consistent with an eating disorder should be evaluated immediately. Brochures and pamphlets related to eating disorders prominently displayed in the health office or counseling office will let students know that these issues can be discussed in these settings and might facilitate their seeking help.

Medication Administration

There has been a dramatic increase in the use of psychotropic medications during the last 10 years, primarily in conjunction with increased numbers of students diagnosed with ADHD.[31] These students should be monitored using clear, written protocols. Consideration should be given to the following:

- Routine assessment for adverse reactions and effects;
- Assessment of efficacy (are symptoms improving?);
- Compliance regarding dosage and timing;
- Potential for overdosing and emergency response protocols; and
- Compliance with the treatment plan in general.

Concerns should be reported to the prescribing physician following written guidelines that protect confidentiality and privacy.

Crisis Response

The tragic school shooting events during the late 1990s helped raise awareness of the connection between youth violence and mental health. Since then, increased federal and state resources have been identified to prevent and address violence-related problems among youth. There is much that schools can do to prevent and reduce violent behavior and to assist youth exposed to violence as victims, as witnesses, or through the experiences of friends and family members. Recommended actions include the following:

- Ensure that schools have clear rules that are consistently enforced and that students are closely monitored and supervised.

- Implement skill training and violence prevention programs for students and staff, including conflict negotiation training, leadership, and mentoring programs.
- Develop crisis management plans and grief response plans in case a death occurs on campus.
- Link school staff members who work with at-risk students with community professionals who can provide additional services.
- Provide mental health assessments for students with recognized behavior problems and refer for treatment as needed.
- Create safeguards that ensure buildings are free of weapons and work with local law enforcement and emergency personnel to respond to violent events.

Guidelines for Linking With Community Professionals (See also School-Based Health Centers, Chapter 6)

For many school districts, full-service school-based health centers (SBHCs) represent an optimal approach for providing comprehensive physical and mental health services for students. Emotional and behavioral problems often rank as the number 1 or number 2 reason for referral to the center.[32] Many students seek care because of both somatic and emotional behavioral needs, calling for a coordinated approach between health care professionals specializing in both areas. Fortunately, the typical SBHC staff includes nurse practitioners and consulting physicians, as well as mental health staff. The medical staff often recognizes students who have physical health needs that are masking emotional or behavioral issues, and in turn, mental health staff often identify unaddressed medical issues. The physical proximity of the staff in SBHCs ensures timely and appropriate care.

Nowhere is this collaboration more needed than in addressing substance abuse problems. When schools and SBHC staff work collaboratively, substance abuse problems in a school can be reduced. SBHCs also can link students to other community outreach programs that promote youth development, thus decreasing their likelihood of substance involvement. They also can link students to needed inpatient care.

For many communities or districts without SBHCs, having community-based mental health professionals come to campuses to provide on-site mental health services has been shown to be feasible. As with SBHCs, communication with a student's medical home is critical. Community mental health agencies have a critical role in augmenting school-based services. Two national centers that can provide technical assistance for establishing mental health programming in schools are the Center for School Mental Health Assistance at the University of Maryland and the Center for School Mental Health Policies at the University of California at Los Angeles.

Transition Plans After Treatment

Schools should set up agreements with medical and mental health inpatient facilities in their regions so that discharge planning includes a school transition plan. Returning students often are faced with questions, fears, and suspicion from fellow classmates, particularly when the absence is known to have been for mental health issues. It is important that outpatient and inpatient mental health professionals coordinate services and collaborate with parents, the student, and appropriate school representatives (school counselor, nurse, principal). The student should not be expected to handle the transition alone but should have the assistance of school staff.

Certain maladaptive behaviors should be anticipated on return to a regular school environment from a protected home or hospitalized environment. Establishing open communication between school staff and community-based mental health professionals is important so that students' mental heath care professionals are updated on their progress. The particular diagnosis need not be disclosed to school staff, but school staff must be able to respond appropriately to potential maladaptive behaviors, emotional states that can interfere with academic learning or school-related social functioning, and potential adverse effects of medication the student is taking.

Principles of Care

Four important principles of care are central to the provision of quality mental health services in schools:

- Involve all community stakeholder groups (youth, families, school staff, child mental health staff, other agency staff, neighborhood leaders, clergy) in assessing the needs of youth in the school or community.
- Apply interdisciplinary approaches that are developmentally and culturally sensitive.
- Offer evidence-based programs and a range of services that build on school and community assets to maximize available resources.
- Emphasize quality assurance and evaluation.

Emerging Issues
Individualized Education Programs

The issue of whether students with chronic emotional and behavioral problems should receive special education services and have individualized education programs (IEPs) is controversial. If mental health problems interfere with their ability to make satisfactory progress in school, students are entitled to special educational services to ensure that programs are in place to address their problems and optimize their ability to learn. However, many students with significant emotional and behavioral concerns are able to function in school and resist being categorized as receiving special education services. In addition, few schools have sufficient resources and staff to adequately provide services for students with emotional disorders, and linking schools to community mental health care professionals is necessary. These programs help reduce the costs of care, provide more specialized services, and eliminate the stigma sometimes associated with special education services.

Recommendations for Pediatricians

The movement toward comprehensive mental health programs in schools is still in its early phases, and as such, much work remains to be done. Pediatricians can contribute to these efforts in the following ways:

- Establish a genuine collaborative relationship with various mental health professionals in the community as well as at the school site.
- Identify mechanisms to include mental health assessments as an integral part of the school's screening services.
- Advocate for school mental health services using a framework that goes beyond a focus on problems (eg, one that acknowledges the roles of stress, risk, and protective factors in contributing to or decreasing problems).
- Include mental health professionals in assessments of available community health resources.
- Promote the role of mental health in student achievement and social function.
- Encourage a full spectrum of behavioral health services, including prevention, intervention, and treatment (eg, school mental health services linked to outpatient community-based mental health professionals and psychiatric hospitals).
- Support recognition of institutional approaches that focus on youth strengths and empirically supported interventions that have proven to be effective.
- Develop support within the medical community for mental health programs in schools.
- Explore creative funding mechanisms to support behavioral health services as part of the school health services.

- Suggest ways of improving systems of quality assurance and program evaluation that include behavioral health issues.
- Insist that schools and school-based mental health professionals encourage parents to allow communication with students' primary health care professionals.

References

1. National Advisory Mental Health Council, Workgroup on Child and Adolescent Mental Health Intervention, Development, and Deployment. *Blueprint for Change: Research on Child and Adolescent Mental Health.* Bethesda, MD: National Institute of Mental Health; 2001
2. Burns BJ, Costello EJ, Angold A, et al. Children's mental health service use across service sectors. *Health Aff (Millwood).* 1995;14:147-159
3. Dryfoos JG. *Safe Passage: Making It Through Adolescence in a Risky Society.* New York, NY: Oxford University Press; 1998
4. Leaf PJ, Alegria M, Cohen P, et al. Mental health service use in the community and schools: results from the four-community MECA Study. Methods for Epidemiology of Child and Adolescent Mental Disorders Study. *J Am Acad Child Adolesc Psychiatr.* 1996;35;889-897
5. Graczyk PA, Domitrovich CE, Zins JE. Facilitating the implementation of evidence-based prevention and mental health promotion efforts in schools. In: Weist M, Evans S, Lever N, eds. *Handbook of School Mental Health: Advancing Practice and Research.* New York, NY: Kluwer Academic/ Plenum Publishers; 2003:301-318
6. American Medical Association. *Guidelines for Adolescent Preventive Services (GAPS): Recommendations and Rationale.* Elster AB, Kuznets NJ, eds. Baltimore, MD: Williams & Wilkins; 1994
7. Lucas CP, Zhang H, Fisher PW, et al. The DISC Predictive Scales (DPS): efficiently screening for diagnoses. *J Am Acad Child Adolesc Psychiatry.* 2001;40:443-449
8. Jellinek MS, Murphy JM, Robinson J, Feins A, Lamb S, Fenton T. Pediatric symptom checklist: screening school-age children for psychosocial dysfunction. *J Pediatr.* 1988;112:201-209
9. Gall G, Pagano ME, Desmond MS, Perrin JM, Murphy JM. Utility of psychosocial screening at a school-based health center. *J Sch Health.* 2000;70:292-298
10. Knight JR, Shrier L, Bravender T, et al. A new brief screen for adolescent substance abuse. *Arch Pediatr Adolesc Med.* 1999;153:591-596

11. American Psychiatric Association. *Diagnostic and Statistical Manual of Mental Disorders, Fourth Edition (DSM-IV)*. Washington, DC: American Psychiatric Association; 1994

12. American Academy of Pediatrics. *The Classification of Child and Adolescent Mental Diagnoses in Primary Care: Diagnostic and Statistical Manual for Primary Care (DSM-PC), Child and Adolescent Version.* Wolraich ML, ed. Elk Grove Village, IL: American Academy of Pediatrics, 1996

13. Vitiello B, Jensen P. Disruptive behavior disorders. In: Kaplan HI, Sadock BJ, eds. *Kaplan and Sadock's Comprehensive Textbook of Psychiatry.* 6th ed. Baltimore, MD: Williams & Wilkins; 1995:2311–2319

14. American Academy of Pediatrics, Committee on Quality Improvement, Subcommittee on Attention-Deficit/Hyperactivity Disorder. Clinical practice guidelines: diagnosis and evaluation of the child with attention-deficit/hyperactivity disorder. *Pediatrics.* 2000;105:1158–1170

15. American Academy of Child and Adolescent Psychiatry. Practice parameters for the assessment and treatment of children and adolescents with anxiety disorders. *J Am Acad Child Adolesc Psychiatry.* 1997;36:69S–84S

16. US Department of Health and Human Services. *Surgeon General's Report on Mental Health.* Washington, DC: US Government Printing Office; 1999

17. Merikangas KR, Mehta RL, Molnar BE, et al. Comorbidity of substance use disorders with mood and anxiety disorders: results of the International Consortium in Psychiatric Epidemiology. *Addict Behav.* 1998;23:893–907

18. Centers for Disease Control and Prevention. Youth Risk Behavior Surveillance: United States, 2001. *MMWR Surveill Summ.* 2002;51(SS-04):1–64

19. Shaffer D, Greenberg T. Teen Suicide Fact Sheet. New York, NY: Columbia College of Physicians and Surgeons/New York State Psychiatric Institute; 2002. Available at: http://www.teenscreen.org/pdfs/SuicideFacts080902.pdf. Accessed July 28, 2003

20. Department of Health and Human Services, US Public Health Service. *The Surgeon General's Call to Action To Prevent Suicide.* Washington, DC: US Government Printing Office; 1999

21. Fisher M, Gordon NH, Katzman DK, et al. Eating disorders in adolescents: a background paper. *Adolesc Health.* 1995:16:420–437

22. Becker AE, Grinspoon SK, Klibanski A, Herzog DB. Eating disorders. *N Engl J Med.* 1999;340:1092–1098

23. Kreipe RE, Uphoff M. Treatment and outcome of adolescents with anorexia nervosa. *Adolesc Med.* 1992;3:519–540

24. Fisher M. Medical complications of anorexia and bulimia nervosa. *Adolesc Med.* 1992;3:487–502

131

25. Christophersen ER, Mortweet SL. *Treatments that Work with Children: Empirically Supported Strategies for Managing Childhood Problems.* Washington, DC: American Psychological Association; 2001

26. Kasdin AE, Wassell G. Therapeutic changes in children, parents, and families resulting from treatment of children with conduct problems. *J Am Acad Child Adolesc Psychiatry.* 2000;39:414–420

27. Velosa JF, Riddle MA. Pharmacologic treatment of anxiety disorders in children and adolescents. *Child Adolesc Psychiatr Clin North Am.* 2000;9:119–133

28. Howard B, Kendall PC, Chu BC, Krain AL, Marrs-Garcia AL. *Cognitive-Behavioral Family Therapy for Anxious Children Therapist Manual.* 2nd ed. Ardmore, PA: Workbook Publishing; 2000

29. Kendall PC, Southam-Gerow MA. Long-term follow-up of a cognitive-behavioral therapy for anxiety-disordered youth. *J Consult Clin Psychol.* 1996;64:724–730

30. Dadds MR, Holland DE, Laurens KR, Mullins M, Barrett PM, Spence SH. Early intervention and prevention of anxiety disorders in children: results at 2 year follow-up. 1999. *J Consult Clin Psychol.* 1999;67:145–150

31. Zito JM, Safer DJ, DosReis S, et al. Psychotropic practice patterns for youth: a 10-year perspective. *Arch Pediatr Adolesc Med.* 2003;157:17–25

32. Anglin TM, Naylor KE, Kaplan DW. Comprehensive school-based health care: high school student's use of medical, mental health, and substance abuse services. *Pediatrics.* 1996;97;318–330

Chapter 6
School-Based Health Centers

No educational reform initiative will succeed where health fails.
National School Boards Association

Health remains a significant factor in both academic and personal
success. The need to address health care remains critical, particularly
for the growing number of children without insurance or access to
care.[1] School-based health centers (SBHCs) were developed to provide
care to students without health insurance or who have other barriers
to receiving health care. SBHCs are health clinics based on the school
campus that provide services to students during the school day. There
is no uniform SBHC model; however, most centers provide both
health and mental health services during all or part of the school
week. Centers are located in elementary, middle, and high schools
and generally are collaborative projects between the schools and a
local community health care professional.

School-based health centers developed in the early 1970s as a way
for schools and communities to meet the physical and emotional
health needs of students from medically underserved families. With
funding from local community foundations, local health care organizations, and a few national foundations, SBHCs were established in a
few high-risk urban areas. As public funds increased, the number of
centers grew. Today there are approximately 1135 SBHCs in 45 states.[2]
Most centers are located in high schools (41%), while elementary
schools represent 30% of centers. Middle school SBHCs and schools
with mixed grades represent the remainder. School-based health centers are located in urban (56%), rural (30%), and suburban (14%)
schools.[2] Parents generally must give consent for their children to

access SBHC services and for the SBHC to release records. School-based health centers strive to enhance a community's capacity to respond to the needs of its children and youth.

Characteristics of School-Based Health Centers

School-based health centers are distinguished from each other by the types of services offered on site, the types of professionals who provide the services, and the on-site availability of these services and staff from day to day. The presence of staff members on site can range from a half day a week to 2 full-time equivalents, depending on need, size of population, and availability of resources. Differences between SBHCs are influenced by the perceived primary care and mental health care needs of the school-aged population, the availability of funding, and community politics. Despite these differences, what is most telling about SBHCs are their common characteristics. SBHCs are:

- *Located in school settings.* Immediate access and convenience are important and necessary to serve youth effectively. Consequently, SBHCs strive to be where students spend the majority of their day—in schools. In some cases, SBHCs are housed in retrofitted classrooms, specially designated "health suites" near the central health office, portable units outside the building, or in some cases, areas that used to be used for storage.
- *Sponsored by community health organizations in partnership with the school district.* Most SBHCs are sponsored by health care organizations: 31% by hospitals, 23% by public health departments, 19% by community health centers, and 27% by other community agencies.[2] Sponsorship provides important advantages, including technical and financial support, clinical backup, and consultation. The type of backup needed depends on the types of services offered. An SBHC that offers comprehensive primary physical and mental health services or substance abuse services must arrange for after-hours coverage and for emergency services.

In some cases, this might mean specialty services, inpatient care for medical or mental health problems, or detoxification facilities.

School-based health centers should also be:

- *Supportive of the district's educational mission.* School-based health centers rely on their host schools for space and access to students. The SBHC staff must respect and appreciate the unique culture of public education and its administrative structure and work to maintain effective collaborative relations. Generally, SBHCs include school staff and administrators on their advisory committees. In addition, most SBHCs are guided by an advisory committee comprising school staff and administrative personnel, community members, parents, and students to help ensure continued responsiveness to the community served. Schools receiving federal funding through the Healthy Schools/Healthy Communities program that is sponsored by the Bureau of Primary Health Care[3] are required to have a consumer-dominant board providing direction to the health center.

- *Concerned with unmet health needs that create barriers to learning.* Poor health directly affects students' attendance and their ability to learn. Students who attend school when they are sick, scared, hungry, or in pain will not benefit fully from their educational experience. Because health is so important to student achievement, particularly during the formative years, SBHCs and school districts have a mutual interest in meeting students' health needs. SBHCs permit teachers to concentrate on academics and make it easier for students to keep medical appointments.

- *Partnered with community service agencies to ensure access to services beyond the center's scope.* It is essential that health services provided by the educational sector are integrated with health education, social services, and health services provided elsewhere in the community. Local primary care professionals, managed care organizations, social agencies, public and private mental health care agencies, and representatives of local government and local business, cultural, ethnic, and religious communities should participate in the planning of SBHCs. It is important that school-based services not supplant services that could be delivered elsewhere, unless that is part of the agreed-on design.[4] Successful SBHCs recognize and acknowledge the complementary roles and functions of the school district's health care professionals and community health care professionals who provide technical and financial support, clinical backup, after-hours coverage for emergency and specialty services, inpatient care for physical and emotional problems including detoxification, and consultation on complex cases. By working collaboratively with these partners, SBHCs can provide quality health care services and convenient access to a larger framework of health care services for students, their families, and school staff.

- *Committed to introducing each student and family to a traditional medical home.* Whenever this is possible in a community, students should be taught to use health services that are available. An integrated school health program must include activities that prepare the large portion of students who will inevitably graduate or transfer from school each year. Examples of such activities are those that assist families with health insurance eligibility determinations, applications for insurance, selection of a non–school-based primary care professional, and registration in a community-based clinical practice that will serve as the students' medical homes. Even if students receive most services at a school health center, families should be taught when and how to make preventive health appointments, to travel to their medical-home site independently, and to become familiar with a permanent primary care professional of their choice.[4]

- *Committed to multidisciplinary practice.* SBHCs are typically staffed in 1 of 3 patterns:

  (1) A primary care team, including physician and nurse practitioner or physician assistant, with clinical support from a registered nurse and/or medical assistant (40%);

  (2) A primary care team that includes a mental health professional (35%); or

  (3) A primary care and mental health staff that also includes health education and social services (25%).

- *Motivated to perform ongoing evaluation.* Evaluation should be incorporated into all integrated school health programs. Quality assurance and improvement are important parts of the evaluation. Systematic evaluation should provide information about whether the integrated school health services approach is effective and worth the investment.[4]

According to the National Assembly on School-Based Health Care, most SBHC services are provided by nurse practitioners or physician assistants, although physicians work full-time in a few centers.[2] Typically, physicians consult on and review complex cases. Clinical social workers, mental health therapists, and substance abuse counselors provide most of the mental health services, although a few centers receive services from psychiatrists or clinical psychologists. Nurses and health aides provide clinical support; clerical staff perform administrative tasks.

Health Services

Most SBHCs provide basic comprehensive primary and preventive health and mental health services.[5] The services are convenient, confidential, affordable, and provided in a supportive environment. For students with an established medical home, the SBHC provides an additional access point for services, such as immunizations, health supervision, minor acute illness care, and management of stable chronic health conditions, in conjunction with the student's primary care physician. When the SBHC serves primarily as an access point, the SBHC and the primary care physician must establish clear mechanisms and protocols for consent for treatment and the exchange of clinical information. Under a state's minor treatment laws, independently operated SBHCs can serve "mature minors" for certain needs, such as emergency care, substance abuse treatment, or treatment of sexually transmitted diseases without parental consent.[6]

Primary Health Care

The majority of SBHCs (89%) offer minor acute illness care as well as prescriptions for medications.[2,7,8] Many offer comprehensive health assessments, anticipatory guidance, vision and hearing screening, and immunizations. In addition, more than 80% provide treatment of chronic health conditions, limited laboratory services, and medication administration. Approximately 50% screen for dental problems, but fewer than 15% provide either preventive or restorative dental services.[2] Pregnancy testing is offered in 90% of the SBHCs located in high schools and middle schools. More than 70% provide diagnosis of, counseling for, and treatment of sexually transmitted diseases, including human immunodeficiency virus infection. Two thirds offer reproductive health counseling, but only 25% provide female contraceptive devices on site, and only 30% offer condoms.[9]

> Increase the proportion of sexually active, unmarried adolescents aged 15 to 17 years who use contraception that both effectively prevents pregnancy and provides barrier protection against disease (*Healthy People 2010*, Objective 9-10).

Mental Health Services

Students are confronted with a wide range of psychosocial problems, and the importance of providing emotional and social support services as part of a comprehensive health program is increasingly recognized. Fortunately, the stigma often associated with mental health problems seems to be reduced when students have access to care through SBHCs.[7] In fact, emotional issues are the second most common reason students visit SBHCs. Most SBHCs (79%) provide crisis intervention, and 69% provide comprehensive mental health evaluation and treatment. A slight majority (57%) offer counseling for substance abuse. In addition, some (39%) offer assessment and treatment of learning problems.[10] Some SBHCs offer peer support groups and health counseling.

> Increase the number of persons seen in primary health care who receive mental health screening and assessment (*Healthy People 2010*, Objective 18-6).

Prevention and Intervention Services

One of the keys to SBHCs' effectiveness is the opportunity, seldom possible in other health care settings, to detect and address emotional and psychological issues that often are masked by routine medical complaints. School-based health centers routinely administer student health risk assessment questionnaires. The nurse practitioner or physician assistant uses the questionnaire to identify students at social or emotional risk and those engaging in risky health behaviors. Identified students are referred for mental health counseling and other risk-reduction activities available in the school or through community agencies. These expanded health education programs target high-risk behaviors, such as violence and premature or unsafe sexual practices.[11]

> Increase the proportion of persons appropriately counseled about health behaviors (*Healthy People 2010*, Objective 1-3).

Social Services

Some SBHCs also serve as the locus for a variety of human services programs that support families, including food distribution sites and employment assistance. The SBHCs often provide case management services to coordinate and integrate care to optimize resources, improve continuity of care, reduce fragmentation, prevent duplication, and maintain affordable services. In addition, they often serve as application centers for Medicaid and the State Children's Health Insurance Program (SCHIP).[12]

Administration

Day-to-day management of the SBHC frequently is shared between an off-site medical director (often a pediatrician) or administrator from the sponsoring medical institution and/or an on-site center coordinator.

Financing

Most SBHCs are supported by a combination of private and public health grants. Schools typically contribute space, security, janitorial services, and utilities. The median operating costs for an SBHC approach $125 000 annually, and funding is received from a variety of sources.[13,14] Private funding sources include foundations and third-party reimbursement through insurance. The bulk of funding, however, is from state and local human and social service funds, Maternal and Child Health Block Grants, and Medicaid. At the beginning of 2002, the federal Healthy Schools/Healthy Communities program supported 78 grantees that operate 158 SBHCs in the United States.[3]

Accountability

Most SBHCs are established through a contract or binding "memorandum of understanding" signed by the district and the various partners providing services through the center. The memorandum should clearly articulate the assignment of responsibilities and detail the type of services that can and cannot be offered at the center.

Privacy and Confidentiality

When the SBHC is operated by an outside agency, the SBHC is subject
to the Health Insurance Portability and Accountability Act (HIPAA)
of 1996. One part of this law requires uniform national standards for
how health information should be formatted, shared, and protected.
Another part of the law establishes national standards for protecting
the privacy of health information[15] (45 CFR Parts 160 and 164 RIN
0991-AB08). The privacy rules establish significant restrictions on
the use and release of medical records, describe privacy safeguard
standards that must be met, give individuals several important rights,
and provide for significant penalties for misuse of health information.
Information can be disclosed only with the parent's or individual's
consent (depending on age) and can be used only for treatment, payment, and health care operations. More information on regulations
related to HIPAA is available on the Office for Civil Rights Web site
at http://www.hhs.gov/ocr/hipaa/.

Physicians and staff at SBHCs or other community health care
professionals often are asked to send confidential information to the
school. Such requests must be accompanied by an informed consent
statement from parents giving permission to release the information
and also should indicate the status of the information once it becomes
part of the student's school health records. The request should specify
the particular information needed and why it is needed for educational purposes. Only the requested information should be sent to the
school, preferably to a school health care professional, even if it is
requested by a teacher or administrator. It is most helpful to send
either a summary or selected excerpts from medical records that
include the relevant physical, emotional, or psychological data needed
to promote learning or provide appropriate related services, not the
entire record. Once referral or treatment information is documented
in the school health record, or once confidential health information
is transferred from an independently run SBHC to the school, the

medical record is considered a school record that is covered under the Family Educational Rights and Privacy Act (FERPA). Under this act, all health records can be accessed by parents (see Chapter 2 for additional information).

Emerging Issues

Funding for SBHCs is always an issue. According to the US General Accounting Office, health care costs are expected to increase an average of 4.1% per year through 2007. At the same time, the US Census Bureau estimates that the number of children younger than 19 years will increase 2.2%. In addition, anticipated slowdowns in economic growth will affect states' willingness to fund public health services. Without dependable long-term support, SBHCs constantly are forced to piece together the necessary funds to operate. Unfortunately, such financial constraints hamper the ability of SBHCs to realize their potential to provide needed health services for students.[13,14]

Recommendations for Pediatricians

Pediatricians are essential partners in the design, implementation, and operation of SBHCs. Pediatricians can provide medical supervision, consultation, and treatment recommendations for complex cases. Perhaps most important, pediatricians can forge effective and successful links between the SBHC and the broader health care community. As advocates at federal, state, and local levels, pediatricians can:

- Help raise awareness about the unmet health care needs of children and youth and the potential for SBHCs to increase access to care;
- Advise about accountability systems and develop clinical practice guidelines;
- Provide on-site consultation and off-site backup for the SBHC;
- Develop protocols for allied health care professionals;
- Assist SBHC staff in managing complex cases;

- Encourage SBHCs to enroll students in Medicaid or other public health insurance programs; and
- Advocate for public and private health insurance reimbursement for SBHC services.

Resources

Detailed information on SBHCs, national trends and models, quality standards, how to develop an SBHC, and examples of state standards is available from the National Assembly on School Based Health Care at http://www.nasbhc.org and the Center for Health and Health Care in Schools at http://www.healthinschools.org. Additional help is available from the Bureau of Primary Health Care at http://bphc.hrsa.gov/.

References

1. Ku L. The number of Americans without health insurance rose in 2001 and continued to rise in 2002. *Int J Health Serv.* 2003;33:359–67
2. Schlitt J, Santelli J, Juszczak L, et al. *Creating Access to Care for Children and Youth: School-Based Health Center Census 1998–1999.* Washington, DC: National Assembly on School-Based Health Care; 2000
3. Bureau of Primary Health Care, Health Resources and Services Administration. Healthy Schools, Health Communities Program. Available at: http://bphc.hrsa.gov/HSHC/Default.htm. Accessed July 28, 2003
4. American Academy of Pediatrics, Committee on School Health. School health centers and other integrated school health services. *Pediatrics.* 2001;107:198–201
5. Santelli J, Morreale M, Wigton A, Grason H. School health centers and primary care for adolescents: a review of the literature. *J Adolesc Health.* 1996;18:357–366
6. Loxterman J. *A Guide to School-Based Health Centers. Volume V: Introduction to Legal Issues.* Washington, DC: Advocates for Youth; 1996
7. Anglin TM, Naylor KE, Kaplan DW. Comprehensive school-based health care: high school students' use of medical, mental health, and substance abuse services. *Pediatrics.* 1996;97:318–330
8. Kaplan D, Calonge B, Guernsey BP, Hanrahan MB. Managed care and school-based health centers. Use of services. *Arch Pediatr Adolesc Med.* 1998;152:25–33

9. Fothergill K, Feijoo A. Family planning services at school-based health centers: findings from ad national survey. *J Adolesc Health.* 2000;27: 166–169

10. Kaplan DW, Brindis C, Naylor KE, Phibbs SL, Ahlstrand KR, Melinkovich P. Elementary school-based health center use. *Pediatrics.* 1998;101(6). Available at: http://www.pediatrics.org/cgi/content/full/101/6/e12

11. Dryfoos JG. *Full-Service Schools: A Revolution in Health and Social Services for Children, Youth, and Families.* San Francisco, CA: Jossey-Bass, 1994

12. Council of Chief State School Officers. *Building Bridges to Healthy Kids and Better Students: School-based Outreach and Enrollment for the State Children's Health Insurance Program and Medicaid.* Washington, DC: Council of Chief State School Officers; 2001

13. Schlitt J. *Critical Issues in School-based Health Care Financing.* Washington, DC: National Assembly on School-Based Health Care; 1999

14. Morone JA, Kilberth EH, Langwell KM. Back to school: a health care strategy for youth. *Health Aff (Millwood).* 2001;20:122–136

16. Park E, Ku L, Broaddus M. OMB estimates indicate that 900,000 children will lose health insurance due to reductions in federal SCHIP funding. *Int J Health Serv.* 2003;33:369–81

17. More pediatricians participating in Medicaid: AAP survey results. *AAP News.* 2000;17:115

15. Bergren MD. HIPAA hoopla: privacy and security of identifiable health information. *J Sch Nurs.* 2001;17:336–340

Chapter 7
Nutrition, Dietary Practices, and School Food Service Programs

The link between good nutrition and good education is clearly demonstrated by higher test scores, better attendance, and fewer behavior problems in school.
B. Dan Glickman, Secretary, US Department of Agriculture

From the moment of conception, inadequate nutrition threatens the behavioral and cognitive development of young children.[1] Calories consumed are first used for the maintenance of the body, second for growth, and third for cognitive development. The link between nutrition and cognitive development in children[2] is based on compelling research that undernutrition during any period of childhood, even in its milder forms, can have detrimental effects on cognitive development and later productivity. In ways not previously known, undernutrition affects the behavior of students, their school performance, and their overall cognitive development. These findings are extremely sobering in light of the existence of hunger among millions of American children.[3]

One of the US Department of Education's national education goals is that children will come to school ready to learn.[4] Yet, it is estimated that more than 3 million students attend school each day without having eaten breakfast.[5] Many more consume an inadequate one. Children who attend school hungry have diminished attention spans and are unable to perform tasks as well as their nourished peers. In these cases, the full value of the education provided is lost.[2] Teachers increasingly complain of numerous nutrition-related concerns: short attention span, disruptive classroom behavior, irritability, hyperactivity, and below-grade-level proficiency skills.[4]

Unfortunately, the scientific literature on the connection between nutrition and achievement is not widely disseminated in the educational community or the medical profession. To redress this, the American Academy of Pediatrics collaborated with the American Dietetic Association, US Department of Agriculture, American Academy of Family Physicians, National Hispanic Medical Association, and National Medical Association to develop a program titled Promoting Healthy Eating Behaviors: The Role of the School Environment.[5] Included in the program are the following recommendations, titled "Prescription for Change: Ten Keys to Promote Healthy Eating in Schools," which schools can use to evaluate their current nutrition environment.

- Students, parents, educators, and community leaders will be involved in assessing the school's eating environment, developing a shared vision and an action plan to achieve it.
- Adequate funds will be provided by local, state, and federal sources to ensure that the entire school environment supports the development of healthy eating patterns.
- Behavior-focused nutrition education will be integrated into the curriculum from pre-K through grade 12. Staff who provide nutrition education will have appropriate training.
- All students will have designated lunch periods of sufficient length to enjoy eating healthy foods with friends. These lunch periods will be scheduled as near the middle of the school day as possible.
- Schools will provide enough serving areas to ensure student access to school meals with a minimum of wait time.
- Space that is adequate to accommodate all students and pleasant surroundings that reflect the value of social aspects of eating will be provided.
- Students, teachers, and community volunteers who practice healthy eating will be encouraged to serve as role models in the school dining areas.

- If foods are sold in addition to National School Lunch Program meals, they will be from the 5 major food groups of the Food Guide Pyramid. This practice will foster healthy eating patterns.
- Decisions regarding the sale of foods in addition to the National School Lunch Program meals will be based on nutrition goals, not on profit making.

Nutritional Problems Facing American Students
Problems of Deficiency
Iron

One of the most striking examples of the interaction of health and educational progress is iron deficiency anemia. Iron deficiency, with or without manifest anemia, is associated with fatigue, shortened attention span, delayed psychomotor development, and irritability during the first years of life; these are problems that, if untreated, can extend into school age.[6,7] Deficiency occurring in the preschool-aged child might result in poor performance on developmental and memory tests.[8] In the school-aged child, educational achievement, especially in reading, vocabulary, and memorization, often is jeopardized by low iron status if it is left untreated for a long interval.[9] Investigation of and treatment for iron deficiency are crucial roles of pediatricians in promoting students' academic success.

> Increase the proportion of persons aged 2 years and older who meet dietary recommendations for calcium (*Healthy People 2010*, Objective 19-11).

Calcium

Peak bone mass is achieved by the age of 20 years, and nearly 90% of bone density is accrued by 17 years of age.[10,11] There are 10 million cases of osteoporosis in the United States, contributing to 1.5 million fractures per year.[10] Nutrition experts estimate that if the current trends in calcium consumption continue until 2030, there might be 40 million cases of osteoporosis. Nutrition education and exposure to calcium-rich foods are important to help students identify various sources of calcium. Although dairy products are an excellent source of calcium, intake of dairy products has decreased 40% during the past 20 years.[12] One of the factors cited for this decline is the 300% increase in the consumption of carbonated beverages.[12] Jacobson[13] and the Center for Science in the Public Interest noted that this liquid candy is dispensed in more than 2.8 million vending machines, some of them in schools. Males 12 to 19 years of age average 868 cans per year, or more than 2 cans per day or 9% of their total daily calories; for girls, such intake represents 8%.[14]

Reading food labels and deciphering their meanings should be included in the district's nutrition curriculum.[15] For example, some fruit drink choices are better than others. Several brands are fortified with vitamins A and C, and some have added calcium. However, many fruit drinks are little better than carbonated beverages. In many, the primary ingredient is high-fructose corn syrup, with actual fruit juice accounting for no more than 10% of the content. Pediatricians can encourage districts to establish policies that limit access to carbonated beverages and promote consumption of calcium-rich foods and beverages.

Problems of Nutritional Excess
Dental Disease

Dental caries is the most common chronic disease among children,[16] and dietary practices are a significant contributing factor. Untreated dental caries results in pain and infection, leading to missed school days and loss of teeth. The infectious agents that contribute to dental caries also can affect the gums, resulting in gingivitis. Counseling students about the role of diet in oral health is twofold. Students should obtain recommended amounts of calcium, vitamin D, and vitamin C. On the other hand, carbohydrates, which should constitute at least half of a person's daily energy source, also are the preferred food for mutant streptococci. It is not realistic to eliminate sugars from the diet or school menus, but students should limit the frequency and duration of exposure to simple sugars. Frequent between-meal snacking of foods high in simple sugars or that stay in the mouth for longer periods, such as suckers, should be discouraged. Healthful snack choices should be available at school.

> Reduce the proportion of children and adolescents who have dental caries experience in their primary or permanent teeth (*Healthy People 2010*, Objective 21-1) and reduce the proportion of children, adolescents, and adults with untreated dental decay (*Healthy People 2010*, Objective 21-2).

Obesity

Obesity has reached epidemic proportions among US youth[17]; the proportion of obese youth has doubled in 25 years.[18] This is a serious concern because of obesity's link with heart disease, hypertension, and insulin-resistant diabetes.[19] More than 1 in 4 students are overweight. Studies of concordant twins and certain racial groups, especially black and Hispanic individuals, confirm that genetics predispose some people to obesity, but this does not explain the dramatic increase.[20] A significant decline in the daily expenditure of calories is a likely contributing factor as daily participation in physical education classes decreased from 42% in 1991 to 27% in 1997.[4,21]

Obese students sometimes are viewed more negatively than students with physical disabilities or students without a weight problem. Physicians can collaborate with school counselors, psychologists, and mental health professionals to identify and manage problems, such as low self-esteem, social isolation, and poor relations with or rejection by peers. Conversely, children with psychological, behavioral, and learning problems are at risk of obesity.[22] Intervention goals should include increased physical activity, weight management plans that do not place the student at risk of nutritional and caloric insufficiency, and nutrition education.

Physicians and school health care staff can work together to prevent and treat obesity and minimize secondary medical conditions and the social and emotional issues that often accompany the condition. Asking young students to count calories is not a useful strategy. Family support and positive modeling by teachers and influential adults, however, are helpful strategies.

Problems Linked With Dietary Practices

The Food Guide Pyramid (Fig 7.1) is intended to help people achieve a diet with 30% of calories from fat (no more than 10% from saturated fats), increased intake of complex carbohydrates, fruits and vegetables, and sufficient calcium intake. Only 1 child in 100 fulfills the daily recommendations.[23]

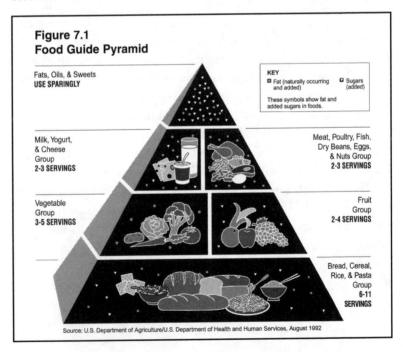

Figure 7.1
Food Guide Pyramid

Fats, Oils, & Sweets
USE SPARINGLY

KEY
▧ Fat (naturally occurring and added)   ▣ Sugars (added)
These symbols show fat and added sugars in foods.

Milk, Yogurt, & Cheese Group
2-3 SERVINGS

Meat, Poultry, Fish, Dry Beans, Eggs, & Nuts Group
2-3 SERVINGS

Vegetable Group
3-5 SERVINGS

Fruit Group
2-4 SERVINGS

Bread, Cereal, Rice, & Pasta Group
6-11 SERVINGS

Source: U.S. Department of Agriculture/U.S. Department of Health and Human Services, August 1992

Fruit and Vegetable Consumption

The Food Guide Pyramid recommends daily consumption of 2 servings of fruit and 3 servings of vegetables ("five a day"). Only 3% of Americans older than 2 years consume more than 3 servings per day of fruits or vegetables. Even multicomponent interventions that are successful in changing eating behaviors struggle to influence vegetable intake, especially among boys.[24] Of adolescents surveyed in 1999, fewer than half ate a cooked vegetable and fewer than one third ate salad on the day before the survey, but nearly two thirds ate French fries or potato chips.[25] Without potatoes, few students would consume vegetables at all, but the dominance of potatoes diminishes the likelihood of introducing variety and balance into their diets. Pediatricians can work with families and school food service staff to provide foods that meet the dietary guidelines and are acceptable to students.

Vegetarian Diets

There are many types of vegetarian diets that vary in their strictness regarding consumption of nonanimal foods. The American Dietetic Association has stated that vegetarian diets are healthful and nutritionally adequate when appropriately planned. Both vegetarian and nonvegetarian diets have the potential to be beneficial or detrimental to health.[26] However, because vegetarianism requires considerable nutrition information and careful meal planning, there is concern about young children or adolescents meeting their own dietary needs through a vegetarian diet. The more restrictive the diet, the more highly educated and skilled the individual must be to meet nutrient needs. The vegan diet, for example, restricts dairy, meat, eggs, seafood, and poultry, making it challenging for vegans to obtain sufficient daily energy (calories), protein, vitamin B12, vitamin D, calcium, and zinc. The school food service can offer meat-free alternative entrees for students who choose a vegetarian diet for personal, religious, or cultural reasons.

Weight Management Practices

Almost half of American students in grades 1 through 3 indicate that they wish to be thinner.[27] Of children older than 10 years, 80% are afraid of becoming fat. Adolescents are easily influenced by media and advertising hype. Fruitarian diets, macrobiotic diets, juice-based diets, and, most recently, a carbohydrate-restricted, protein-based (ketogenic) diet have all had excessive media exposure. Some diets are harmless and some are dangerous, but dieting can become a trap. One third of dieters develop pathologic dieting behaviors, and one quarter of that group displays characteristics of an eating disorder. All adults involved with schools—parents, teachers, coaches, nurses, and physicians—need to reinforce the concept that weight control can be achieved only in the long-term with a reasonable blend of moderate daily intake and physical activity. The most powerful influence is modeling of reasonable behavior by adults.

Nutrition Education

Pediatricians can encourage districts to implement nutrition education programs that help students adopt eating practices that promote health and reduce disease risk. Students who receive more lessons on nutrition have more positive behavioral changes than students who have fewer lessons.[28] Establishing stable and positive eating behaviors requires adequate time and exposure to developmentally appropriate information and skills from preschool through secondary school. In addition, the context in which students learn about healthy eating behaviors and the feelings they associate with healthful foods are key factors in determining their receptivity to nutrition education. Students are more likely to adopt healthy eating behaviors when:

- They learn about these behaviors through fun, participatory activities rather than through lectures;
- Lessons emphasize the positive, appealing aspects of healthful eating rather than the negative consequences of unhealthful eating;

- The benefits of healthy eating behaviors are presented in the context of what is already important to the students; and
- The students have repeated opportunities to taste foods during their lessons.[29]

The US Dietary Guidelines

The US Dietary Guidelines are designed to help individuals choose foods that meet their nutritional needs, promote health, support active lifestyles, and serve as the central theme throughout a district's nutrition education program:

- Aim for fitness
    - Aim for a healthy weight.
    - Be physically active each day.
- Build a healthy base
    - Use the Food Guide Pyramid to guide food choices.
    - Choose a variety of grains daily, especially whole grains.
    - Choose a variety of fruits and vegetables daily.
    - Keep food safe to eat.
- Choose sensibly
    - Choose a diet that is low in saturated fat and cholesterol and moderate in total fat.
    - Choose beverages and foods that limit intake of sugars.
    - Choose and prepare foods with less salt.

School Food Service Programs
The National School Lunch Program

In 1933, in the midst of the Great Depression, the US Secretary of Agriculture was directed by Congress to distribute surplus agricultural commodities to schools. Distribution steadily increased until shortly before World War II, when 450 million pounds of food were given to 5.3 million children in 78 000 schools. After the war, the National School Lunch Act of 1946 distributed commodities as part of an effort to address child hunger. In the 1950s, the Special Milk Program provided free milk to students who were eligible for free lunch. The Child Nutrition Act of 1966 was intended to strengthen and expand food service programs for students and distribute agricultural commodities, equipment, and nonfood assistance. It also created the school breakfast program.[30] Today, students from families with incomes at or below 130% of the poverty level receive meals free, while those between 130% and 185% of the poverty level pay a reduced price. Uniform national guidelines, which are available from the USDA Web site, are issued yearly to determine eligibility for free or reduced-price meals. The National School Lunch Program reimburses school districts based on the number of full-price, reduced-price, and free meals served. This income provides the financial base for districts' food service programs.

School Breakfast Program

The School Breakfast Program also is administered by the USDA. One fourth or more of the Recommended Dietary Allowances (RDAs) are provided through funding in breakfast programs in schools and residential child care settings. During the 1999-2000 school year, 7.6 million children participated, 84% at reduced price or no cost.[31] Currently, 75% of all schools participate in the program.[30]

For both the National School Lunch Program and School Breakfast Program, food service staff develop the district's menu on the basis of available commodities from the USDA and purchases from local vendors. The National School Lunch Program permits food service staff to chose from 4 menu patterns: traditional, enhanced, NuMenus, and NuMenus Assist. The former 2 are based on food group components— meat/meat alternative, vegetable/fruit, grains/bread, and milk—served in specific amounts on the basis of age, grade, and food group. The enhanced format has additional guidelines to improve balance. NuMenus and NuMenus Assist are planned and analyzed using nutrient standards on the basis of age and grade. The meal must include a minimum of 3 items classified as entrée, side dishes, and milk. The menu must meet appropriate caloric, fat (<30%), and saturated fat (<10%) guidelines and minimums for protein, iron, and vitamins A and C. Although the commodities offer reasonable quality at minimal costs, they are not sufficient to supply all nutrient needs. Consequently, the food service program must purchase other items, especially foods such as fresh fruits and vegetables, in bulk. Most costly are brand-name foods, such as pizza from local vendors.

Food Service Vendors

School food service finances are complex and vary between school districts, but in every district, financial decisions strongly influence the foods offered. Many districts contract for some or all of their food services to save money and cut administrative and personnel costs. Such contracts offer the convenience of a single full-service vendor and a single payment. These arrangements are permitted under the National School Lunch Program, provided that the vendor adheres to the same nutritional standards as the school food service. Contracts with full-service vendors can be customized to the district, permitting control of many facets of service, including menu creation. For vendors that provide a single item, such as brand-name pizza, the school food service must incorporate that item into the weekly menu, maintaining the same dietary standards that pertain to daily operations.

Special Issues and Concerns
Food Allergies

An estimated 2 million school-aged children have potentially life-threatening food allergies. In children, most allergic reactions involve peanuts, tree nuts, eggs, milk, soy, and wheat. The risk of accidental exposure to foods can be reduced in the school setting if physicians work with students, families, and school staff to minimize risks and provide a safe educational environment for students with food allergies. Recently developed guidelines suggest that the pediatrician can encourage families to do the following[32]:

- Notify the school of the student's allergies.
- Work with the school team to develop a plan that accommodates the student's needs throughout the school, including in the classroom, in the cafeteria, in after-care programs, during school-sponsored activities, and on the school bus, as well as a food allergy action plan.
- Provide written medical documentation, instructions, and medications as prescribed by a physician as well as a photo of the child on a written form.
- Replace medications after use or when the medication or prescription is outdated.
- Educate the student in the self-management of the food allergy, including the following:
  - Safe and unsafe foods and the risks of sharing lunches
  - Strategies for avoiding exposure to unsafe foods
  - Identification of symptoms of allergic reactions
  - How and when to tell an adult the student may be having an allergy-related problem
  - How to read food labels (age-appropriate instruction)
- Review policies and procedures with the school staff, the physician, and the child (if age is appropriate) after a reaction has occurred. Pediatricians also can educate school nurses and other staff about applicable federal laws including the Americans With Disabilities Act, Individuals with Disabilities Education Act, Section 504 (of the Rehabilitation Act of 1973), and the Family Educational Rights and Privacy Act of 1974 and any state laws or district policies that apply. In turn, school nurses should:
  - Review the health records submitted by parents and physicians.
  - Ensure that students with food allergies are not excluded from school activities based solely on the food allergy.

- Identify a multidisciplinary team to work with students and their families to establish a food allergy management plan that includes prevention.
- Ensure that all staff understand food allergy, can recognize symptoms, and know what to do in an emergency, and work with other school staff to eliminate the use of potential food allergens in students' meals, educational tools, arts and crafts projects, or incentive rewards.
- Implement food allergy action plans before an allergic reaction occurs to ensure the efficiency and effectiveness of the plans.
- Store medications appropriately and ensure that an emergency kit is available that contains a physician's standing order for epinephrine. Keep medications easily accessible in a secure location central to designated school personnel.
- Designate and train school personnel to administer medications during the school day regardless of time or location in accordance with the state nursing and Good Samaritan laws governing the administration of emergency medications.
- Review policies and the prevention plan with team members, the student, and the family after a reaction has occurred.
- Work with the district transportation administrator to ensure that all school buses have communication devices in case of an emergency and that drivers have training in symptom identification and emergency procedures.
- Recommend a no-eating policy on school buses with exceptions made only to accommodate special needs under pertinent laws or school district policy.
- Discuss field trips with the families of children with food allergies to determine appropriate strategies for managing the food allergy.
- Follow federal, state, and district laws and regulations regarding sharing medical information about the student.
- Take threats or harassment against a child with allergies seriously.

More detailed suggestions for implementing these objectives and creating a specific plan for each student to address his or her particular needs are available in the Food Allergy & Anaphylaxis Network's School Food Allergy Program (http://www.foodallergy.org/school.html). The School Food Allergy Program has been endorsed or supported by the Anaphylaxis Committee of the American Academy of Allergy, Asthma, and Immunology; the National Association of School Nurses; and the Executive Committee of the Section on Allergy and Immunology of the American Academy of Pediatrics. The Food Allergy & Anaphylaxis Network can be reached at 800/929-4040 or http://www.foodallergy.org.

Competitive Foods

Competitive foods are foods or drinks served on school grounds that are not part of the meals served by the school food service. Although regulations state that the school lunch program must provide meals consistent with the Dietary Guidelines for Americans, the same is not true for competitive foods. The only prohibition for this food category is the prohibition of sales in the cafeteria during school lunch hours.[33] Competitive foods are available in vending machines, in á la cart lines, in school stores and snack bars, and in other venues that are popular in high schools. Generally, the drinks and foods offered lack the ingredients that permit students to make healthful selections.[33] Carbonated soft drinks, certain candies, gum, and water ices fall into a category called foods of minimal nutritional value, meaning that they contain less than 5% of the RDA of protein, vitamin A or C, niacin, riboflavin, thiamin, calcium, or iron. Competitive offerings dilute the impact of the school food service and decrease students' interest in nutritious foods.

Pediatricians can work with the district food service director to eliminate foods of minimal nutritional value, as has been done in West Virginia, or increase the price of these foods and use the funds to subsidize the purchase of more healthful food selections through the food service program. Such pricing strategies also can shift behavioral patterns away from foods of minimal nutritional value.

Emerging Issues
The Commercialization of School Food Programs

In an era of shrinking resources, many enterprising school administrators have turned to corporate sponsorships as a means of increasing resources. In exchange for money, districts permit exclusive rights to food and beverage companies to distribute their products, set up vending machines, and advertise on book jackets and posters. In many cases, these vendors compete directly with the nonprofit school food service program for student lunch money. This situation highlights several areas in which school policy is critical.

Recommendations for Pediatricians

District food service programs are becoming increasingly complex, requiring clear and comprehensive policies.[34,35] Food service policies should complement other district policies that promote healthful eating through both classroom instruction and a supportive school environment. The challenge for many districts is to remain financially stable while offering acceptable and nutritious foods to students and staff. Besides identifying and treating nutrition-related illnesses that limit attendance and academic performance, the pediatrician also can educate students and their families about the role of nutrition in health and illness and raise the district's awareness of the important work of the school food service. As members of district or school health advisory councils, pediatricians can develop policies that encourage districts to implement effective nutrition education and food service programming that helps students stay healthy, fit, and ready to learn. For example:

• Clearly state in the district's nutrition policy the purpose and intent of all nutritional offerings provided by the district.

- Educate district staff, parents, and youth that good nutrition promotes healthy growth, development, and academic achievement.
- Include in policies the mission and mandate of the district's food service program to serve all students.
- Recommend that district guidelines and regulations acknowledge the *Healthy People 2010* objectives in addition to federal and state regulations.
- Suggest that the school food service director, not the business manager, be designated as the individual responsible for contracting with commercial food vendors.
- Provide a rationale for permitting or not permitting students to leave campus during meal periods.
- Define where, when, and how many vending machines can be placed in school buildings and what can be sold.
- Require that breakfast and lunch programs offer a variety of foods low in fat, sodium, and added sugars and high in vitamins, minerals, and fiber.
- Develop policies that provide a helpful framework for the school food service program to meet accepted dietary guidelines and remain financially sound.
- Create curriculum development criteria that ensure that nutrition education is developmentally appropriate, culturally relevant, fun, and participatory and involves social learning strategies.[28]
- Participate in training for school staff.
- Ensure that nutrition programming links nutrition education in the classroom, opportunities to practice healthful eating in the cafeteria, and lifetime fitness opportunities with timely access to school health care and mental health professionals.
- Encourage family and community involvement that supports and reinforces nutrition education and participation in school food programs.

• Support program evaluation that determines the effectiveness of
the educational and service components in promoting healthful
eating and suggest how the program can be changed to increase
effectiveness.

Resources

American Dairy Association:
  http://www.adadcmideast.com/
American Dietetic Association:
  http://www.eatright.org
American Food Service Association:
  http://www.asfsa.org
Centers for Disease Control and Prevention:
  http://www.cdc.gov/health/nutrition.htm
CNN (Cable News Network):
  http://www.cnn.com/health
Dietsite:
  http://www.dietsite.com
Medicine and Science in Sports and Exercise:
  http://www.ms-se.com
National Association of State Boards of Education
  http://www.nasbe.org
National Eating Disorders Association:
  http://www.edap.org
National Institute of Child Health and Development:
  http://www.nichd.nih.gov
National Institutes of Health:
  http://health.nih.gov/search.asp?category_id=29
Nutrition for Kids:
  http://www.nutritionforkids.com
Team Nutrition:
  http://www.fns.usda.gov/tn

Tufts Nutrition Navigator:
   http://www.navigator.tufts.edu
USDA Food and nutrition service:
   http://www.fns.usda.gov/fncs/
Vegetarian Resource Group:
   http://www.vrg.org
Weight Control Information Network:
   http://www.niddk.nih.gov/health/nutrit/win.htm
What We Eat in America:
   http://www.barc.usda.gov/bhnrc/foodsurvey

Text Resources

American Academy of Pediatrics. *Guide to Your Child's Allergies and Asthma.* Welch MJ, ed. Elk Grove Village, IL: American Academy of Pediatrics; 2000

American Academy of Pediatrics. *Guide to your Child's Nutrition.* Dietz WH, Stern L, eds. Elk Grove Village, IL: American Academy of Pediatrics; 1999

Bogden JF. *Fit, Healthy, and Ready to Learn: A School Health Policy Guide. Part I: Physical Activity, Healthy Eating, and Tobacco Use Prevention.* Alexandria, VA: National Association of State Boards of Education; 2000. Available at: http://www.nasbe.org. Accessed January 29, 2003.

References

1. Center on Hunger, Poverty, and Nutrition Policy. Nutrition-Cognition National Advisory Committee. *Statement on the Link Between Nutrition and Cognitive Development in Children.* Medford, MA: Tufts University; 1993
2. Troccoli KB. *Eat to Learn, Learn to Eat: the Link Between Nutrition and Learning in Children.* Washington, DC: National Health Education Consortium; 1993

3. Marx E, Wooley SF, Northrop D, eds. *Health is Academic: A Guide to Coordinated School Health Programs.* New York, NY: Teacher's College Press; 1998

4. Siega-Riz AM, Popkin BM, Carson T. Trends in breakfast consumption for children in the United States from 1965–1991. *Am J Clin Nutr.* 1998;67(suppl):748S–756S

5. *Call to Action. Healthy School Nutrition Environments: Promoting Healthy Eating Behaviors.* Washington, DC: US Department of Agriculture; 1999. Available at: http://www.fns.usda.gov/tn/Healthy/calltoaction.html. Accessed July 28, 2003

6. Walter T. Impact of iron deficiency on cognition in infancy and childhood. *Eur J Clin Nutr.* 1993;47:307–316

7. Lozoff B, Jimenez E, Wolf AW. Long-term developmental outcome of infants with iron deficiency. *N Engl J Med.* 1991;325:687–694

8. Pollitt E, Saco-Pollitt S, Leibel Rl, Viteri FE. Iron deficiency and behavioral development in infants and preschool children. *Am J Clin Nutr.* 1986;43:555–565

9. Soemantri AG, Pollitt E, Kim I. Iron deficiency anemia and educational achievement. *Am J Clin Nutr.* 1985;42:1221–1228

10. Golden NH. Osteoporosis prevention: a pediatric challenge. *Arch Pediatr Adolesc Med.* 2000;154:542–543

11. Bonjour JP, Theintz G, Buchs B, Slosman D, Rizzoli R. Critical years and stages of puberty for spinal and femoral bone mass accumulation during adolescence. *J Clin Endocrinol Metab.* 1991;7:555–563

12. Calvadini C, Siega-Riz AM, Popkin BM. US adolescent food intake trends from 1965 to 1996. *Arch Dis Child.* 2000;83:18–24

13. Jacobson MF. *Liquid Candy: How Soft Drinks Are Harming America's Health.* Washington, DC: Center for Science in the Public Interest; 1998

14. Harnack L, Stang J, Story M. Soft drink consumption among US children and adolescents: nutritional consequences. *J Am Diet Assoc.* 1999;99:436–441

15. American Academy of Pediatrics, Committee on Nutrition. The use and misuse of fruit juice in pediatrics. *Pediatrics.* 2001;107:1210–1213

16. Edelstein BL, Douglass CW. Dispelling the myth that 50 percent of US school children have never had a cavity. *Public Health Rep.* 1995;110:522–530

17. Centers for Disease Control and Prevention. Update: prevalence of overweight among children, adolescents, and adults—United States, 1988–1994. *MMWR Morb Mortal Wkly Rep.* 1997:46:198–202

18. Must A, Spadano J, Coakley EH, Field AE, Colditz G, Dietz WH. The disease burden associated with overweight and obesity. *JAMA*. 1999;282:1523–1529

19. Dietz WH. Health consequences of obesity in youth: childhood predictors of adult disease. *Pediatrics*. 1998;101:518–525

20. Mokdad AH, Serdula MK, Dietz WH, Bowman BA, Marks JS, Koplan JP. The spread of the obesity epidemic in the United States, 1991–1998. *JAMA*. 1999;282:1519–1522

21. American Academy of Pediatrics, Committee on Sports Medicine and Fitness and Committee on School Health. Physical fitness and activity in schools. *Pediatrics*. 2000;105:1156–1157

22. Mellbin T, Vuille JC. Further evidence of an association between psychological problems and increase in relative weight between 7 and 10 years of age. *Acta Paediatr Scand*. 1989;78:576–580

23. Munoz KA, Krebs-Smith SM, Ballard-Barbash R, Cleveland LE. Food intakes of children and adolescents compared with recommendations. *Pediatrics*. 1997;100:323–329

24. Perry CL, Bishop DB, Taylor G, et al. Changing fruit and vegetable consumption among children: the 5-a-Day Power Plus Program in St. Paul, Minnesota. *Am J Public Health*. 1998;88:603–609

25. Centers for Disease Control and Prevention. Youth risk behavior surveillance—United States, 1999. *MMWR CDC Surveill Summ*. 2000;49(SS-05):1–96

26. American Dietetic Association Web site. Available at: http://www.eatright.org. Accessed July 28, 2003

27. Eating Disorder Awareness and Prevention Web site. Available at: http://www.edap.org. Accessed July 28, 2003

28. Devine CM, Olson CM, Frongillo EA Jr. Impact of the Nutrition for Life program on junior high students in New York State. *J Sch Health*. 1992;62:381–385

29. Centers for Disease Control and Prevention. Guidelines for school health programs to promote lifelong healthy eating. *MMWR Recomm Rep*. 1996;45(RR-9):1–33

30. US Department of Agriculture, Food and Nutrition Service Web site. Available at: http://www.fns.usda.gov/fns/. Accessed July 28, 2003

31. Food Research and Action Center. School Breakfast Scorecard. Washington, DC: Food Research and Action Center; 2000. Available at: http://www.frac.org/html/publications/pubs.html. Accessed July 28, 2003

32. American Academy of Pediatrics. *Guide to Your Child's Allergies and Asthma.* Welch MJ, ed. Elk Grove Village, IL: American Academy of Pediatrics; 2000.

33. National Association of State Boards of Education. *Fit, Healthy, and Ready to Learn: A School Health Policy Guide.* Alexandria, VA: National Association of State Boards of Education; 2000

34. Story M, Hayes M, Kalina B. Availability of foods in high schools: is there a cause for concern? *J Am Diet Assoc.* 1996;96:123–126

35. Griffith P, Sackin B, Bierbauer D. *School Meals: Benefits and Challenges.* Alexandria, VA: American School Food Service Association; 2000

Chapter 8
Physical Education, Physical Activity, and School Sports

Exercise and recreation are as necessary as reading. I will rather say more necessary, because health is worth more than learning.
Thomas Jefferson

Rates of coronary artery disease, cancer, hypertension, obesity, and type 2 diabetes mellitus are increasing in the United States. These serious health problems have roots in our population's sedentary lifestyle.[1,2] Exercise, in conjunction with other interventions, has been shown to successfully manage these and other chronic diseases in adults.[3] For example, regular activity is associated with high bone mineral mass, low levels of body fat, stabilized blood glucose levels, and low levels of tobacco and alcohol use.[1]

Adult habits of regular physical activity are established in childhood, and schools can have a critical role in providing opportunities for physical activity and helping establish regular habits of daily exercise. A primary goal of physical education (PE) programs is to promote a physically active lifestyle that can persist for a lifetime.[4-6] Unfortunately, fewer than 8% of US schools provide daily PE or its equivalent.[7] This is in part because of intense public pressure on educators to focus on literacy, competency in math and science, and short-term educational objectives. Consequently, pediatricians and others who want to promote health through the school will have to adopt messages that pertain closely to schools' teaching mission.

Promoting Physical Activity Programs to Educators and Administrators

A number of beneficial academic outcomes are associated with regular physical activity. Regular physical activity during the school day promotes cognitive function through improvement in general circulation and increased blood flow to the brain. Significant differences in academic performance have been demonstrated for students who participate in aerobic activity during the school day, and this difference is most pronounced for low-achieving students.[8] In addition, physical activity raises levels of norepinephrine and endorphins, resulting in stress reduction, an antidepressant effect, and a calming effect after exercise.[9,10] Such effects may improve students' ability to concentrate and learn.

There are also a variety of social benefits. Team activities provide students with opportunities to socialize and to learn to cooperate, share, and abide by rules of appropriate social interaction. Individual activities permit students to discover and test their physical abilities. Such positive effects have been found across the entire age spectrum from kindergarten through high school. When given an opportunity, most students elect to participate in various school physical activities, because they want to be with friends and learn new skills. The social benefits of PE and after-school physical activity help students feel connected to their school and community, two factors shown to reduce high-risk behaviors. Physically active adolescents are less likely to drop out of school, attempt suicide, adopt risk-taking behaviors, or become pregnant.[11,12]

Opportunities for PE at School
Free Play and the Role of Recess

In the early 20th century, many youth participated in physical activities that were generally spontaneous, unstructured, and without adult involvement. Today, some neighborhoods are unsafe, and the schedules of working families are such that there is little time for free play. School recess is one of the few remaining opportunities for students to engage in free play. For preschool and elementary students, free play can positively affect self-esteem and support language development,[13] although unstructured recess periods during the school day require adult supervision. Playground equipment frequently is used improperly, and aggressive behaviors can be a factor. More injuries and bullying occur during recess, particularly for boys, than during participation in structured activities.[14,15] As important as recess is to student development, it is not a substitute for physical education and other structured opportunities for physical activity.

> Increase the proportion of adolescents who participate in daily school physical education (*Healthy People 2010*, Objective 22-9).

> Increase the proportion of the nation's public and private schools that require daily physical education for all students (*Healthy People 2010*, Objective 22-8).

Physical Education Programs
The American Academy of Pediatrics (AAP),[3] the Centers for Disease Control and Prevention, and the Council for Physical Education for children[16,17] recommend that schools adopt specific characteristics that make physical education programs effective.

> **Recommendations for PE Programs in Schools (modified and adapted from the AAP statement[8])**
> - Promote enjoyable, lifelong physical activity.
>   - Develop students' knowledge, attitudes, motor skills, behavioral skills, and confidence.
>   - Require comprehensive, daily PE programs from kindergarten through grade 12.

(continued on page 170)

Recommendations for PE Programs in Schools (modified and adapted from the AAP statement[8]), *continued*

- – Coordinate PE with health education and life science at each grade.
- – Employ appropriately trained PE teachers for PE classes.
- – Educate all members of the school community about the benefits of physical activity and encourage them to participate.
- – Offer a variety of activities for students and staff.
- – Provide opportunities for students and families to participate in physical activities together.
- – Accommodate the needs and interests of all students, including those with illness, injury, disability, obesity, sedentary lifestyles, and disinterest in team or competitive sports.
- Provide a safe, supportive environment for a variety of physical activities. Offer staff development on injury prevention, first aid, and equipment and facilities maintenance. Require appropriate use of protective equipment.
- Commit to adequate resources, including program funding, personnel, safe equipment, and facilities.
- Regularly evaluate the district's physical activity programs, including classroom instruction, the nature and level of student activity, and the adequacy and safety of athletic facilities.
- Establish complementary relationships with community recreation agencies and youth sports programs. Encourage student and family participation in these extracurricular programs.

Goal and Structure of Physical Education Programs

The goal of physical education programs is to expose students to all components necessary for a lifetime of continued physical activity. Such programs build and strengthen psychomotor, cognitive, affective, safety, and motor skills. Motor skills include muscle strength and endurance, flexibility, coordination, and cardiac strength and endurance. Physical education programs that actively engage students in a variety of enjoyable individual and group experiences that result in increased competency will improve the chances that students will adopt lifelong habits of physical activity.[3]

The National Association for Sport and Physical Education has identified national standards for physical education that form the structure of a sound, sequential curriculum that builds students' knowledge and skills from year to year in developmentally appropriate ways. Teaching or expecting skills to develop before students are developmentally ready is more likely to cause frustration than long-term success.[18,19]

Safety accommodations for younger students include smaller playing fields, shorter contest times, pitch counts for pitchers, softer balls, and adjusting play for extreme climatic conditions.[15] Most preschool students have short attention spans and are easily distracted; therefore, exercise sessions should be short and emphasize playfulness, experimentation, and exploration of a wide variety of movement experiences. A reasonable format is no longer than 20 minutes of structured activity combined with 30 minutes of free play. Concentration is maximized if instructional sessions take place in a setting with minimal distraction. Instructing younger students using a show-and-tell format with physical demonstration is more effective than verbal instruction alone.

Elementary school students should not compete against each other but work to improve previous performance. Judgment should be based on improvement. Rules should be flexible enough to promote success, action, and participation of all students. For example, when playing with a soccer ball, young students do not take positions or use basic strategies but tend to swarm around the ball as it travels around the field. Weightlifting is not appropriate for prepubertal students.

Once students are in middle school, activities should promote muscle strength, cardiac endurance, flexibility, and healthy bones. Some districts promote fitness to their staff and students using the "FITT Principles" for cardiovascular endurance. This is an acronym for Frequency, Intensity, Time (duration), and Type of activity. Frequency should be daily, and the intensity should consist of vigorous activity at least 3 times each week. The time goal is 30 to 60 minutes of activity daily. Multiple sessions of 10 to 15 minutes each provide nearly the same health benefits as sustained activity of 30 to 60 minutes, permitting some flexibility for activity periods. Type of activity is particularly important, because students need to explore various ways that they can enjoy being fit.

Activities that involve a significant amount of physical contact should be avoided. There is little evidence that more injuries occur in coeducational activities; of greater concern is the athletic dominance of postpubertal boys over prepubertal boys and girls, which can make it difficult for other students to feel successful. Under such circumstances, less physically mature students might misperceive themselves as less athletic or adept, which might discourage continued interest and involvement in physical activity.

To maximize variety and opportunity for aerobic activity, some districts combine 2 or more classes for a PE period. Large class sizes are a barrier to a quality PE program; therefore, PE classes should be no larger than academic classes, preferably 25 students. Ample equipment and supplies are important to prevent excessive waiting in line, which is inconsistent with beneficial activity.

> Increase the proportion of adolescents who spend at least 50 percent of school physical education class time being physically active (*Healthy People 2010*, Objective 22-10).

In addition to well-structured, developmentally appropriate curricula, districts need well-trained, credentialed PE teachers if they are to succeed in promoting skills and fitness, providing safe activities, and making physical activity fun. Professionally prepared physical educators can establish individualized exercise plans that focus on skill development, self-improvement, cooperation, participation, and goal setting.

Episodic Exclusion From PE for Health Reasons

Some students complain of headache, flu symptoms, menstrual pain, asthma exacerbation, and other symptoms to avoid participation in PE classes. Physical education teachers need guidelines and information to respond when students frequently have an acute complaint. Working with school staff, the pediatrician can suggest appropriate guidelines and assist them in educating students and their families about the value of regular physical activity. For example, district guidelines should require that families of students with repetitive complaints and absence from regular physical activity obtain medical verification of need.

Physicians should be cautious about complying with requests for long-term excuses from PE without a thorough medical history and discussion with both the student and the family. Although in many cases no medical reason is justified, underlying concerns such as fear of ridicule, embarrassment about body type, bullying, or ignorance about the value of activity can be addressed.

When there is a valid medical reason to consider, the physician should first assess whether participation in a modified program might be appropriate. For example, perhaps a student should avoid aerobic activity for 2 weeks but continue with strength training, or for a sprain, the student should avoid activity that taxes the relevant extremities for 2 weeks. When in doubt about whether or how long to keep a student out of participation in PE or sports, a collaborative approach often is helpful. The student, parent, school nurse, and the PE teacher or coach can participate in a shared decision-making process. Building alliances makes the health care professional part of a team, thus increasing understanding of and compliance with rules and recommendations.

Modified and Adapted PE Programs

Ideally, students with physical disabilities or chronic health conditions should participate in physical activities with their age peers to the extent possible. Students without disabilities gain a better understanding of their peers with disabilities and learn to appreciate individual differences. In fact, the Individuals With Disabilities Education Act requires school districts to provide PE programs for students with physical disabilities in the least restrictive environment. Modifying the regular PE classroom can range from exempting a student with a modest coagulation problem from contact sports and games to specially designed physical activities to meet a student's particular needs. Often in the latter circumstance, the PE teacher follows a tailored curriculum for a particular student or teaches the skills differently. Often, an adaptive PE specialist collaborates with the regular physical educator to design a program that can be implemented in the regular PE classroom and meets the requirements for physical activity written in a student's individualized education program. Guidelines are available for pediatricians who wish to have more information on what to recommend in regard to participation in physical activities for many specific chronic disabilities.[20-28]

In some cases, the need for accommodation cannot be met in the regular PE classroom. Students with cerebral palsy, severe to moderate developmental delay, osteogenesis imperfecta, severe vision impairments, or other sensory deficits often need adaptive programs. Ideally, an adaptive PE specialist designs and implements an alternative program. Adaptive specialists receive training to address multiple special needs, special behavioral and educational strategies, and planning and implementation skills for carrying out the adapted PE program. Not surprisingly, these specialists also exhibit more positive attitudes toward students with disabilities than do regular physical educators.[29] Unfortunately, not all states require certified adaptive PE specialists. However, national standards exist,[30] and physicians can advocate that districts meet them.

In the absence of adaptive specialists, physical and occupational therapists can collaborate with PE teachers in altering equipment, modifying playing areas, and developing adaptive PE programs.[31] It is important to clarify, however, that physical therapy is not a substitute for PE. The aim of PE is to improve fitness, whereas therapy is designed to improve function.

Role of the Physician in Adaptive PE Programs

Modifying a PE program or referring a student to an adapted PE program usually occurs without physician intervention in most districts; however, physicians should not assume that this will always occur. If a pediatrician believes a student requires modification or referral into an adaptive PE program, it is important to communicate this information, with permission, to the appropriate school staff. Physicians can offer valuable insights to adaptive PE specialists and families for identifying appropriate physical activity goals, considering long-range needs, and identifying motivational rewards for students when they achieve their "personal best" performance. Pediatricians should describe as accurately as possible in functional terms all limitations regarding body contact, highly aerobic activity, or activity involving upper or lower extremities and specify whether the student has musculoskeletal or coagulation disorders, is dependent on technology, or is at risk of respiratory compromise or predisposed to infection. When working with school staff, pediatricians should create transition plans as students advance from elementary to middle school or when a student moves from one district to another. Clear, specific instructions written by a physician after discussion with a PE program specialist, school nurse, or both usually are welcomed and can be incorporated into a student's individual health care plan (see Chapter 2, Health Services). When precautions are written, they are less likely to slip through the cracks when a change in PE staff or a change of schools occurs.

School Athletic Programs

Reasonable goals for preadolescents participating in any school-sponsored competitive sport include acquisition of basic motor skills, increasing physical activity levels, learning social skills necessary to work as a team, learning good sportsmanship, and having fun.[32] Despite many potential benefits, however, there is no consensus regarding the overall value of organized sports for students before high school.

> Increase the proportion of the nation's public and private schools that provide access to their physical activity spaces and facilities for all persons outside of normal school hours (that is, before and after the school day, on weekends, and during summer and other vacations) (*Healthy People 2010*, Objective 22-12).

More than 6 million high school students participate in organized sports each year. High school athletic programs offer numerous physical and social benefits. Physicians should advocate for well-trained, credentialed coaches and athletic trainers prepared in certification programs that meet the standards for coaching competency.[33] These individuals can provide fitness assessments and establish individualized exercise plans that focus on skill development, self-improvement, cooperation, participation, and goal setting. They can ensure fairness in choosing teams,[34] matching competitors,[35] and enforcing rules that are the basis of safe play, cooperation, and fairness. Consistent enforcement of the rules reduces injuries stemming from dangerous practices, such as head-first sliding in baseball[36] and body checking in hockey.[37]

Participation in athletic programs can provide many opportunities for students to develop important social skills. There is a strong association between high rates of athletic participation and decreased risk taking and suicidal behaviors, decreased drop-out rates, and fewer pregnancies.[11,12] Sharing a team uniform and a logo, traveling with friends to other schools, and having a sense of belonging to one's school and team is akin to the gains that some students otherwise might seek in gangs.

Family involvement in school athletic programs usually is desirable, enriching the experience for all. It is important, however, that districts develop rules and guidelines that clarify the extent of desired involvement; inappropriate or overzealous parental influences can have negative effects. When demands and expectations of the sport exceed the maturation or readiness of the participant, benefits of participation are offset. Some families tie parental love and acceptance to their students' successful participation in sports and focus intensely on the importance of winning.

It is important that pediatricians support district efforts that limit negative effects of overzealous adults. Physicians can encourage district policies that maintain congruity between coaching philosophies and behavioral management techniques, parental expectations, and students' temperament and developmental stage. Pediatricians are encouraged to help assess developmental readiness and medical suitability for participation in a district athletic program and assist in matching a student's physical, social, and cognitive maturity with appropriate sports activities.[38] In addition, districts should be discouraged from exempting students from PE classes who participate in extracurricular activities, such as marching band or athletic teams. Participation in athletics or other physically demanding activities should complement, not replace, daily PE.

Physical Assessments Related to Physical Activity

Optimally, physical examinations should be required annually or every 2 years for all students. Despite their enormous potential benefit, annual medical assessments for school attendance are unlikely to be mandated. Nevertheless, many districts require medical assessment before participation in physical education or athletic activities.

Several chronic medical conditions, including asthma, seizure disorders, and hemophilia, justify a medical assessment before participation in physical education classes or athletic activity.

Asthma

Most students with asthma can participate in physical activity without restrictions. In fact, individualizing the intensity of training for students with asthma has been shown to result in a rapid and marked increase in cardiovascular fitness.[39] In some districts, physicians need to educate school staff, because exercise-induced asthma often is unrecognized—it often is self-limiting and its symptoms frequently occur after, rather than during, exercise. It is important that physicians include information about the PE period in their patient's history. As far as treatment for exercise-induced asthma in school, students in middle school and higher grades usually are responsible enough to carry their own quick-acting metered-dose inhalers. It is helpful if the PE teacher, classroom teacher, or school nurse reminds younger students to take their preexercise medications.

Pediatricians can inform families and school staff of a particular student's needs by including specific exercise instructions, along with the student's medication instructions, on the asthma action plan. Notes on optimal hydration, relaxation techniques, and warm-up exercises can be written into the student's preexercise plan. Teachers should know that when cool, dry air triggers asthma, tying a scarf around a student's nose and mouth can help warm and humidify the air. When coordinating with the school nurse and physical educator, physicians can request reports about the number of days or periods of physical activity that are missed because of asthma. Sometimes this is the best or only history indicative of a child's real degree of asthma severity.

Seizure Disorders

Students with known seizure disorders should have regular medical visits for this condition. Although there are no absolute contraindications to PE, district staff often need information on general precautions. For example, extra vigilance is required when students with known seizure disorders are in a swimming pool or hanging upside down from gymnastic bars. Precautions and physical activity restrictions, if necessary at all, depend to some degree on the student's level of control, adherence to a medical regimen, and the time interval since the most recent seizure.

Hemophilia

Students with hemophilia are less likely to have bleeding symptoms when they are physically fit. Generally, with the exception of high-contact, collision sports, participation in most physical activities is preferential to tight restrictions, even if there are occasional minor bleeding episodes. The degree of restriction depends largely on each student's individual situation and level of clotting factor. Consultation with each student's hematologist and family is required. In addition to specifying the desired level of contact, the school's written plan should include descriptions of protective clothing, protective equipment, quick access to cold compresses after an injury, and a plan to transport the student promptly to a facility where clotting factor can be replenished.

Preparticipation Physical Examinations for Sports

Preparticipation physical examinations should involve thorough medical assessments, a careful history, and patient education. The AAP publication *Care of the Young Athlete,* published in conjunction with the American Academy of Orthopaedic Surgeons,[40] has an excellent review of the preparticipation physical examination. It includes history-taking strategies and special points of emphasis on the orthopedic, neurologic, and cardiac examinations (as well as their interpretations) and provides physicians an opportunity to promote physical activity, address issues of readiness, discuss barriers to fitness, and educate students on safety practices such as hydration, equipment, supplements, and diets.

Unfortunately, most assessments typically are limited to high school students with an already established interest in a particular sport. A private office where student and practitioner can talk is best for conducting such an examination. Too frequently, however, less desirable practices occur, such as lining students up to be examined in the locker room or having them rotate through a series of stations staffed by various individuals with and without medical training. Another concern is that some districts require presports medical assessments within weeks of playing. This places enormous pressure on physicians and students, and it has never been proven to be important from a medical perspective. Individual physicians, but more effectively, local chapters of the AAP and other medical societies should educate athletic directors who establish such needlessly restrictive policies.

Nutrition and Physical Activity

Physical educators and coaches should encourage students to keep a record of what they eat and how they exercise or train. This record is a good base for discussion and education. Active adolescents generally require 1500 to 3000 more kilocalories per day than the recommended daily allowance for adults.[41] Recommending that students follow the serving guide advocated by the US Department of Agriculture's Food Guide Pyramid is the best way for students to fulfill their energy requirements: 55% to 60% of total energy should come from carbohydrates, 12% to 15% from protein, and 25% to 30% from fat. Any extra calories needed by rapidly growing and physically active adolescents should come from the grain family: bread, cereal, rice, and pasta—

the base of the food pyramid. High-carbohydrate beverages, such as Gatorade, can boost carbohydrate calories and are safe but should not be used to replace regular foods. Physicians should try to detect whether their patients are fasting or omitting carbohydrate-rich foods from their diets and discourage them from doing so.

Students beginning a training program, those participating in endurance and resistance sports, and those consuming calorie-restricting diets might require 50% to 60% more protein than is recommended for daily intake, but many athletes already have this excess in their current diets. Protein supplements and specific amino acids have not shown any benefit over regular foodstuffs. School athletic staff members need to explain that any excessive protein not used for energy expenditure or muscle repair eventually is converted to fat and can lead to weight gain. It also can lead to dehydration and increased calcium loss. Vegetarian athletes should consume a wide variety of grains and vegetables as additional sources of protein.

Fruit juices and low-fiber fresh fruit are readily available foods that make good snacks 1 to 2 hours before activity. Students should avoid high-bran and high-fiber foods and gas-forming foods such as cauliflower (to avoid cramping) and high fat foods (to avoid delayed gastric emptying and sluggishness). A more complete meal made up of complex carbohydrates, fruit, and lean proteins is best consumed 3 or more hours before competition or training.

Nutrition-Related Problems

Active students generally have less fat and lower body weight than their less active counterparts.[42] Participation in physical activity can be an effective way to help students maintain their ideal body weight. Unfortunately for students participating in activities such as ballet, dance, wrestling, gymnastics, swimming, diving, long-distance and sprint running, rowing, and figure skating, body weight can become an irrational focus. These students often attempt to modify their weight inappropriately. Physicians can work with district health educators, physical educators, and coaches to educate students about nutritional misconceptions and inappropriate behaviors. All youth coaches should receive education in sports nutrition and the consequences of excessive weight control in young athletes.[41] Detection of symptoms and early intervention can prevent recalcitrant problems such as anorexia nervosa and bulimia. For elite female athletes, early detection and intervention might help prevent the "female athletic triad," (menstrual irregularities [primary or secondary amenorrhea], osteoporosis, and eating disorders), which has become a significant and dangerous syndrome.[43]

Student Safety and Injury Prevention

Some risk always is present with physical activity. However, risk can be minimized through careful surveillance studies, injury prevention programs, and optimal care and management of injuries.[44] Physical education teachers and coaches should be certified in cardiopulmonary resuscitation (CPR) and first aid as a matter of policy. Unfortunately, there is wide variability in compliance and enforcement. Some districts' policies require athletic trainers, nurses, sports physicians, or team doctors at sporting events. If districts do not have their own staff, they can contract with athletic trainers and physicians in the community.

In addition to having staff trained in safety and injury prevention, districts should have clearly written policies and protocols for handling and reporting injuries. Particularly for head injuries, it is essential that families be notified. The seriousness of missing delayed sequelae of some injuries is ominous. Recommendations for students experiencing pain also should be clarified. Most coaches encourage students to report pain and are sensitive to students' concerns; however, in a few instances, staff members encourage students with pain to "play it out." Physicians consulting with schools can help districts develop appropriate written policies. The publication *Care of the Young Athlete*[40] provides 4 chapters of worthwhile information for physicians writing such protocols.

Suggested Injury-Related Policy Items

- Encourage students to report pain, and assure young athletes that their position on a team is rarely in jeopardy because of an injury.
- Prohibit students in pain from continued participation in any activity that might exacerbate the injury. If pain relievers are required to continue playing, the activity should not be permitted.
- Develop alternative activities that help maintain fitness or develop skills without involving an injured limb or body system for students who temporarily cannot participate because of an injury.
- Require parent notification about injuries. Do not rely on a student's self-report. This is particularly important for head, chest, and abdominal injuries.
- Record all injuries, including data on time of day, nature of the sport, site of injury, nature of collision or other description, level of supervision, age and sex of the injured student, and the geographic location within the school or off-campus activity.
- Routinely monitor the following:
  - Students' level of conditioning and nutritional practices, particularly hydration;
  - Status of previous injuries, particularly those that might not have completely healed;
  - Students' psychological and motivational status;
  - Number of available, experienced adult supervisors with CPR and first aid training;
  - Availability, status, and use of personal protective equipment; and
  - Status of district equipment and field facilities.
- Establish an effective communication system with emergency paramedic help.

Protective Equipment

The use of approved equipment to prevent injury is essential. Only protective eye wear and mouth guards recommended by the American Academy of Ophthalmology and the American Dental Association should be used. Bicycle helmets should by approved by the Snell Memorial Foundation or the American National Standards Institute. The American Society for Testing Materials and the National Operating Committee on Standards for Athletic Equipment also critically evaluate, rate, and approve sports equipment. A detailed listing of sport-specific suggestions for injury prevention is included in the American Academy of Orthopaedic Surgeons and American Academy of Pediatrics publication *Care of the Young Athlete*.[40] For more information, see Chapter 9, Injury Prevention and School Safety.

> Increase the proportion of public and private schools that require use of appropriate head, face, eye, and mouth protection for students participating in school-sponsored physical activities (*Healthy People 2010*, Objective 15-31).

Injury Reports

The National High School Sports Injury Surveillance System, the University of North Carolina National Center for Catastrophic Sports Injury Research, the US Consumer Product Safety Commission, the Centers for Disease Control and Prevention, and other federal agencies collect data regarding sports-related injuries. These reports affect future decisions about recommended or required equipment modifications, sports surfaces, coach and athlete preparation, and education.

Dehydration, Heat, and Cold

School personnel sometimes undervalue the importance of hydration, particularly during high temperatures, high-intensity exercise, or long duration of exercise. Younger students are at greater risk than adolescents because of their relatively high heat loss and low sweating capability. As a matter of policy and procedure, students should have free access to fluids, a period of acclimatization to heat conditions, rest periods, and reminders to drink before, during, and after activities.[45] Muscle cramps can occur in all weather conditions, but they are more prevalent at extreme temperatures. Improved fitness might prevent cramping in the future,[45] so students experiencing cramping should be permitted to participate in future events.

School staff members who oversee PE, recess, and athletics should have guidelines on the symptoms of heat exhaustion (fatigue, mild fever, muscle cramping, confusion, headache, dizziness, chills, and nausea) and be able to initiate management (move child to a cool and shady location, remove unnecessary clothing, hydrate using cold water, contact emergency medical services). High body temperature, abnormal mental status, and reduced sweating might indicate heat stroke, a condition that staff must know to treat with the same urgency as drowning or cardiac arrest.[45,46]

Potential Problems Associated With Physical Activity and Sports
Stress
One of the benefits of regular physical activity is improved mood and reduction in depression. For some students, however, participation in physical education classes or sports can increase stress. Students at risk of increased stress are those who are overly concerned about failure, those who see sports as work rather than fun, and those who are perfectionists in evaluating their own performance and the performance of others. Pediatricians can educate their patients regarding strategies to minimize stress and offer guidance to district staff on how to identify stress responses, when to intervene, and when to refer.

Substance Abuse
Physicians, along with PE teachers and coaches, can have an important role in preventing substance abuse. Physicians who want to familiarize

themselves and school staff about abused substances can refer to excellent review articles on the subject[47-49] and to Chapter 10 of *Care of the Young Athlete.*[40] The federal Office of Juvenile Justice and Delinquency Prevention has excellent resources for coaches that pediatricians can and should promote. *The Coach's Playbook Against Drugs* is available online at no cost at http://www.playclean.org/coach-a-thon.pdf or by mail to Juvenile Justice Clearinghouse, PO Box 6000, Rockville, MD 20849-6000. The manual helps coaches prevent drug use by players. It outlines the coach's role, teaches how to get a message across effectively, and offers other useful information.

Students who participate in regular physical activity and athletic programs tend to engage less in substance abuse than their nonactive peers.[50,51] However, athletes are more likely to abuse certain substances to increase endurance, speed, muscle strength, and performance. Fortunately, unlike prevention messages among the general student population, when student athletes are informed about the negative consequences of substance abuse, they generally respond positively by changing their behavior.[52]

Stimulants

Nicotine found in smokeless tobacco (snuff, quid, chaw) is particularly prevalent among youth who play baseball; otherwise, athletes tend to use nicotine less than their peers. More common is the use of caffeine and ephedrine, stimulants purported to increase endurance and speed.[53] Some athletes also use ephedrine and other amphetamines to lose weight. Caffeine has diuretic properties, but it also can cause dehydration, which might lead to reduced strength, stamina, and hyperthermia. Ephedrine is found in such common substances as herbal teas, cold medications, commercially available weight loss supplements, and traditional medicines, such as ginseng and gingko biloba. Serious reactions, including cardiovascular events, seizures, and even death are possible and typically underappreciated.

Creatine

Creatine is a legal, easy-to-find nutritional supplement used increasingly (8%-25% among middle and high school athletes in some geographic regions).[54,55] Although studies with adults using a very narrow dose range have found some mild benefits of creatine,[56] there have been no safety studies with young people. Adverse effects in adults have been assessed only after brief periods of use.

Steroids

Anabolic steroids and androstenedione are used by 5% to 6% of students (by injection or oral ingestion) to increase muscle size and strength. The popularity of androgenic steroids is believed to be related to the high prevalence of muscular male images in the media.[57] Adolescents abusing anabolic steroids have poorer health-related attitudes. They often are preoccupied with their weight and build.[58] Diuretics sometimes are abused to reduce fluid retention secondary to anabolic-androgenic steroid abuse. Adrenocorticotropic hormone, human growth hormone, and human chorionic gonadotropin are used to increase height, muscle mass, and body weight. They are expensive and not readily available. However, counterfeits of these substances are widely advertised.[59] Beta blockers, such as propanolol, can enhance fine motor control, but they have negative cardiovascular effects. Fortunately, there is no evidence that high school students are abusing them.

Emergining Issues
Automated External Defibrillators

Sudden cardiac death sometimes is attributed to tobacco use, other drug use, obesity, lack of conditioning, or a combination of these factors. In children and youth, sudden cardiac death is a consequence of myocarditis, hypertrophic cardiomyopathy, congenital long QT syndrome, and arrhythmias.[60] It rarely is attributable to ischemic heart disease and very often occurs without a known cause. Most students at risk of sudden cardiac death do not experience symptoms and have not been identified to be at risk. One of the most significant factors for survival of a sudden cardiac event is delayed application of cardiopulmonary resuscitation or defibrillation. There is only an 8- to 10-minute window of opportunity, with the greatest chance of survival within the first 3 minutes. For each minute that passes without defibrillation, the chance of survival decreases 7% to 10%.[61]

During the last several years, automated external defibrillators have been increasingly recognized for their efficacy and ease of use in resuscitation. Automated external defibrillators now are found in airports, golf courses, professional sports arenas, workplaces, and schools. Many districts are debating whether they should be available at school sporting events, contemplating who should be trained to use them, and exploring the potential liability of staff. The devices are not retrofitted for use with young children but would be appropriate for adolescents and staff. Although the costs of this technology are greatly reduced from previous years, at several thousand dollars each, they are still well beyond the reach of many districts. Relative to the many other unmet health needs of schools and students, automated external defibrillators might be considered a good thing but a low priority.

Recommendations for Pediatricians

Pediatricians and other health care professionals are encouraged to support districts in their efforts to promote physical activity and fitness by:

- Helping them adapt programs to meet the physical activity needs of students who have limitations because of temporary or chronic illness, injury, or disability;
- Encouraging them to implement effective kindergarten through grade 12 curricula that provide information and skills for lifetime fitness;
- Advocating for policies that require students to use appropriate safety equipment for sports and physical activities in all settings;

- Educating members of the school community about current activity patterns, obesity, and other chronic illnesses linked to physical activity and offering strategies for increasing daily activity levels;
- Encouraging families to engage in physical activities together;
- Advocating for funding and personnel resources that would offer opportunities for all students to be physically active and to receive appropriate direction and supervision from well-trained, knowledgeable adults;
- Joining school health advisory boards and advocating for more physical education during the school day in addition to increased opportunities after school; and
- Adopting a physically active lifestyle. Physicians who exercise regularly are more likely to promote it to their patients.[62]

Text Resource

Bogden JF. *Fit, Healthy, and Ready to Learn: A School Health Policy Guide. Part I: Physical Activity, Healthy Eating, and Tobacco Use Prevention.* Alexandria, VA: National Association of State Boards of Education; 2000. Available at: http://www.nasbe.org. Accessed January 29, 2003.

References

1. Centers for Disease Control and Prevention. Guidelines for school and community programs to promote lifelong physical activity among young people. *MMWR Morb Mortal Wkly Rep.* 1997;46(RR-6):1–36
2. US Department of Health and Human Services. *Physical Activity and Health: A Report of the Surgeon General.* Atlanta, GA: Centers for Disease Control and Prevention, US Department of Health and Human Services; 1996
3. American Academy of Pediatrics, Committee on Sports Medicine and Fitness and Committee on School Health. Physical fitness and activity in schools. *Pediatrics.* 2000;105:1156–1157
4. Sallis JF, ed. Physical activity guidelines for adolescents. *Pediatr Exerc Sci.* 1994;6:299–463

5. Simons-Morton BG, Parcel GS, O'Hara NM, Blair SN, Pate RR. Health-related physical fitness in childhood: status and recommendations. *Annu Rev Public Health.* 1988;9:403–425

6. Bar-Or O. Childhood and adolescent physical activity and fitness and adult risk profile. In: Brouchard C, Shephard RJ, Stephens T, eds. *Physical Activity, Fitness, and Health: International Proceedings and Consensus Statement.* Champaign, IL: Human Kinetics Publishers; 1994:931–942

7. Burgeson CR, Wechsler H, Brener ND, Young JC, Spain CG. Physical education and activity: results from the School Health Policies and Programs Study 2000. *J Sch Health.* 2001;71:279–293

8. Crist RW. The effects of aerobic exercise and free-play time on the self-concept and classroom performance of sixth-grade students [dissertation]. Lexington, KY: University of Kentucky; 1994

9. Fleshner M. Exercise and neuroendocrine regulation of antibody production: protective effect of physical activity on stress-induced suppression of the specific antibody response. *Int J Sports Med.* 2000; 21(suppl 1):S14–S19

10. Morgan WP. Physical activity, fitness, and depression. In: Bouchard C, Shephard RJ, Stephens T, eds. *Physical Activity, Fitness, and Health: International Proceedings and Consensus Statement.* Champaign, IL: Human Kinetics Publishers; 1994:851–867

11. Brown DR, Blanton CJ. Physical activity, sports participation, and suicidal behavior among college students. *Med Sci Sports Exerc.* 2002;34:1087–1096

12. Patel DR, Luckstead EF. Sport participation, risk taking, and health risk behaviors. *Adolesc Med.* 2000;11:141–155

13. Dickinson DK. Large-group and free-play times: conversational settings supporting language and literacy development. In: Dickinson DK, Tabors PO, eds. *Beginning Literacy with Language: Young Children Learning at Home and School.* Baltimore, MD: Paul H Brookes Publishing Co; 2001:223–255

14. Menckel E, LaFlamme L. Injuries to boys and girls in Swedish schools: different activities, different results? *Scand J Public Health.* 2000;28:132–136

15. Coppens NM, Gentry LK. Video analysis of playground injury-risk situations. *Res Nurs Health.* 1991;14:129–136

16. National Association for Sport and Physical Education. *Physical Activity for Students: A Statement of Guidelines.* Reston, VA: National Association for Sport and Physical Education; 1998:1–21

17. National Association for Sport and Physical Education. *Appropriate Practices for Elementary School Physical Education.* Reston, VA: National Association for Sports and Physical Education; 2000

18. Stryker BK, Toffler IR, Lapchick R. A developmental overview of child and youth sports in society. *Child Adolesc Psychiatr Clin North Am.* 1998;7:697–724

19. Rowland TW. Clinical approaches to the sedentary child. In: *Exercise and Children's Health.* Champaign, IL: Human Kinetics Books; 1990:259–274

20. National High Blood Pressure Education Program, Working Group on Hypertension Control in Children and Adolescents. Update on the 1987 Task Force Report on High Blood Pressure in Children and Adolescents: a working group report from the National High Blood Pressure Education Program. *Pediatrics.* 1996;98:649–658

21. 26th Bethesda Conference: recommendations for determining eligibility for competition in athletes with cardiovascular abnormalities. *J Am Coll Cardiol.* 1994;24:845–899

22. American Academy of Pediatrics, Committee on Sports Medicine and Fitness. Mitral valve prolapse and athletic participation in children and adolescents. *Pediatrics.* 1995;95:789–790

23. Dorsen PJ. Should athletes with one eye, kidney, or testicle play contact sports? *Phys Sportsmed.* 1986;14:130–133, 137–138

24. American Academy of Pediatrics, Committee on Sports Medicine and Fitness and American Academy of Ophthalmology, Committee on Eye Safety and Sports Ophthalmology. Protective eyewear for young athletes. *Pediatrics.* 1996;98:311–313

25. American Medical Society for Sports Medicine and American Academy of Sports Medicine. Human immunodeficiency virus and other blood-borne pathogens in sports. *Clin J Sports Med.* 1995;5:199–204

26. Wojtys EM, Hovda D, Landry G. Concussion in sports. *Am J Sports Med.* 1999;27:676–687

27. Colorado Medical Society, Sports Medicine Committee. *Guidelines for the management of concussion in sports, revised.* Denver, CO: Colorado Medical Society; 1991

28. Kerle KK, Runkle GP. Sickle cell trait and sudden death in athletes. *JAMA.* 1996;276:1472

29. Folsom-Meek SL. Licensure of adapted physical education teachers and undergraduates' attitudes toward children with disabilities. *Precept Mot Skills.* 1998;86:1117–1118

30. National Consortium for Physical Education and Recreation for Individuals with Disabilities. *Physical Education.* Available at: http://ncperid.usf.edu/page2.html. Accessed July 28, 2003

31. Cicirello N. The therapist's role in adapted physical education. In: *Therapy in Educational Settings*. Washington, DC: Office of Special Education and Rehabilitative Services; 1989

32. Martens R, Seefeldt V, eds. *Guidelines for Children's Sports*. Reston, VA: National Association for Sport and Physical Education; 1979

33. National Association for Sport and Physical Education. *National Standards for Athletic Coaches: Quality Coaches, Quality Sports*. Dubuque, IA: Kendall/Hunt Publishing Co; 1995

34. Kamm RL. A developmental and psychoeducational approach to reducing conflict and abuse in little league and youth sports. The sport psychiatrist's role. *Child Adolesc Psychiatr Clin North Am*. 1998;7:891–918

35. Roemmich JN, Rogol AD. Physiology of growth and development. Its relationship to performance in the young athlete. *Clin Sports Med*. 1995;14:483–502

36. American Academy of Pediatrics, Committee on Sports Medicine and Fitness. Risk of injury from baseball and softball in children. *Pediatrics*. 2001;107:782–784

37. American Academy of Pediatrics, Committee on Sports Medicine and Fitness. Safety in youth ice hockey: the effects of body checking. *Pediatrics*. 2000;105:657–658

38. American Academy of Pediatrics, Committee on Sports Medicine and Fitness and Committee on School Health. Organized sports for children and preadolescents. *Pediatrics*. 2001;107:1459–1462

39. Varray AL, Mercier JG, Terral CM, Perfaut CG. Individualized aerobic and high intensity training for asthmatic children in an exercise readaptation program. Is training always helpful for better adaptation to exercise? *Chest*. 1991;99:579–586

40. American Academy of Pediatrics, American Academy of Orthopaedic Surgeons. *Care of the Young Athlete*. Sullivan JA, Anderson SJ, eds. Elk Grove Village, IL: American Academy of Pediatrics/American Academy of Orthopaedic Surgeons; 2000

41. Steen SN, Bernhardt DT. Nutrition and weight control. In: Sullivan JA, Anderson SJ, eds. *Care of the Young Athlete*. Elk Grove Village, IL: American Academy of Pediatrics/American Academy of Orthopaedic Surgeons; 2000:81–94

42. Landry GL. Benefits of sports participation. In: Sullivan JA, Anderson SJ. *Care of the Young Athlete*. Elk Grove Village, IL: American Academy of Pediatrics/American Academy of Orthopaedic Surgeons; 2000:1–7

43. Yurko-Griffin L, Harris SS. Female athletes. In: Sullivan JA, Anderson SJ, eds. *Care of the Young Athlete.* Elk Grove Village, IL: American Academy of Pediatrics/American Academy of Orthopaedic Surgeons; 2000:137–148

44. Rice SG. Risks of injury during sports participation. In: Sullivan JA, Anderson SJ, eds. *Care of the Young Athlete.* Elk Grove Village, IL: American Academy of Pediatrics/American Academy of Orthopaedic Surgeons; 2000:9–18

45. Coyle JF. Thermoregulation. In: Sullivan JA, Anderson SJ, eds. *Care of the Young Athlete.* Elk Grove Village, IL: American Academy of Pediatrics/American Academy of Orthopaedic Surgeons; 2000:65–80

46. American Academy of Pediatrics, Committee on Sports Medicine and Fitness. Climatic heat stress and the exercising child and adolescent. *Pediatrics.* 2000;106:158–159

47. Griesemer BA. Performance enhancing substances. In: Sullivan JA, Anderson SJ. *Care of the Young Athlete.* Elk Grove Village, IL: American Academy of Pediatrics/American Academy of Orthopaedic Surgeons; 2000:95–104

48. Ahrendt DM. Ergogenic aids: counseling the athlete. *Am Fam Physician.* 2001;63:913–922

49. American Academy of Pediatrics, Committee on Sports Medicine and Fitness. Adolescents and anabolic steroids: a subject review. *Pediatrics.* 1997;99:904–908

50. Read JP, Brown RA, Marcus BH, et al. Exercise attitudes and behaviors among persons in treatment for alcohol use disorders. *J Subst Abuse Treat.* 2001;21:199–206

51. Collingwood TR, Sunderlin J, Reynolds R, Kohl HW. Physical training as a substance abuse prevention intervention for youth. *J Drug Educ.* 2000;30:435–451

52. MacKinnon DP, Goldberg L, Clarke GN, et al. Mediating mechanisms in a program to reduce intentions to use anabolic steroids and improve exercise self-efficacy and dietary behavior. *Prev Sci.* 2001;2:15–28

53. Graham TE. Caffeine, coffee, and ephedrine: impact on exercise performance and metabolism. *Can J Appl Physiol.* 2001;26

54. Metzl JD, Small E, Levine SR, Gershel JC. Creatine use among young athletes. *Pediatrics.* 2001;108:421–425

55. Smith J, Dahm DL. Creatine use among a select population of high school athletes. *Mayo Clin Proc.* 2000;75:1257–1263

56. Lawrence ME, Kirby DF. Nutrition and sports supplements: fact or fiction. *J Clin Gastroenterol.* 2002;35:299–306

57. Labre MB. Adolescent boys and the muscular male body ideal. *J Adolesc Health.* 2002;30:233–242

58. Irving LM, Wall M, Newmark-Sztainer D, Story M. Steroid use among adolescents: findings from Project EAT. *J Adolesc Health.* 2002;30:243–252

59. Rogol AD. Sex steroid and growth hormone supplementation to enhance performance in adolescent athletes. *Curr Opin Pediatr.* 2000;12:382–387

60. Maron BJ. The young competitive athlete with cardiovascular abnormalties: causes of sudden death, detection by preparticipation screening, and standards for disqualification. *Cardiol Electrophysiol Rev.* 2002;6:100–103

61. Berger S. Sudden cardiac death in children and adolescents: can we prevent it? *Sch Nurse News.* 2001;18:42–46

62. Long BL. Promoting physical activity. In: Sullivan JA, Anderson SJ, eds. *Care of the Young Athlete.* Elk Grove Village, IL: American Academy of Pediatrics/American Academy of Orthopaedic Surgeons; 2000:33–42

Chapter 9
Injury Prevention and School Safety

If some infectious disease came along that affected students [in the pro-portion that injuries do], there would be a huge public outcry and we would be told to spare no expense to find a cure and to be quick about it. C. Everett Koop, February 9, 1989

More than 10 years after C. Everett Koop, MD, then US Surgeon General, made the foregoing statement, it remains true. Injury accounts for more deaths of students and youth than all childhood diseases combined.[1] Approximately 10% to 20% of all injuries to students and adolescents occur in and around schools,[2] and injury is the most common health problem treated by school health personnel.[3] Most school injuries are minor and unintentional. Fatalities at school are rare; approximately 1 in 400 injury-related fatalities among students 5 to 19 years of age occur at school.[4] However, school districts may be liable for injuries that occur during school hours and might find that reducing injuries is less expensive than litigation.

No national reporting system exists for school-associated injuries or violence.[5] In 31% of states and 90% of districts, schools are required to write an injury report when a student is seriously injured on school property, but only 2 states require districts to report data to the state education agency or state health department.[6] Available data on school-related injuries are based on statistics from those seeking medical attention, a serious underestimate of the number of preventable, nonfatal school-based injuries that occur in schools on a daily basis. Nevertheless, more than $3 billion is spent annually on medical care to treat school-related injuries, one fifth of all reported injuries to students.[7]

Injury prevention efforts generally address several factors: the environment, individual behavior, products, social norms, legislation, and policy. Passive injury prevention strategies that require little or no action on the part of individuals are often most effective. For example, environmental changes, such as adding soft surfaces under playground equipment, usually result in fewer injuries than strategies requiring voluntary, consistent, and frequent individual protective behaviors, such as asking students to follow playground safety rules. The most effective injury prevention efforts use multiple approaches simultaneously. For example, legislation requiring use of bicycle helmets accompanied by an educational campaign for students and parents, police enforcement, and discounted sales of helmets by local merchants has been more successful than legislation alone.[8]

The responsibility for injury control in schools typically is ill defined, delegated at times to administrative personnel, school health personnel, school transportation personnel, or athletic department personnel. With increasingly limited funds, comprehensive injury prevention plans and programs in schools are rarely a priority. School personnel often are forced to address problems as they arise rather than plan for their prevention. Systematic surveillance of injury patterns within school districts is not routinely performed, which is particularly unfortunate given the seeming complexity of injuries resulting from multiple mechanisms, occurring in multiple settings within the school framework, and affecting multiple age groups.[9,10]

The school setting offers some unique advantages for injury control efforts. The public expectation for school safety is high. Parents and others expect students to be safe at school, if nowhere else. The activities and curricula of schools are overseen by school boards that are accountable to the public. Schools are subject to enforceable regulations and routine inspection. Also, in keeping with the educational mission, school curricula can integrate safety education with safety practice. In districts where family involvement is actively encouraged, the safety practices learned by students in school can have a positive influence on safety in the home.

Students With Special Health Care Needs

Studies that define the types of injuries to which students with special needs are predisposed are extremely limited. Students with attention–deficit/hyperactivity disorder, seizure disorder, and general cognitive deficits, however, are at increased risk, and attention to requirements necessary to prevent injury should be considered on an individual basis.[8] The school environment should be designed to ensure the safety of all students during an emergency. Students who have difficulty with ambulation, use a wheelchair, or require equipment such as oxygen or a ventilator should receive services on the ground floor of the building or be able to be transported down stairwells quickly and safely during an emergency evacuation. Prevention of injury to students with special health care needs, as for all students, requires the supervision and support appropriate for the developmental, behavioral, and emotional needs of each individual child.

Reduce deaths caused by unintentional injuries (*Healthy People 2010*, Objective 15-13) and reduce nonfatal unintentional injuries (*Healthy People 2010*, Objective 15-14).

Safety in the School Setting

School buildings should be safe havens where careful attention is given to reducing the risk of unintentional injuries. Smoke detectors, emergency exits, and a regularly practiced plan for orderly evacuation of a building are necessary. Stairways should be well lit and unobstructed. Outdoor stairs, walkways, and landings should be unobstructed and free of water, ice, and snow. Carpeting on indoor stairs should be well secured and free of any debris. Carts used to transport audiovisual equipment may be top-heavy and should not be moved by students;

temporary power cords lying across floors (through traffic paths) should be taped down. Folding chairs and heavy folding tables, such as those used in school cafeterias, should be set up and stored by older students or adults. Electrical equipment, plugs, power cords, and fans should be out of the reach of young students. Toxic chemicals used in science laboratories, art classes, and industrial arts classes should be used and stored, under direct adult supervision, with adequate protection and ventilation.[11]

Playground Safety

Playground equipment is the leading cause of injuries to students.[12] The majority (70%) of injuries are the result of falls from climbing apparatuses, such as monkey bars, jungle gyms, swings, and slides.[13] Injuries to the head and face account for 60% of these injuries. Playground injuries are only slightly more likely to involve boys than girls (53% vs 46%).

Several factors contribute to playground injuries. As with many types of unintentional injuries, lack of supervision is problematic; students 5 to 12 years old need adult supervision. Students should not play on equipment that is inappropriate for their age, size, strength, and decision-making ability. Play equipment appropriate for use by students with disabilities should be available and accessible to all students to encourage play in an inclusive environment.

Age-appropriate equipment for students 5 to 12 years old includes rope or chain climbers, horizontal bars, tire swings, seesaws, and merry-go-rounds. Lack of a suitable fall surface is associated with fatal head injuries. Even a 1-foot fall onto asphalt or concrete or a 4-foot fall onto packed earth or grass can be deadly. The surface beneath each piece of playground equipment should be covered and maintained with shock-absorbent materials such as wood chips, sand, or rubber outdoor mat.

Inadequate equipment maintenance can cause injuries. Continual inspection, regular maintenance, and repair of all equipment and surfaces are essential. Inspection should involve looking for sharp points, corners, and edges; protrusions and projections; missing or damaged protective caps or plugs; potential clothing entanglement hazard, such as gaps; pinch or crush points; and exposed moving parts. Aged playground equipment should be replaced or repaired. General procedures to minimize risk also include routine removal of miscellaneous debris and trash, broken glass, needles, litter, and obstacles. Playgrounds located near streets should have circumferential fencing to prevent students from running into traffic.

Transportation Safety

Reduce deaths caused by motor vehicle crashes (*Healthy People 2010*, Objective 15-15) and reduce nonfatal injuries caused by motor vehicle crashes (*Healthy People 2010*, Objective 15-17).

School systems and local governments can collaborate to improve the safety of students traveling to and from school and school-related activities. An analysis of student injury and fatality rates by mode during normal school travel hours from 1991 to 1999 revealed that injuries and fatalities per 100 million miles were highest for passenger vehicles with an adolescent driver, followed by bicycling and then walking.

School Bus Safety

Increase use of safety belts (*Healthy People 2010*, Objective 15-19).

School bus safety, particularly the issue of safety belts, is one of the most controversial transportation topics. Each year approximately 450 000 public school buses transport 23.5 million students to and from school and school-related activities over an estimated 4.3 billion miles. There are more than 26 000 school bus crashes per year, result-ing in more than 8000 injuries to passengers. On average, 10 school bus occupants die each year in crashes, for a fatality rate of 0.2 fatali-ties per 100 million vehicle miles traveled (1.5 per 100 million vehicle miles traveled for all motor vehicles).[14]

Despite this low rate of injury and death, many experts suggest that using safety belts on buses would further reduce school bus-related injuries and deaths. In 1999, the National Transportation Safety Board found that compartmentalization (keeping passengers confined to a padded compartment in a crash) as a means of occupant protection on school buses is incompletely effective. Passenger fatalities and seri-ous injuries can occur away from the area of vehicle impact. The National Transportation Safety Board recommended the development of seat restraint systems to restrain passengers in all types of crashes.[15] In a 2002 study on school bus safety, the National Highway Traffic Safety Administration determined that lap-shoulder belt restraint sys-tems on school buses performed best in crash testing compared with no belts, compartmentalization, and lap belts. Head injury measure-ments were significantly lower than with compartmentalization and lap belts results. The severity of neck injuries was below threshold for all sizes of dummies when lap and shoulder belts were worn properly. In crash tests, the lap-shoulder belt restraint systems effectively kept the dummies in their seats. Head injury severity values were low for all dummy sizes.[14] The American Academy of Pediatrics (AAP) has a long-standing policy recommending seat belts on school buses.[16]

Several additional issues affect the safety of bus occupants. First, many districts still use buses manufactured before 1977, when the current motor vehicle safety standards became effective. The need to remove these buses from service is urgent; they should not be sold or donated to camps or youth groups. Second, not all the buses have enough seats for all passengers, requiring some passengers to stand, which is hazardous. Last, school bus drivers should be subject to various licensing requirements, such as training in medical emergencies and annual physical examinations, including vision screening.[11]

The larger fatality problem in school bus-related crashes occurs outside of the bus, where approximately 30 pedestrians and 86 occupants of other vehicles are killed each year.[17] Although the number of pedestrian injuries is far fewer than the number of passenger injuries, pedestrian injuries are more likely to be serious or fatal. Students and their parents should be taught safe school bus behavior, with pedestrian training having a high priority. Students should be taught to stay clear of the bus and never be close enough to touch it. Parents and school personnel should monitor younger students at bus stops and at school until they are safely aboard or off the bus. Student monitors or "safety patrols" should be assigned at bus stops where older students and elementary grade students interact.[11]

Transporting Students With Special Needs

School systems are responsible for ensuring that students with special needs are safely transported in federally approved transportation. Guidance to ensure the safest form of transportation to meet the unique needs of all children with specific health care needs, including those with a tracheostomy, those requiring use of car seats, and those transported in wheelchairs, should be included in the individualized education program. Policy and protocol recommendations are available from several resources, including AAP policy statements[15,16] and the publications *Safe Transportation of Children With Special Needs: A Guide for Families*[17] and *Safe Travel for All Students: Transporting Children With Special Health Care Needs Training and Resource Manual.*[18]

All students weighing less than 80 pounds should be secured in an appropriate child restraint. School bus seats with attached restraint systems should have reinforced frames. When possible, students in wheelchairs should be moved to seats with an approved restraint. Otherwise, an occupant restraint system that includes upper and lower torso restraint should be provided for each wheelchair-seated occupant. Wheelchairs should be secured with 4-point tie-down devices from the frame to the floor. Unoccupied wheelchairs and ancillary equipment should be restrained separately.

Pedestrian Safety

Reduce pedestrian deaths on public roads (*Healthy People 2010,* Objective 15-16) and reduce nonfatal pedestrian injuries on public roads (Healthy People 2010, Objective 15-18).

Increase the proportion of trips made by walking (*Healthy People 2010,* Objective 22-14).

In 1998 in the United States, 5220 pedestrians died of traffic-related injuries, and another 69 000 pedestrians sustained nonfatal injuries. During the same year, students 15 years and younger accounted for 30% of all nonfatal pedestrian injuries and 11% of all pedestrian fatalities.[19] School parking lots, driveways, and surrounding streets and sidewalks are particularly dangerous areas. This is especially true during the congested periods before and after school when school buses, automobiles, students, and parents converge on school property.

Pedestrian safety requires careful planning and supervision. Adult supervision is necessary at designated intersections where students cross and at school bus loading and unloading sites. Driver, parent, and student education is necessary, but because of lack of good evidence linking education of students to a reduction in injury,[20] education alone is inadequate. Establishing safe routes to school, enforcing speed limits in school zones, establishing safe parking and drop-off/pick-up practices, establishing a school bus loading zone, improving unclear signs and crosswalks, and posting crossing guards are measures that can be implemented to enhance child pedestrian safety. Extra precautions should be taken when inclement weather reduces visibility and causes slippery streets and sidewalks. Traffic-calming strategies, such as speed bumps and cul-de-sacs, may be helpful.

Bicycle Safety

> Increase use of helmets by bicyclists (*Healthy People 2010*, Objective 15-23).

> Increase the proportion of trips made by bicycling (*Healthy People 2010*, Objective 22-15).

Students are at risk of bicycle-related injury from falls resulting from intrinsic factors, such as exceeding their ability level, or extrinsic factors, such as swerving from or striking a motor vehicle or fixed object. Bicycle-related injuries among students younger than 21 years resulted in approximately 275 deaths and an estimated 430 000 visits to emergency departments in 1998.[21] Among all recreational sports, bicycling injuries are the leading cause of emergency department visits for children and adolescents. Traumatic brain injury accounts for two thirds of all bicycle-related fatalities.[21] An estimated 23 000 students required emergency care after sustaining a traumatic brain injury while bicycling in 1998, accounting for about 5% of all bicycle-related injuries.[22]

If the *Healthy People 2010* objective for bicycling to school is to be achieved without increasing the rate of injury and fatality, strategies to enhance safety must be implemented. All bicyclists should wear properly fitted bicycle or multisport helmets each time they ride.[22,23] A bicycle helmet or multisport helmet manufactured after March 1999 must have certification that it met the US Consumer Product Safety Commission (CPSC) standard, regardless of whether it met the standards of any other organization. If a helmet manufactured before March 1999 meets the standards established by the Snell Memorial

Foundation or American Society for Testing Materials (but not American National Standards Institute alone), it may be used. However, once damaged or outgrown, it should be replaced with a new helmet that has been certified to meet the CPSC standard.

School districts should require mandatory helmet wearing if students ride bicycles to and from school and during school-related bicycle trips. In addition, students should learn all essential aspects of bicycle safety. Helmet use is only one aspect of bicycle safety and does not substitute for the students' knowledge and practice of the rules of the road, sufficient visibility to drivers, and other safety measures. Coalitions of schools, physicians, parents, and community leaders should develop and support community-based and school-based education programs to promote bicycle safety training that emphasizes helmet use.

Adolescent Drivers

Reduce the proportion of adolescents who report that they rode, during the previous 30 days, with a driver who had been drinking alcohol (*Healthy People 2010,* Objective 26-6).

Motor vehicle-related crashes remain the leading cause of death in youth 15 through 20 years of age, resulting in more than 3500 such deaths annually. This age group constitutes less than 9% of the US population but accounts for more than 14% of all drivers involved in fatal crashes.[24] The motor vehicle fatality rate of adolescents is higher than that of any other age group; on a per-mile-driven basis, 16-year-old drivers are more than 20 times as likely to have a crash as is the general population of drivers, and 17-year-old drivers are more than 6 times as likely.[25] Young men are at especially high risk, having nearly twice the risk of fatality as young women.[25] For every adolescent killed in a motor vehicle crash, approximately 100 nonfatal injuries occur.[25,26] Crashes are a leading cause of disability caused by head and spinal cord injuries in this age group. The 2 main factors that account for adolescents' increased risk of crashing are their lack of driving experience and their risk-taking behaviors.

Substantial reductions in fatal crashes among 16-year-olds have been reported in states with graduated licensing laws, which provide drivers' licenses in 3 sequential stages: a learner's permit, a provisional license, and a regular license.[27] School districts can reduce crashes among adolescent drivers by implementing driver education programs that require behind-the-wheel training in addition to classroom instruction. Parent-peer initiatives, such as alcohol-free dances and adult chauffeurs, provide a method for parents and adolescents to encourage alternatives to alcohol consumption and high-risk driving. Other policies that merit further examination include not permitting students to leave the school campus during school hours, a zero-tolerance philosophy for drug and alcohol use, and nighttime driving restrictions for evening school-related events.

Injury Reporting Systems

Establishing an injury surveillance system permits districts to use assessment findings to correct hazards, improve safety, and reduce liability. Data can identify patterns and risks for each type of injury, and the patterns and risks can be reported to a school safety committee or school health council. When implementing a new injury data collection system, the number of injuries often seems to increase temporarily; this is usually an artifact of better reporting, not an actual increase in incidents. Information collected might include the following:

- The date and time of injury;
- Place of injury occurrence (eg, classroom, playground, or off-campus event);
- Number of persons injured;
- Activity during which injury occurred (eg, sports or classroom activity);

- Surface on which injury occurred (eg, grass or concrete);
- Agents of injury (eg, ball, bat, firearm, or playground equipment);
- Contributing factors (eg, alcohol use, drug use, self-inflicted injury, nonuse of protective gear, or lack of supervision);
- Status of injured party and others involved in incident (eg, student, faculty, staff member, visitor, or intruder);
- Names and contact information of witnesses;
- Description of event;
- Type of injury (eg, cut, bruise, gunshot wound, or loss of consciousness);
- Location of injury (eg, face, arm, or foot);
- Relationship of injured party to others involved in incident (eg, relative, member of same gang, or member of rival gang);
- Intent (eg, unintentional, assault, or self-inflicted); and
- Description of action taken (eg, first aid administered, emergency services called, or parent or guardian notified).

Violence Prevention

> Reduce physical assaults (*Healthy People 2010*, Objective 15-37), reduce physical fighting among adolescents (*Healthy People 2010*, Objective 15-38), and reduce weapon carrying by adolescents on school property (*Healthy People 2010*, Objective 15-39).

School violence is defined as "any behavior that violates a school's educational mission or climate of respect or jeopardizes the intent of the school to be free of aggression against persons or property, drugs, weapons, disruptions, and disorder."[28] Clearly, students who fear for their safety are more likely to limit their involvement in school activities and to do less well academically than if they feel safe. The social environment of the school encompasses the formal and informal policies, norms, climate, and mechanisms that can promote safety or increase risk of unintentional injuries, violence, and suicide.[28]

Recent dramatic media coverage of shootings in US schools has raised concern about the safety of the school environment. Although there is no national reporting system for school-associated injuries or violence, national surveys indicate that most schools are free of violent behavior. In 2001, the percentage of students in grades 9 through 12 who reported being injured in a physical fight was 4%.[29] Approximately 6% of the students reported carrying a weapon on school property. Fewer than 1% of all homicides among students are associated with schools. Students are twice as likely to be victimized away from school than at school.[28] Nevertheless, aggressive behavior in schools is an important problem that continues to challenge many students, teachers, and school administrators.

Risk and Protective Factors for Youth Violence

There is no simple answer to the question of why some youth become violent and others do not. However, researchers have determined that some factors put young people at greater risk of violence and other factors seem to protect them. Table 9.1 presents risk and protective factors grouped into 5 different domains: individual, family, school, peer group, and community.[28]

Recommendations to Prevent Unintentional Injuries and Violence

The Centers for Disease Control and Prevention recommends 8 strategies to prevent unintentional injury and violence in schools.[3] Each recommendation includes guidelines for implementation and a rationale for action. They address the school environment, classroom instruction, and needed supportive services for both students and staff. These recommendations, guiding principles, and strategies represent the state-of-the-science in school-based unintentional injury and violence prevention. Every recommendation might not be feasible for every school, but districts should determine which recommendations have the highest priority on the basis of their needs and available resources.

Table 9.1
Early and Late Risk Factors for Violence at Age 15 to 18 and Proposed Protective Factors, by Domain*

Domain	Risk Factor		Protective Factor[†]
	Early Onset (age 6-11)	**Late Onset (age 12-14)**	
Individual	General offenses Substance use Being male Aggression[‡] Psychological condition Hyperactivity Problem (antisocial) behavior Exposure to television violence Medical, physical Low IQ Antisocial attitudes, beliefs Dishonesty[‡]	General offenses Psychological condition Restlessness Difficulty concentrating[‡] Risk taking Aggression[‡] Being male Physical violence Antisocial attitudes, beliefs Crimes against persons Problem (antisocial) behavior Low IQ Substance use	Intolerant attitude toward deviance High IQ Being female Positive social orientation Perceived sanctions for transgressions
Family	Low socioeconomic status or poverty Antisocial parents Poor parent-child relations Harsh, lax, or inconsistent discipline Broken home Separation from parents Other conditions Abusive parents Neglect	Poor parent-child relations Harsh, lax discipline; poor monitoring, supervision Low parental involvement Antisocial parents Broken home Low socioeconomic status or poverty Abusive parents Other conditions Family conflict[‡]	Warm, supportive relationships with parents or other adults Parents' positive evaluation of peers Parental monitoring

| Domain | Risk Factor | | Protective Factor† |
	Early Onset (age 6-11)	Late Onset (age 12-14)	
School	Poor attitude, performance	Poor attitude, performance Academic failure	Commitment to school Recognition for involvement in conventional activities
Peer Group	Weak social ties Antisocial peers	Weak social ties Antisocial, delinquent peers Gang membership	Friends who engage in conventional behavior
Community		Neighborhood crime, drugs Neighborhood disorganization	

* Reprinted from US Department of Health and Human Services. *Youth Violence: A Report of the Surgeon General.* Rockville, MD: US Department of Health and Human Services, Centers for Disease Control and Prevention, National Center for Injury Prevention and Control; Substance Abuse and Mental Health Services Administration, Center for Mental Health Services; and National Institutes of Health, National Institute of Mental Health; 2001:58.

† Age of onset not known.
‡ Males only.

Recommendation 1: Establish a Social Environment That Promotes Safety and Prevents Unintentional Injuries and Violence

Health and academic success are reciprocal. School districts should establish a mission statement in cooperation with students, faculty, families, and community members that promotes a set of core beliefs that includes responsible, safe, and ethical behavior and recognizes the need for a supportive and safe school environment. Guiding principles for establishing a social environment that promotes safety and prevents unintentional injuries, violence, and suicide include the following:

- Ensure high academic standards and provide faculty, staff members, and students with the support and administrative leadership to promote the academic success (ie, achievement), health, and safety of all students.
- Encourage students' feelings of connectedness to school.
- Designate a person with responsibility for coordinating safety activities.
- Establish a climate that demonstrates respect, support, and caring and that does not tolerate harassment or bullying.
- Develop and implement written policies regarding unintentional injury, violence, and suicide prevention.
- Infuse unintentional injury, violence, and suicide prevention into multiple school activities and classes.
- Establish unambiguous disciplinary policies; communicate them to students, faculty, staff members, and families; and implement them consistently.
- Assess unintentional injury, violence, and suicide prevention strategies and policies at regular intervals.

Recommendation 2: Provide a Physical Environment, Inside and Outside School Buildings, That Promotes Safety and Prevents Unintentional Injuries and Violence

The physical environment, inside and outside school buildings including equipment, can affect unintentional injuries and violence. Schools should ensure that the physical environment is safe by implementing the following guidelines:

- Conduct regular safety and hazard assessments.
- Maintain structures, playground and other equipment, school buses and other vehicles, and physical grounds; make repairs immediately after hazards have been identified.
- Actively supervise all student activities to promote safety and prevent unintentional injuries and violence.
- Ensure that the school environment, including school buses, is free of weapons.

Recommendation 3: Implement Health and Safety Education Curricula and Instruction That Help Students Develop the Knowledge, Attitudes, Behavioral Skills, and Confidence Needed to Adopt and Maintain Safe Lifestyles and to Advocate for Health and Safety

Health instruction is an important component of district efforts to prevent unintentional injuries, violence, and suicide. Guiding principles that help students develop the knowledge, attitudes, behavioral skills, and confidence needed to adopt and maintain safe lifestyles and to advocate for health and safety include the following:

- Choose prevention programs and curricula that are grounded in theory or that have scientific evidence of effectiveness.
- Implement unintentional injury and violence prevention curricula consistent with national and state standards for health education.
- Use active learning strategies, interactive teaching methods, and proactive classroom management to encourage student involvement in learning about unintentional injury and violence prevention.

- Provide adequate staffing and resources, including budget, facilities, staff development, and class time to provide unintentional injury and violence prevention for all students.

Recommendation 4: Provide Safe Physical Education and Extracurricular Physical Activity Programs

Physical education and extracurricular physical activity programs offer many opportunities to teach skills that can promote lifelong involvement in physical activity and prevent activity-related injury. Physical activity programs can also be positive alternatives to risky behaviors and increase school connectedness. Guiding principles for providing safe physical education and extracurricular physical activity programs including the following:

- Develop, teach, implement, and enforce safety rules.
- Promote unintentional injury prevention and nonviolence through physical education and physical activity program participation.

Recommendation 5: Provide Health, Counseling, Psychological, and Social Services to Meet the Physical, Mental, Emotional, and Social Health Needs of Students

Students' risk for unintentional injury, violence, and suicide is affected by various factors that can be improved by meeting their health needs through supportive services.

- Coordinate school-based counseling, psychological, social, and health services; and the educational curriculum.
- Establish strong links with community resources and identify providers to bring services into the schools.
- Identify and provide assistance to students who have been seriously injured, who have witnessed violence, who have been the victims of violence or harassment, and who are being victimized or harassed.
- Assess the extent to which injuries occur on school property.

- Develop and implement emergency plans for assessing, managing, and referring injured students and staff members to appropriate levels of care.

Recommendation 6: Establish Mechanisms for Short- and Long-term Responses to Crises, Disasters, and Injuries That Affect the School Community

Guiding principles include the following:

- Establish a written plan for responding to crises, disasters, and associated injuries.
- Prepare to implement the school's plan in the event of a crisis.
- Determine appropriate short-term responses and services after a crisis.
- Identify long-term responses and services after a crisis.

Recommendation 7: Integrate School, Family, and Community Efforts to Prevent Unintentional Injuries, Violence, and Suicide

Schools cannot prevent unintentional injuries, violence, and suicide in isolation from the communities and families they serve. Guiding principles include the following:

- Involve parents, students, and other family members in all aspects of school life, including planning and implementing prevention programs and policies.
- Educate, support, and involve family members in child and adolescent risk reduction and prevention efforts.
- Coordinate school and community services.

Recommendation 8: For All School Personnel, Provide Regular Staff Development Opportunities That Give Them the Knowledge, Skills, and Confidence to Effectively Promote Safety and Prevent Unintentional Injury, Violence, and Suicide, and Support Students in the Efforts to Do the Same

Trained staff members are essential to implementing effective prevention programs. Guiding principles include the following:

- Ensure that staff members are knowledgeable about unintentional injury, violence, and suicide prevention and have the skills needed to prevent injuries, violence, and suicide at school, at home, and in the community.
- Train and support all personnel to be positive role models for a healthy and safe lifestyle.

Recommendations for the Pediatrician

Parents look to pediatricians for guidance on injury prevention. Counseling patients and their families should emphasize key injury prevention messages. In addition, pediatricians should make parents aware of specific injury prevention issues in schools and urge families to insist on appropriate safety measures. As a consultant to the schools, the pediatrician should be knowledgeable about injury prevention and collaborate with the local health department, emergency medical and hospital services, families, and school staff to establish an injury surveillance system that provides epidemiologic data to facilitate development and implementation of targeted injury countermeasures.[11]

When pediatricians are asked to speak to school groups, to advise school boards, and to serve as school physicians and health consultants, they can help ensure the safest school environment possible and encourage the best use of schools' resources to educate and influence students and staff. Pediatricians should publicly support community safety initiatives and should volunteer for school-based activities.

Pediatricians should become advocates for injury prevention by participating in community coalitions, educating public policy makers, and becoming recognized as advocates and experts on pediatric injury prevention.[11] In summary, pediatricians should:

- Become familiar with any violence-related problems or concerns their patients might be facing in school, in their family, with peers, or in the community;
- Be prepared to intervene on behalf of their patients by notifying the appropriate individuals or institutions;
- Become familiar with injury and violence data in the community;
- Identify risk and protective factors within their patients' immediate environments;
- Establish relationships with schools that their patients are attending and introduce themselves to the principals and mental health staff;
- Become familiar with the types of programs being implemented in the schools to reduce injury, substance abuse, and violence; and
- Participate on the district's health council and advocate for research-based, effective injury and violence prevention programs.

References

1. Murphy SL. Deaths: final data for 1998. *Natl Vital Stat Rep.* 2000;48:1–105
2. Student's Safety Network. *Injuries in the School Environment: A Resource Packet.* 2nd ed. Newton, MA: Education Developmental Center Inc; 1994
3. Centers for Disease Control and Prevention. School health guidelines to prevent unintentional injuries and violence. *MMWR Recomm Rep.* 2001;50(RR-22):1–73
4. Miller TR, Spicer RS. How safe are our schools? *Am J Public Health.* 1998;88:413–418
5. US Office of Technology Assessment. *Risks to Students in Schools.* Washington, DC: US Government Printing Office; 1994. Publication No. OTA ENV-633
6. Brener ND, Burstein GR, DuShaw ML, Vernon ME, Wheeler L, Robinson J. Health services: results from the School Health Policies and Programs Study 2000. *J Sch Health.* 2001;71:294–304

7. Scheidt PC, Harel Y, Trumble AC, Jones DH, Overpeck MD, Bijur PE. The epidemiology of nonfatal injuries among US children and youth. *Am J Public Health.* 1995;85:932–938

8. DiScala C, Lescohier I, Barthel M, Li G. Injuries to children with attention deficit hyperactivity disorder. *Pediatrics.* 1998;102:1415–1421

9. American Academy of Pediatrics, Committee on Injury and Poison Prevention. *Injury Prevention and Control for Children and Youth.* Widome MD, ed. Elk Grove Village, IL: American Academy of Pediatrics; 1997

10. Laflamme L, Menckel E. Pupil injury risks as a function of physical and psychosocial environmental problems experienced at school. *Inj Prev.* 2001;7:146–149

11. National Highway Traffic Safety Administration. *Report to Congress. School Bus Safety: Crashworthiness Research, April 2002.* Washington, DC: 2002. Available at: httw://www-nrd.nhtsa.dot.gov/departments/nrd-11/schoolbus.html. Accessed July 28, 2003

12. National Transportation Safety Board. *Highway Special Investigation Report: Bus Crashworthiness Issues.* Washington, DC: National Transportation Safety Board; 1999. Publication No. NTSB/SIR-99/04. Available at: http://www.ntsb.gov/publictn/1999/SIR9904.htm. Accessed July 28, 2003

13. American Academy of Pediatrics, Committee on School Health and Committee on Injury and Poison Prevention. School transportation safety. *Pediatrics.* 1996.97:754–757

14. National Highway Traffic Safety Administration. *Traffic Safety Facts 1999: School Buses.* Washington, DC: National Highway Traffic Safety Administration; 1999. Available at: http://www.nhtsa.dot.gov/people/. Accessed July 28, 2003

15. American Academy of Pediatrics, Committee on Injury and Poison Prevention. Transporting children with special health care needs. *Pediatrics.* 1999;104:988–992

16. American Academy of Pediatrics, Committee on Injury and Poison Prevention. School bus transportation of children with special health care needs. *Pediatrics.* 2001;108:516–518

17. American Academy of Pediatrics. *Safe Transportation of Children With Special Needs: A Guide for Families.* Elk Grove Village, IL: American Academy of Pediatrics; 2002

18. Indiana University School of Medicine. *Safe Travel for all Students: Transporting Children With Special Health Care Needs Training and Resource Manual.* Indianapolis, IN: Automotive Safety Program, James Whitcomb Riley Hospital for Children, Indiana University School of Medicine; 2000

19. Centers for Disease Control and Prevention. Pedestrian Injury Prevention. Available at: http://www.cdc.gov/ncipc/factsheets/pedes.htm. Accessed July 28, 2003

20. Duperrex O, Bunn F, Roberts I. Safety education of pedestrians for injury prevention: a systematic review of randomized controlled trials. *BMJ.* 2002;324:1129

21. Centers for Disease Control and Prevention, National Center for Health Statistics. *1998 Mortality Tapes.* Hyattsville, MD: National Center for Health Statistics; 2000

22. US Consumer Product Safety Commission. National Electronic Injury Surveillance System [database]. Bethesda, MD: US Consumer Product Safety Commission; 1999

23. Centers for Disease Control and Prevention. Injury-control recommendations: bicycle helmets. *MMWR Recomm Rep.* 1995;44(RR-1):1–17

24. National Highway Traffic Safety Administration. *Traffic Safety Facts 2000: Young Drivers.* Washington, DC: National Highway Traffic Safety Administration; 2000. Available at: http://www.nhtsa.dot.gov/people/. Accessed July 28, 2003

25. Cerrelli EC. *Research Note: Crash Data and Rates for Age-Sex Groups of Drivers, 1994.* Washington, DC: US Department of Transportation, National Highway Traffic Safety Administration; 1995

26. Insurance Institute for Highway Safety. *Crash Problem on a Per Mile Basis.* Washington, DC: Insurance Institute for Highway Safety; 1992:11:1–8

27. Shope JT, Molnar LJ, Elliot MR, Waller PF. Graduated driver licensing in Michigan: early impact on motor vehicle crashes among 16-year-old drivers. *JAMA.* 2001;286:1593–1598

28. *Youth Violence: Report of the Surgeon General.* Washington, DC: US Department of Health and Human Services; 2001. Available at: http://www.surgeongeneral.gov/library/youthviolence/default.htm. Accessed July 28, 2003

29. Centers for Disease Control and Prevention. Youth Risk Behavior Surveillance—United States, 1999. *MMWR CDC Surveill Summ.* 2000;49:1–32

Chapter 10
Comprehensive Health Education

No knowledge is more crucial than knowledge about health. Without it, no other life goal can be successfully achieved.[1]

More than 50 million young people attend more than 100 000 schools across the United States.[2] School health programming represents one of the most efficient means to improve the health of children and youth. As part of a coordinated school health program, comprehensive health education is classroom instruction that:

- Addresses the physical, emotional, intellectual, social, and ethical dimensions of health;
- Develops health knowledge, attitudes, and skills tailored to each age level for which it is designed; and
- Motivates and assists students in establishing healthy habits, reducing health-related risk behaviors, and preventing disability and disease.[3]

Although it has been stated on numerous occasions and is well demonstrated that health and learning are inextricably linked,[3] when working with school districts, this concept must be repeated and reinforced continuously. Schools are held accountable for the educational outcomes of their students, not students' health status. Although it is obvious that a student who is ill or has poor vision or hearing cannot perform well in school, it often is less obvious how risky health behaviors interfere with academic success. Health education holds enormous potential for positively influencing both health and academic outcomes, and there is widespread support among school administrators, students, and their families for teaching more health information and disease prevention skills.[4] Nevertheless, few schools offer truly comprehensive and effective health education. A pediatrician can be a strong advocate for comprehensive health education and coordinated health programming in schools.

Increase the proportion of middle, junior high, and senior high schools that provide comprehensive health education to prevent health problems in the following areas: unintentional injury; violence; suicide; tobacco use and addiction; alcohol or other drug use; unintended pregnancy; human immunodeficiency virus/acquired immunodeficiency syndrome (HIV/AIDS) and sexually transmitted disease (STD) infection; unhealthy dietary patterns; inadequate physical activity; and environmental health (*Healthy People 2010*, Objective 7-2).

Written Course of Study

Health education is not mandated at the national level, although 9 of 10 states (90%) and districts (90.8%) require schools to offer health instruction.[5] Some states mandate that certain topics be covered. For example, most states require instruction to prevent infection with HIV and other STDs and to prevent the use of alcohol, other drugs, and tobacco. Some states require discussion of nutrition and other dietary behaviors. Even in states in which health instruction is mandated, implementation is highly variable.

Districts that include health instruction are required to have a written course of study outlining what students should know and be able to do for every grade level from preschool through high school. There are 3 basic approaches to framing the course of study. Some districts include 10 "traditional" content areas:

- Personal health
- Family health
- Community health
- Environmental health

- Growth and development
- Emotional health
- Injury prevention and safety
- Nutrition
- Prevention and control of disease
- Prevention of substance use and abuse

A second framework uses the 6 priority risk categories identified by the Centers for Disease Control and Prevention that are linked to the leading causes of morbidity and mortality among youth: intentional and unintentional injuries; alcohol and other drug use; tobacco use; unhealthy dietary behaviors; inadequate physical activity; and sexual behaviors. A third structure is based on the National Health Education Standards developed in 1995 by the Joint Committee on National Health Education Standards. These standards state that students will:

- Comprehend concepts related to health promotion and disease prevention;
- Demonstrate the ability to access valid health information and health-promoting products and services;
- Demonstrate the ability to practice health-enhancing behaviors and reduce health risks;
- Analyze the influence of culture, media, technology, and other factors on health;
- Demonstrate the ability to use interpersonal communication skills to enhance health;
- Demonstrate the ability to use goal-setting and decision-making skills to enhance health; and
- Demonstrate the ability to advocate for personal, family, and community health.

Whatever framework the district uses, the course of study should be reviewed every 3 to 5 years by a committee that includes family representatives and interested community members. The committee should ensure that the framework includes current scientific knowledge and best practices.

> Increase the proportion of young adults who have received formal instruction before turning age 18 years on reproductive health issues, including all of the following topics: birth control methods, safer sex to prevent HIV, prevention of sexually transmitted diseases, and abstinence (*Healthy People 2010,* Objective 9-11).

Effective Curricula

Curricula, including texts and supplemental health education materials, are used by teachers to meet the goals and objectives outlined in the course of study. Local schools are given autonomy for selecting the health curriculum. Curriculum review committees should review and select age-appropriate curricula based on written selection criteria. Suggested criteria have been identified in a meta-analyses[6] of curricula that were successful in reducing or delaying tobacco, alcohol, and other drug use; violence; and sexual risk behaviors. These curricula had the following characteristics:

- Research based and theory driven;
- Provision of basic, accurate, age-appropriate information;
- Use of interactive, experiential activities that actively engaged students;
- Students given opportunities to model and practice relevant social skills;
- Social or media influences on behaviors addressed;
- Strengthening of individual values and group norms supportive of positive health behaviors;
- Sufficient duration to permit students to master needed information and skills; and
- Professional development for teachers to enhance implementation.

Professional development for teachers is essential to produce results similar to those found in evaluation studies. Success rates will vary to the extent that the curricula are implemented with fidelity to the parameters used in the original evaluation.

When selecting any curriculum, written guidelines should be in place before the review process. These might vary depending on the topic under consideration. When considering materials addressing sexual issues or other controversial topics, it is essential that approved, written criteria be in place. Again, meta-analyses of effective curricula are helpful.

For example, curricula that reduced sexual risk behaviors were found to have the following shared characteristics[7]:

- A narrow focus on reducing specific risk-taking behaviors that can lead to HIV infection, other STDs, or unintended pregnancy;
- Behavioral goals, teaching methods, and materials appropriate to the age, sexual experience, and culture of the students;
- Use of theoretic approaches shown to be effective in influencing other health-related behaviors (eg, social cognitive theory, social influence theory, social inoculation theory, cognitive behavioral theory, and the theory of reasoned action);
- Sufficient number of lessons (time) to complete important activities adequately;
- Teaching methods designed to actively involve students and personalize the information;
- Basic, accurate information about risks associated with unprotected intercourse and methods of avoiding them;
- Activities that help students think critically about social and media influences on sexual behaviors;
- Opportunities to model and practice communication, negotiation, and refusal skills; and
- Teachers who are trained in the use of the particular curricula and are committed to using them.

Increase the age and proportion of adolescents who remain alcohol and drug free (*Healthy People 2010*, Objective 26-9), increase the proportion of adolescents who disapprove of substance abuse (*Healthy People 2010*, Objective 26-16), and increase the proportion of adolescents who perceive great risk associated with substance abuse (*Healthy People 2010*, Objective 26-17).

Reduce the proportion of persons engaging in binge drinking of alcoholic beverages (*Healthy People 2010*, Objective 26-11), reduce steroid use among adolescents (*Healthy People 2010*, Objective 26-14), and reduce the proportion of adolescents who use inhalants (*Healthy People 2010*, Objective 26-15).

Reduce tobacco use by adolescents (*Healthy People 2010*, Objective 27-2) and increase tobacco use cessation attempts by adolescent smokers (*Healthy People 2010*, Objective 27-7).

Reduce initiation of tobacco use among children and adolescents (*Healthy People 2010*, Objective 27-3) and increase adolescents' disapproval of smoking (*Healthy People 2010*, Objective 27-17).

Skill Orientation

In addition to scientifically correct information, an important curriculum selection criterion should be the inclusion of a variety of reality-oriented activities that provide students with opportunities to practice needed cognitive and behavioral skills. These skills include how to access health information; how to analyze influences on health; and effective communication, decision-making, and other skills to advocate for personal, family, and community health.

Sufficient Time

Research suggests that a minimum of 50 hours of instruction over 2 to 3 years is necessary to establish a single positive health behavior.[3] Districts can prescribe the amount of time devoted to health instruction at each grade level. Health is an academic subject that needs and deserves a place in the curriculum if schools are to produce healthy and health-literate citizens.

Health Coordinator

Management and coordination by a qualified professional is necessary to plan, implement, and evaluate all facets of the school health program. Without consistent leadership, school health programs seldom achieve their goals and objectives. Health education is an academic course, and there often is a department chairperson who serves on the district curriculum committee. This person also might be responsible for the physical education curriculum. Alternatively, some districts include health education as one of several content areas for which a district-level curriculum supervisor is responsible. This person might have no special training in health education. A district advisory council can help guide program development and assist the coordinator.

Qualified Teachers

The key to effective instruction lies in the training and preparation of the teacher. Although health education requires separate certification in some states, in other states many teachers responsible for teaching health have limited or no preservice preparation in health content or the interactive teaching strategies that are at the heart of effective health education. Many middle schools and most high schools have health teachers who are trained and certified in health education. At the elementary level, the classroom teacher is responsible for health along with all other subjects. Unfortunately, few states mandate that elementary teachers have any training or preparation in health education and offer little in the way of in-service education in health.

Family and Community Involvement

Schools cannot, nor should they be expected to, provide everything students need to learn and be healthy. Health education that attempts to provide students with necessary information and skills to establish life-long healthy habits requires positive modeling from teachers and family members as well as significant reinforcement in the home.

Performance Assessment

Health instruction programming, like all other aspects of school health programming, should establish mechanisms that provide qualitative and quantitative data to assess progress in meeting stated objectives. This information should be used to continually improve and update the course of study, suggest professional development needs, and demonstrate accountability. With the growing state and national interest in school assessments, pediatricians should advocate for the inclusion of health education on the assessment measures. The State Collaborative on Assessment and Student Standards has a health education assessment project to help guide this process (more information available at http://www.ccsso.org/scass).

Emerging Issues

Sex education is one aspect of health education that invokes a great deal of concern and discussion in school districts. Nationally representative surveys of parents consistently document that most support sexuality and HIV education in the schools. In fact, a 1994 Gallup poll sponsored by the American Cancer Society found that 80% of those surveyed considered sex education and information about HIV and AIDS equal to or more important than other courses taught in school, and 96% rated it at least as important, if not more important. Of all the topics covered in health education, topics related to sexuality were rated the most important.

School districts rely on influential community members and vocal parents to advise and inform them about sensitive issues. Pediatricians can help educate concerned individuals about adolescent sexual development; provide current rates of adolescent pregnancy, birth, and STDs locally, in the state, and nationally; offer available technology to prevent pregnancy and STDs, including HIV; and facilitate discussions about whether to include information about these technologies in schools. There often is confusion about what is meant by "abstinence-only" and "abstinence-based" sex education. Abstinence-only sex education includes only information and skills on how to abstain from sexual intercourse and other risky sexual behaviors. It does not provide information on how to prevent pregnancy or STDs among sexually active individuals. Abstinence-based sex education emphasizes abstinence but includes information on protective technologies.

Recommendations for Pediatricians

- Contact the district administrator responsible for health education and learn about the course of study, curricula, and materials used in the elementary, middle, and high schools and the processes used to select them.
- Offer to serve on the curriculum review committee.
- Review district policies related to health instruction.
- Volunteer to participate in the professional development in-service for teachers and other school staff.
- Volunteer to talk to families as part of the district's efforts to engage parents.
- Remind school administrators of the link between health and learning at every opportunity.
- Because many policies affecting what schools teach are determined at the state level, either at the state department of education or in the state legislature, work with the American Academy of Pediatrics chapters and the Committee on School Health to ensure that policy makers are well informed of the health education needs of students, and lobby health policy makers to include health education on state proficiency tests.

- Support the use of valid and reliable survey instruments, such as the Youth Risk Behavior Survey, to collect data in your district on student health behaviors that can help inform the district's course of study and curriculum selection process.
- Join other state-level organizations, such as affiliates of the American School Health Association or the National Association of School Nurses, to strengthen their voices.

Resources
Internet
AAP Section on School Health:
  http://www.schoolhealth.org
Centers for Disease Control and Prevention, Division of Adolescent and School Health:
  http://www.cdc.gov/nccdphp/dash
  (800/488-3163; 1600 Clifton Rd, Atlanta, GA 30333)
National School Board Association:
  http://www.nsba.org
Parents and Teachers Association:
  http://www.pta.org

Articles
Centers for Disease Control and Prevention. The School Health Policies and Programs Study (SHPPS): a summary report. *J Sch Health*. 1995;65:289-353

Centers for Disease Control and Prevention. Trends in sexual risk behaviors among high school students—United States, 1991-1997. *MMWR Morb Mortal Wkly Rep*. 1998;47:749-752

Joint Committee on National Health Education Standards. *National Health Education Standards: Achieving Health Literacy*. Kent, OH: American School Health Association; 1995

Kolbe LJ, Collins J, Cortese P. Building the capacity of schools to improve the health of the nation. A call for assistance from psychologists. *Am Psychol.* 1997;52:256-265

Books

Cortese P, Middleton K, eds. *The Comprehensive School Health Challenge: Promoting Health Through Education.* Vol 1 and 2. Santa Cruz, CA: ETR Associates Publishers; 1994

Dryfoos G. *Full Service Schools: A Revolution in Health and School Services for Children, Youth, and Families.* San Francisco, CA: Jossey-Bass Inc; 1994

Marx E, Wooley SF. *Health is Academic: A Guide to Coordinated School Health Programs.* New York, NY: Teachers College Press; 1998

References

1. Boyer EL. *High School: A Report on Secondary Education in America: The Carnegie Foundation for the Advancement of Teaching.* New York, NY: Harper and Row; 1983
2. National Center for Educational Statistics Web site. Available at: http://www.nces.ed.gov. Accessed August 9, 2002
3. Marx E, Wooley SF, eds. *Health is Academic: A Guide to Coordinated School Health Programs.* New York, NY: Teachers College Press; 1998
4. The Gallup Organization. Gallup Poll 1994. Values and opinions of comprehensive school health education in US public schools: Adolescents, parents, and school district administrators. Atlanta, GA: American Cancer Society; 1994
5. Centers for Disease Control and Prevention. The School Health Policies and Programs Study (SHPPS) 2000: a summary report. *J Sch Health.* 2000;71:251–350
6. Dusenbury L, Falco M. Eleven components of effective drug abuse prevention curricula. *J Sch Health.* 1995;65:420–425
7. Kirby D. *No Easy Answers: Research Findings on Programs to Reduce Teen Pregnancy.* Washington, DC: National Campaign to Prevent Teen Pregnancy; 1997

Chapter 11
The School Environment

Students spend up to 50 hours per week for at least 9 months a year in school buildings. If activities before and after regular school hours also are considered, many students are in school or on school grounds for substantially more than half of their waking hours. The school environment includes social and physical elements, both of which contribute to making the school a safe and positive environment for learning.

The Social Environment

The social environment, often referred to as the school climate, affects students' ability to learn in various ways. The psychological atmosphere in a school can influence whether a student feels connected to school and the learning process. Youth who feel connected are more likely to achieve and behave well. Schools that incorporate the characteristics of a positive school environment are more likely to improve academic achievement and staff morale, reduce disciplinary referrals and suspensions, and enhance safety.

Qualities of Safe and Supportive Schools

The following are the fundamental assets of safe and supportive schools[1]:

- Strong leadership, caring faculty, family and community involvement that includes law enforcement officials and representatives of community-based organizations, and student participation in the design of programs and policies;
- A challenging and engaging curriculum for all students;
- Respectful, supportive relationships between and among students, school staff, and parents;

- Frequent opportunities for student participation, collaboration, service, and self-direction;
- Safe physical environment and policies to promote and support responsible behaviors;
- Sustained, coordinated, and comprehensive prevention and intervention programs;
- Interventions based on careful assessment of student needs;
- Use of evidence-based approaches;
- Staff trained and supported so that they can implement programs and approaches; and
- Monitoring and evaluation of interventions to ensure that the programs meet measurable goals and objectives.

A number of strategies have been used to help students feel more connected to school and to improve the social climate of the school, including the following:

- Building school capacity: this is accomplished by modifying the decision-making processes and authority structures within the school to include teachers, school staff, and members of the community. School health councils are typical of this approach because they increase school capacity by involving community members and families in identifying and solving problems within the school. Activities aimed at improving the climate of the school include increasing communication, morale, and cooperation among members of the school community.
- Establishing clear rules and norms for expected behaviors: district-wide efforts to clarify acceptable behavior have been shown to be particularly effective for reducing antisocial behavior and substance abuse. All students are educated about school rules and discipline codes and the consequences for breaking the rules. This strategy is especially successful when students participate in formulating the rules and the consequences.

- Student engagement: activities are designed to increase positive social interaction in the classroom, the larger school community, and the community at large.
- Regrouping students: students are reorganized into smaller classes or units, creating different mixes of students through cooperative learning techniques, or forming teams. An example of regrouping is the development of alternative schools for students who do not adjust well to the typical school environment.

Strategies to Change Student Knowledge, Skills, Attitudes, Beliefs, and Behaviors

High Academic Standards

Engaging in injury-related risk behaviors is associated with poor performance on standardized tests, poor class grades, lower graduation rates, and behavioral problems at school. Conversely, academic success (ie, academic achievement) is associated with a decreased likelihood of engaging in risky health behaviors.[2]

Interactive Instructional Strategies

Life-skills training, the most widely used strategy in schools, incorporates interactive instructional strategies to teach students factual information, increase their awareness of social influences linked to undesirable behaviors, expand their skills for recognizing potentially harmful situations and resisting cues to misbehave, promote appreciation for diversity in society, and emphasize positive character traits.

Behavior Modification and Critical Thinking Strategies

Many of these programs focus directly on changing behavior through techniques that help students identify negative behaviors, formulate personal action plans to change behavior, track and evaluate progress, and use incentives and reinforcements external to the student. Other cognitive-behavioral strategies involve modeling of desired behaviors and practice through role playing and rehearsals with coaching. Students learn to use prompts or cues to slow down and think through a situation instead of acting impulsively.

Peer Programs

Such programs prepare students through structured training programs to serve as peer counselors, mediators, and educators.

Other Counseling Approaches

Student assistance programs might offer one-on-one and small group counseling by trained mental health professionals.

Recreational, Enrichment, and Leisure Activities

Midnight basketball is probably the best known of these approaches, which are intended to offer positive alternatives to delinquent behaviors. This approach includes school dances, after-school programs, and community service activities.

These ideas are consistent with the literature on resilience and promoting positive youth development. Student connectedness and opportunities to serve are related positively to school success. By creating a positive school psychological environment, schools can promote a preventive strategy for school success and avoid having to react to negative behaviors that are discouraging for all involved. Pediatricians should encourage schools to plan and adopt policies that promote positive school climates. A good resource for safe and supportive schools is *Every Child Learning: Safe and Supportive Schools,* published by the Learning First Alliance (available at http://www.learningfirst.org).

The Physical Environment

The school environment might contain a number of physical, biologic, and chemical elements to which students and school staff, nearly 20% of the US population, might be exposed. These elements can result in disease, illness, and poor academic outcomes.

Because an individual's body mass, immune response, stage of de-velopment, and activity level determine the extent of adverse effects, students are at increased risk. For example, young students have high-er metabolic rates and more skin surface per unit of weight than do adults. In addition, their short stature makes them closer to chemicals on floors, in dust, and on playgrounds. Young students also are at greater risk because of the immaturity of their developing organ sys-tems. They cannot detoxify and excrete toxic substances as efficiently as adults.

> Reduce indoor allergen levels (*Healthy People 2010*, Objective 8-16) and increase the number of office buildings that are managed using good indoor air quality practices (*Healthy People 2010*, Objective 8-17).

Air Quality

When indoor air quality is a problem, individuals tend to experience symptoms only when in a particular building or in specific areas within a building. Problems associated with indoor air pollution include asth-ma; increased frequency of respiratory infections; generalized symp-toms such as headaches, fatigue, and poor concentration; and increased absenteeism. Since the early 1980s, the number of children diagnosed with asthma has more than doubled, with an estimated 10 million school days missed each year because of asthma and related illnesses. Because the range of indoor air pollutants is large, school health staff must consider carefully all possible causes of respiratory symptoms, skin reactions, or allergic phenomena. For example, school staff might track locations (particular classrooms) in which students seem to expe-rience difficulties or note particular days of the week or month that seem problematic for individual students. Indoor air pollution can result from contaminants in school buildings or from outdoor air introduced through the ventilating systems. *Sick building syndrome* is the term used to describe the situation in which no specific pollutant or pollutants are identified. Specific problems arise from inadequate air circulation, excessive or inadequate humidity, the presence of fibers, molds, bacteria, gases, and volatile organic compounds in the circulating air, or a combination of these factors.

Inadequate air circulation might be the most common reason for indoor air problems. Because most school buildings are closed to direct ventilation from outside air except for the air intake system, the design, operation, and maintenance of the heating, ventilating, and air conditioning (HVAC) systems are aspects of building construction and maintenance requiring clear and specific guidelines that consider environmental concerns. Outdoor air should be supplied at 15 ft^3 per minute per individual in a ventilated space. Carpets should be vacuumed regularly, but like all cleaning, activities should be performed at night or on weekends. Crowded classrooms, the use of temporary structures, and continuing reductions in funds budgeted for plant maintenance all contribute to the difficulty of maintaining safe school buildings. More detailed discussion of ventilation issues and checklists are provided by the US Environmental Protection Agency (EPA).[3,4]

Excess humidity can arise from improperly functioning HVAC equipment, kitchens, humidifiers, leakage from roofs, basements, wet concrete, damp carpets, and bathrooms and can lead to growth of hazardous bacteria and molds, which release their spores into the air. Damp carpet should be removed and leaks and seepage repaired. Asbestos fibers result from damaged asbestos or asbestos removal without adequate isolation. Without proper air filtration, ordinary dust, dust from chalk, and dust from shop work might remain in the air, and dust mites may proliferate in such environments.

Volatile organic compounds are chemical compounds that produce distinctive odors as they vaporize into the air at room temperature. Examples found in schools include new carpets, air fresheners, bleach, floor care products, toilet cleaners, paints, oven and rug cleaners, paint strippers, copy machines, printers, dry-erase markers, adhesives, and some laboratory and vocational arts supplies. Newly remodeled buildings often have high levels of formaldehyde from plywood, foam insulation, and wallboard. Additional sources include aliphatic hydrocarbons, ketones, and alcohols. Other gases of concern include carbon monoxide resulting from improperly functioning furnaces or hot water heaters, radon from soil, and ozone from office equipment. All paints, solvents, or other chemicals should be stored in closed containers and locked in cabinets in secure locations.

> Reduce the proportion of nonsmokers exposed to environmental tobacco smoke (*Healthy People 2010*, Objective 27-10).

Tobacco smoke contains a variety of chemicals, including carbon monoxide, benzene, hydrogen cyanide, polycyclic aromatic hydrocarbon tars, nicotine, formaldehyde, and nitrous oxide. The effects of exposure to sidestream smoke can last up to 4 hours after exposure. Pediatricians should encourage districts to adopt policies designating all school buildings and grounds smoke-free.

Pesticides

> Reduce exposure to pesticides as measured by urine concentrations of metabolites (*Healthy People 2010*, Objective 8-24).

There are no chemicals considered especially safe for students. No information about developmental toxic effects was available for more than three fourths of 2240 high–production-volume chemicals in 1998. Of the 239 high–production-volume chemicals for which permissible exposure levels have been established, one fourth lacked data on developmental toxic effects.

There are more than 900 chemicals registered as pesticides, including insecticides, herbicides, fungicides, rodenticides, fumigants, and insect repellents. Although pesticides can be useful, there is a growing effort to abolish or greatly diminish their use in school environments. In the past, districts used these compounds on a prophylactic basis; such use is now contraindicated.

> Increase the proportion of the nation's primary and secondary schools that have official school policies ensuring the safety of students and staff from environmental hazards, such as chemicals in special classrooms, poor indoor air quality, asbestos, and exposure to pesticides (*Healthy People 2010,* Objective 8-20).

Insecticides

The major insecticides used in schools are organophosphates and N-methylcarbamates. Both are cholinesterase inhibitors. Because organophosphates are more toxic, their use is increasingly restricted by the EPA. Long-term exposure to these substances affects the central nervous system, a particular concern for pregnant teachers and very young students. Whether there are long-term effects in older students remains unknown. Other insecticides include pyrethrins for treatment of head lice or scabies. The effects are primarily allergic and might manifest as asthma, dermatitis, or paresthesias.

School districts are strongly encouraged to implement an integrated pest management policy.[7] Adopting such a policy requires schools to post a notice regarding pesticide application and to notify parents before the application. In 2000, only 3 states, Maryland, Massachusetts, and Michigan, had statutory requirements for integrated pest management policies, and 21 states had no regulations for any of these.[6]

Other Pesticides

Fungicides, rodenticides, fumigants, and disinfectants also may be encountered in the school setting. Fungicides are not likely to be a serious hazard because of their relatively low toxic effects for mammals. Because of their formulation, they are not absorbed readily, and their actual use is unlikely to result in personal exposures. Exposure might produce skin and mucous membrane irritation. Rodenticides usually are in the form of baits that can be isolated from human contact. The most common ones are anticoagulants of the warfarin class of compounds, and ingestion of these can create bleeding disorders. Fumigants are toxic because of their presence as gases, but their use is highly restricted, and buildings in which they are used remain vacated until all traces of the material have dissipated. Disinfectants include alcohols, hypochlorites (bleach), iodines, hexachlorophene, and pine oil. The major toxic effects of these compounds result when ingested, which would be unlikely in the school setting. Maintaining all chemicals in locked cabinets is the most effective way to avoid accidental exposures.[7]

Insect Repellents

Diethyltoluamide (DEET) is the most effective agent against mosquitoes. It is recommended for use at a 10% to 30% concentration and should be washed off with soap and water after use. It should not be applied to areas around the eyes or mouth or on the hands of young students. It should be used only on exposed skin and never under clothing or on skin that is bruised, abraded, or inflamed. It should not be combined with sunscreens.

Microbiologic Agents

Viruses, bacteria, and molds are all present in the school environment. Bacteria and molds, however, might generate illness from endogenous sources, such as standing water in air conditioners, drip pans, persistently damp carpets or structural materials, poorly ventilated bathrooms, and animals such as insects, arthropods, and mammals. Mycotoxins can create severe skin irritations. In addition, bacterial and fungal spores might be circulated by the ventilation system and may cause mild to severe respiratory illness.

The Outdoor Environment

Elements in the outdoor environment that can produce health effects include air pollution, soil contamination, play equipment made with treated wood, UV light, noise, and herbicides.

> Reduce the proportion of persons exposed to air that does not meet the US Environmental Protection Agency's health-based standards for harmful air pollutants (*Healthy People 2010*, Objective 8-1).

Air Pollution

Outdoor air pollution includes 7 principal substances: ozone, particulate matter, lead, sulfur dioxide, carbon monoxide, nitrous oxides, and other toxins. The degree to which a school experiences exposure to 1 or more of these contaminants depends on its location, weather conditions, and prevailing winds. In areas where air pollution alerts occur frequently, it is advisable that districts provide guidance to teachers, physical educators, and coaches regarding outdoor play, particularly for students with respiratory ailments.

> Reduce the proportion of persons exposed to air that does not meet the US Environmental Protection Agency's health-based standards for ozone (*Healthy People 2010*, Objective 8-1a).

> Eliminate elevated blood lead levels in children (*Healthy People 2010*, Objective 8-11).

Lead and sulfates in outdoor air are generated by industrial sources, such as battery recycling, coal-fired power plants, smelters, and pulp and paper mills.[8] Nearly 1 million of the nation's 22 million children younger than 6 years have blood lead concentrations high enough to impair their ability to think, concentrate, and learn.

Although lead-based paint was banned from residential use in 1978, more than 80% of homes built before 1978 are estimated to contain lead.[9] Because lead does not degrade, many urban students continue to be exposed, and more than one fifth of black children living in housing built before 1946 have elevated blood lead concentrations.[10] Students exposed to low levels of lead can have reading and learning disabilities, impaired hearing, hyperactivity, and behavioral problems. At higher concentrations, lead can damage the kidneys and central nervous system and cause anemia, coma, seizures, and even death. Lead exposure causes reduced IQ, learning disabilities, developmental delays, reduced height, hearing loss, and a variety of other health problems in young children, many of which are believed to be irreversible. Some students with high levels of exposure also experience seizures.[11]

Carbon monoxide and nitrous oxide arise primarily from motor vehicle emissions, so schools located near roadways with heavy traffic are at risk. Other toxic air pollutants include volatile organic compounds, heavy metals, solvents, and combustion products, such as dioxin. Overall, more than 150 substances are considered hazardous air pollutants, and their emissions are regulated by the EPA. The concentration of many outdoor air pollutants might be higher inside than outside because of filtration in school ventilation systems.

Contaminated Soil

Closely related to problems associated with outdoor exposures is the issue of site selection for school buildings. Because land with a low value often is chosen when building schools, the use of abandoned industrial sites called "brownfields" or land in proximity to industrial plants is common. Soil contamination from heavy metals, polychlorinated biphenyls, and leakage from old underground storage tanks is a problem, because students often play in the dirt and have high hand-to-mouth activity. Young students and those with mental impairments sometimes display pica and may ingest up to 50 g of soil in 1 day.[12] Of additional concern is the evidence that soil contaminants can be transported into buildings by foot traffic.[13] This could be an increasing problem as new schools are built to manage the increasing numbers of students. Districts need policies requiring that new building sites meet the standards for individual residential use. Because of the variation in such regulations in different states, caution should be exercised that these regulations are based on safety for students and not only for adults.[14]

Wooden Play Equipment

Wooden play equipment that has been constructed with pressure-treated wood contains chromium and arsenic, which can leach to the surface and also can be deposited on the ground. Students can be exposed while playing on the equipment and by contact with the nearby soil. Protecting current structures with regular use of sealants or paints to cover the surfaces is acceptable, although abolishing the use of such wood for playgrounds is recommended.

Ultraviolet Light

Excessive exposure to ultraviolet (UV) light that results in sunburn is especially harmful to students.[15] The serious effects, which manifest later in life, include melanoma and retinal damage. The most dangerous times of day are from noon to mid-afternoon, which correspond to the lunch period and afternoon recess. Avoiding direct exposure to the sun during these times from late spring to early fall, wearing hats and dark sunglasses, and using sunscreens with a sun protection factor of 15 to 30 are all measures that can help prevent serious UV light exposures.

Noise

Levels of noise greater than 60 dB can be intrusive and annoying; loud noise can interfere with concentration and ability to perform complex tasks and can create physiologic and psychological stress, especially for students with conditions such as attention-deficit/hyperactivity disorder. Examples of 70-dB noises include freeway traffic at a distance of 15 m, noisy offices, and busy urban streets.[16]

Herbicides

Herbicides often are used to control weeds. The most common chemical is glyphosphate. At usual exposure levels, it has a low level of toxic effects, but abdominal pain and vomiting may occur and skin and eye irritation are common. The "inert" ingredient polyethoxylated tallowamine, which is used to improve application, might be more toxic than the glyphosphate.[10]

Symptoms and Clues of Environmental Hazards

Symptoms related to environmental problems are rarely specific, but their repeated occurrence or occurrence in more than 1 individual should alert personnel to the possibility of an environmental hazard. These symptoms include headache, dizziness, fatigue, shortness of breath, coughing, sneezing, repeated upper airway congestion, nausea, and persistent eye, nose, or skin irritation. Recurrent exacerbation of asthma and excessive absenteeism also might suggest problems for individual students.

Clues that suggest problems include symptoms that are widespread in a particular class; occurrence of symptoms only when the student(s) are in school or only on the playground; onset after remodeling or similar alteration in the school building; humidity that is repeatedly greater than 50%; evidence of flooding or leakage in the building, such as damp carpeting, mold growth, or foul odors; pets, rodents, or cockroaches in the building; known problems or deficiencies in the HVAC systems; or recent pesticide applications in or around the building. More specific exposures to office equipment, arts and craft supplies, shop supplies, chemical cleaners, and solvents might affect students in those or nearby rooms.

Prevention and Remediation

Half of the schools surveyed by the US General Accounting Office reported at least 1 unsatisfactory condition in terms of students' health.[17] School health care staff, teachers, administrators, maintenance staff, and school board members should be educated about environmental hazards that might occur in the district.

School nurses should keep careful, detailed, and updated individual health records, noting any known allergies, chemical sensitivities, and the presence of asthma or other chronic illness. A comprehensive logging system, noting symptoms, time, location, and known contact with potentially toxic substances, will be most helpful in identifying and locating specific hazards. School nurses can find helpful information on recognizing symptoms and clues that might indicate environmental health problems from the EPA publication on indoor air quality,[4] which can be obtained by calling 800-438-4318. Other resources include the American Nurses Association Web site at http://www.nursingworld.org (search under "environmental health") and the Healthy Schools Network at http://www.healthyschools.org. Nurses also should educate students and staff about the value of proper hand washing to limit the spread of microbial agents. Schools should have adequate facilities and supplies, and staff and students should wash their hands several times a day.

Recommendations for Pediatricians

Pediatricians can advocate for a specific student, advise the district as a medical consultant, or serve as a citizen member of the school health advisory council that works to improve school environments. When the pediatrician is serving as a specific student's personal physician, the pediatrician should work with the school nurse or nurse-designee to document the time and location of symptom occurrence and determine whether the student has similar complaints outside the school or when school is not in session. Ascertaining whether any changes in the school building or its maintenance occurred just before the onset of symptoms should follow. If possible, the pediatrician should try to determine whether other students experienced related symptoms at the same time or location as the student in question. Contacting other pediatricians in the community to determine whether they have seen similar problems with one or more of their patients can be helpful. If there is a reasonable possibility that the school environment is contributing to the student's problems, remediation by the school should be sought.

If the pediatrician is serving as a medical consultant to the school, a sound background in environmental health issues is helpful. Additional help can be obtained from environmental health specialists at the local health department, the regional Agency for Toxic Substances and Disease Registry, one of the 10 new regional pediatric environmental health specialty units, or an environmental health professional in the state chapter of the American Academy of Pediatrics.

The EPA, the Department of Health and Human Services, and the National Institute of Environmental Health Sciences of the National Institutes of Health have been facilitating investigation of possible linkages between the environment and childhood autism and behavioral problems (such as attention-deficit/hyperactivity disorder). Mercury, PCBs (in ingested fish), and pollutants in the home and neighborhood are some of the potential environmental culprits under investigation.

Pediatricians working directly with a school district soon become advocates for improving school health in the broader context. Enlisting a multidisciplinary group of individuals who feel strongly about the role of the environment in affecting the health and well-being of young people is essential. There are several helpful guides, checklists, and programs for preventing, evaluating, and remediating problems related to environmental hazards in schools. The pediatrician who becomes involved in these situations will find these materials most helpful.[6,18] Other excellent resources are available from the Child Proofing Our Communities Campaign of the Center for Health, Environment, and Justice (Internet, http://www.childproofing.org and e-mail, childproofing@chej.org) and the Healthy Schools Network (http://www.healthyschools.org).

References

1. US Department of Education. *Safeguarding Our Children: An Action Guide.* Washington, DC: US Department of Education; 2000
2. Kellam SG, Mayer LS, Rebok GW, Hawkins WE. Effects of improving achievement on aggressive behavior and of improving aggressive behavior on achievement through two preventive interventions: an investigation of causal paths. In: Dohrenwend BP, ed. *Adversity, Stress, and Psychopathology.* New York, NY: Oxford University Press; 1998:486–505
3. Indoor Air Quality Tools for Schools Kit—IAQ Backgrounder. Washington, DC: US Environmental Protection Agency, Indoor Environmentals Division. Available at: http://www.epa.gov/iaq/schools/tfs/iaqback.html. Accessed July 28, 2003
4. Indoor Air—IAQ Tools for Schools. Washington, DC: US Environmental Protection Agency, Indoor Environmentals Division. Available at: http://www.epa.gov/iaq/schools/index.html. Accessed July 28, 2003
5. Rose RI. Pesticides and public health: integrated methods of mosquito management. *Emerg Infect Dis.* 2001;7:17–23 (See also *Establishing an IPM Program for Schools.* Washington, DC: US Environmental Protection Agency, Office of Pesticide Programs. Available at: http://www.epa.gov/opp00001/ipm/brochure/ipmprograms.htm. Accessed July 28, 2003)
6. Owens K, Feldman J. The schooling of state pesticide laws—2000. *Pesticides and You.* 2000;20:16–23
7. Reigart JR, Roberts JR. *Recognition and Management of Pesticide Poisonings.* 5th ed. Washington, DC: US Environmental Protection Agency; 1999. Publication No. EPA 735-R-98-003. Available at: http://www.epa.gov/oppfead1/safety/healthcare/handbook/handbook.htm. Accessed July 28, 2003
8. US Environmental Protection Agency. *Air Quality Criteria for Lead.* Vol 1-4. Washington, DC: US Government Printing Office; 1996. Publication No. EPA/600/8.83/028
9. US Environmental Protection Agency. *Environmental Health Threats to Children.* Washington, DC: US Government Printing Office; 1996. Publication No. EPA/175-F-96001

10. Centers for Disease Control and Prevention, National Center for Environmental Health, Childhood Lead Poisoning Prevention. *Screening Young Children for Lead Poisoning: Guidance for State and Local Public Health Officials.* Washington, DC; 1997. Available at: http://www.cdc.gov/nceh/lead/guide/guide97.htm. Accessed July 28, 2003

11. US Environmental Protection Agency. *Environmental Health Threats to Children.* Washington, DC: US Government Printing Office; 1996. Publication No. EPA 175 F-96001

12. Calabrese EJ, Stanek EJ, James RC, Roberts SM. Soil ingestion: a concern for acute toxicity in children. *Environ Health Perspect.* 1997;105:1354–1358

13. Nishioka MG, Lewis RG, Brinkman MC, Burkholder HM, Hines CE, Menkekick JR. Distribution of 2,4-D in air and on surfaces inside residences after lawn applications: comparing exposure estimates from various media for young children. *Environ Health Perspect.* 2001;109:1185–1191

14. Center for Health, Environment, and Justice. *Poisoned Schools: Invisible Threats, Visible Actions.* Falls Church, VA: Center for Health, Environment, and Justice; 2001

15. American Academy of Pediatrics, Committee on Environmental Health. Ultraviolet light: a hazard to children. *Pediatrics.* 1999;104:328-333

16. American Academy of Pediatrics, Committee on Environmental Health. Noise. In: Etzel RA, Balk SJ, eds. *Handbook of Pediatric Environmental Health.* Elk Grove Village, IL: American Academy of Pediatrics; 1999:171–179

17. US General Accounting Office. *School Facilities: Conditions of America's Schools.* Report to Congressional Requesters. Washington, DC: US General Accounting Office; 1995. Publication No. HEHS-95-61

18. American Academy of Pediatrics, Committee on Environmental Health. Waste sites. In: Etzel RA, Balk SJ. *Handbook of Pediatric Environmental Health.* Elk Grove Village, IL: American Academy of Pediatrics; 1999:319–328

Chapter 12
Program Evaluation

Pediatricians serving as district consultants or on district health advisory councils sometimes are asked to assist school staff in evaluating programs, policies, and services. This chapter provides a brief review of some of the major elements of program evaluation.

What Is Program Evaluation?

Program evaluation is the systematic collection, analysis, and reporting of information that can help decision makers improve or refine a program. Program evaluation does not need to be expensive or complicated, but its results need to be useful and answer important questions, such as the following:

- Is the program or service being implemented as planned?
- How well is the program meeting the needs of the people it is intended to serve?
- Are the staff sufficiently prepared to implement the program effectively?
- What is going well? What needs to be improved?
- Are scarce resources being used efficiently and effectively?

Why Do Program Evaluation?

Evaluating the school health program is important, because it focuses attention on the health needs of children and youth, provides accountability, and can demonstrate the link between health and improved learning outcomes. As health care professionals, pediatricians have a vested interested in making sure that school health programs are providing the best information and services possible. In addition, the district often looks to the pediatrician for leadership, and the physician should encourage the district to undertake evaluation.

Types of Program Evaluation

- *Process evaluation* answers questions about how the program is implemented and how the outcomes are achieved: What activities were conducted? How many people participated? What materials or services did they receive?
- *Impact evaluation* answers questions about the short-term effects or benefits of a program: Did students' knowledge, attitudes, or skills change after the new curriculum was implemented? Were there fewer days of school missed since the new hand-washing policy went into effect?
- *Outcome evaluation* examines changes in health-related behaviors, illness or injury (morbidity), death (mortality), or organizational culture (systems change): Have there been fewer playground injuries since the volunteer playground aide program began? In general, outcome evaluation is done only after a program has been fully implemented for several years.

Sample Evaluation Questions
- Health instruction: Are teachers knowledgeable and skilled in effective teaching strategies? Are sufficient and appropriate materials and resources on hand? Is health instruction implemented as planned, and if so, what is the effect on health knowledge, attitudes, and behaviors?
- Health services: Are school-based health services (clinical and behavioral health services) provided according to district guidelines and ethical standards of care? What is their effect on morbidity incidence and prevalence? Are appropriate linkages made between health assessments and health services?

- Program coordination: Do the various segments of the district's health program work together efficiently to provide timely and appropriate services? Can health data be linked to effect on academic indicators, such as absenteeism or number of disciplinary incidents?
- Policy: Do district policies and procedures enable students to take full advantage of existing health services or programs?

Steps in Program Evaluation
Step 1: Engage Stakeholders
Useful evaluations take time and resources to conduct. It is essential that these efforts yield useful information to stakeholders, the people who care about what will be learned and who are in a position to use the information to make changes. In general, there are 2 groups of stakeholders: those involved in implementing the program (funders, provider partners, staff) and those served or affected by the program (clients, family members, other school staff). From these 2 groups, a smaller subset is identified: the primary users of the evaluation—the decision makers. These individuals are the ones who will determine how the evaluation findings will be used. Their opinions and perspectives focus the questions that are to be answered. From the primary stakeholders group, it often is helpful to organize a small representative group that can work closely with the evaluators. This group should include both supporters and critics of the program. Care should be taken to identify the major concerns and issues of each stakeholder group.

Step 2: Describe the Program

It is essential to gather information from key informants that can accurately describe the program under consideration. How a program is described is critical. Elements about which the evaluators must be clear include the following:

- Program goals and objectives;
- Essential components intended to achieve objectives;
- Resources and capacity to change;
- The program's stage of development or implementation; and
- The environment in which the program functions.

Different stakeholders might have different ideas about what a program is supposed to achieve and how it is supposed to accomplish its objectives. For example, in a program whose goal is to reduce adolescent pregnancy, some might believe this means increasing access to contraceptives, and others might believe that emphasizing abstinence is the way to achieve the objectives. It is difficult to conduct a useful evaluation if there is disagreement about what the program should be doing.

Step 3: Develop Data Collection Plans and Instruments

This step identifies the necessary sources of information and the methods that will be used to collect the data. Indicators should be selected that will enable answering a few focused questions. Indicators should measure areas in which changes are expected. For example, service delivery might be measured by satisfaction level or increases in the number of individuals served; improvements in knowledge, skills, or behavior might be measured by pre- and post-test scores; health status might be measured by injury rates or days absent from school.

Sources of evidence include previously collected survey data, written questionnaires, interviews, observations, document analysis, logs, journals, charts, diaries, and expert opinion. Information should be obtained from multiple sources. Sufficient data are needed to detect program effects and inspire confidence in the findings.

The evaluation should be simple. Program evaluations are better when they are clear and focused; examining a single element well is better than trying to understand too much at one time. Sometimes separating elements of a program to determine which one has more impact or is more cost-effective will serve the program more than trying to lump everything together and examine the overall effect.

Once the indicators that will provide the necessary information have been determined, a plan should be developed for collecting the information systematically. Methods should be acceptable within a given community's cultural norms and should protect confidentiality. The timeframe for collection of data should be specified.

It saves time to use valid and reliable instruments that might already be available, but it is sometimes necessary to create data collection instruments or questionnaires. An evaluation consultant often can help identify appropriate instruments.

Step 4: Obtain the Data

This step involves assembling the raw materials that can answer the evaluation questions. The information obtained must be credible, and it must come from multiple sources and be in multiple forms. It might be helpful to obtain information from a nearby school district for comparison purposes.

Step 5: Analyze the Findings

Analysis of the data does not necessarily require sophisticated statistical knowledge, but it often is helpful to consult with university faculty with evaluation expertise. There are many easy-to-use computer programs that can be used to make simple calculations such as Excel (Microsoft, Redmond, Wash), Access (Microsoft, Redmond, Wash), Quattro Pro (Corel, Dallas Texas), and others.

Conclusions should be based on the evidence obtained and the opinions of various stakeholders. Frequently, analysis begins with the stated objectives and the performance benchmarks; however, other important stakeholder values, such as social equity and collaboration, might be considered.

Evaluators often are asked to make judgments about the worth or merit of a particular program or program aspect. To strengthen any judgments made, it often is useful to compare the findings observed with similar program findings in similar places, or it might be necessary to review the scientific literature. Identifying a norm group that is acceptable to the stakeholders is important, for many communities believe they are unique. Often the norm group is the same community but at a previous point in time. Whether the stakeholders agree with the judgments will determine whether the evaluation findings are used. For this reason, stakeholders should be involved in the interpretative process so that the practical significance of improving the program is defined.

Step 6: Make Needed Changes

Before undertaking an evaluation, it is good practice to get a commitment from key decision makers that the findings will be considered when making program-related decisions. The evaluation report must be written in clear language, in a timely manner, and with impartiality. Including a brief executive summary is helpful; making a brief oral presentation to stakeholder groups also is useful. It also is essential that the evaluators guard against misuse of the evaluation. Program evaluations are not intended to find fault or lay blame. Instead, they should be focused on solving problems and improving programs. Failure to guard against misuse can result in negative feelings that can hinder all subsequent evaluation efforts.

By using the evaluation findings, program staff should be able to make changes to improve the program. If evidence suggests that the program has met its goals and objectives, it might mean new goals and objectives should be formulated. Alternatively, findings might indicate that some services are being implemented as planned but that others need fine tuning. Other evidence might suggest that to improve performance, staff development or additional resources are required. The evaluation findings serve as a basis for beginning the planning cycle anew.

Current Evaluation Practices
Health Education

The most common method of assessing educational activities is through pre- and post-test information. As schools align their instructional materials with national and state standards, many are using standardized assessment tools as well. In addition, evaluators will want to determine whether the curriculum is being implemented as planned, whether students are attending, and whether the teacher is covering lessons in the amount and sequence recommended for effectiveness.

Student Health Practices

Several national surveys have been developed to assess youth behavior, such as the Centers for Disease Control and Prevention's Youth Risk Behavior Survey, Safe and Drug-Free Schools surveys, PRIDE surveys (http://www.pridesurveys.com), or others.

Health Services

Several computerized data collection programs are designed to track student office visits.[1,2] The computer programs include forms that can capture information about student sex, age, grade, insurance status, risk factors, chief complaint, diagnosis, referrals, laboratory tests done and their results, and counseling or anticipatory guidance. If such software is not available, chart audits can be used. There is an abundance of information available in the school health record or clinic medical record, but it is useful only if there is a way of selecting the charts to be reviewed. In general, this is accomplished through queries of the patient-care or billing databases. Many factors, such as risk status (eg, smoking status, sexual activity), are not routinely entered into the computer database. Sometimes a surrogate diagnosis can be identified that will work. For other studies, it is necessary to either code files on data entry or keep a manual log of the charts that will be reviewed in the future. Health center databases can be linked with school databases to examine, for example, absenteeism of students who use the school-based health center. Emergency department data can be obtained to study the effect on community resources of having a school-based health center. To assess the quality of care provided, chart audits can be conducted to compare diagnosis and treatment against standards of care. There are an ever-growing number of established instruments for collecting information and evaluating quality of care. Simple assessment of hours and days the clinic is open and numbers of students registered can help to examine access and utilization. Surveys of students and parents can assess knowledge about the health center, and surveys of patients can assess satisfaction with services provided.

School Policy and Resource Evaluation
Examining school policies related to violence, suspension, expulsion, access to contraceptives, dispensing of medications, and other health-related issues can reveal whether students are able to take advantage of resources, whether there are specific barriers that need to be addressed, or whether the way policies are enforced will make it difficult to demonstrate change. For example, if the objective is to reduce the number of adolescent pregnancies, students will need a comprehensive program that includes sex education, access to contraceptives, access to pregnancy testing and detection and treatment of sexually transmitted diseases, and a school culture that acknowledges that adolescents have sexual desires and encourages students to discuss these issues with trusted adults in their lives. Policies that limit access to contraceptives, sex education, and treatment for sexually transmitted diseases make attaining this objective unrealistic.

Emerging Issues
Accountability
School health programs, like the district's academic programs, use precious resources and must demonstrate their worth.

Cost-effectiveness
In school health services, as in all health services, there is enormous pressure to measure and improve cost-effectiveness in the provision of services. In a time of dwindling resources, providers are increasingly forced to choose between a service that is needed by more students and can be provided more efficiently and a service that may be limited to a smaller group of students or may be costly. Cost-effectiveness evaluation has 2 basic components: the numbers of students affected (coverage) and the cost of the service that will provide the best cost-student ratio. Included in this calculation will be "effectiveness," the definition of which often is difficult.

Definitions of Success
What exactly does the district expect to achieve by providing school health services, programs, or improved policies? Does it expect to see changes in access, utilization, health outcomes, prevention, educational outcomes, or community health resources?

Recommendations for Pediatricians
Make sure key stakeholders are engaged and invested. The more stakeholders understand the value of program evaluation, the more helpful they can be. Data quality can be vastly improved by stakeholder buy-in.

Ask helpful questions. The program evaluation should be relevant and important to the stakeholders. Ask them what they want to know; do not assume you know what is important. There are a multitude of ways to choose the questions that the evaluation will attempt to answer. The decision is best made in a democratic process within the district health council.

Focus on best practices. Program evaluation has evolved rapidly since the early 1970s. Unless you have special training in this area, it is best to link the school district with university resources or specialists in the community.

Be an advocate for program evaluation. Pediatricians have significant authority in district health councils. Good programming requires ongoing evaluation. Pediatricians can advocate for, and educate other members of the school community about, the program evaluation process and the reasons for the program.

References
1. Kaplan DW. Clinical Fusion [computer program]. Denver, CO: National Center for School-Based Health Information Systems; 2001
2. Helitzer D. SBHC-Pro, V4 [database]. Albuquerque, NM: Office of Evaluation, University of New Mexico; 2001

Appendix A
School Health Program Models

Most school health programs are based on models that have evolved over the past 100 years. The models discussed below represent original and new models used in the United States and internationally. This list does not include all school health models but does represent the major ones.

A) Three-Component Model: This model has been around since the early 1900s and serves as the basis for most of the expanded newer models.

1) Health education
2) Health services in schools
3) Healthy environment at school

B) Eight-Component Model: This expanded model emerged in the mid-1980s and is the major model in existence in the United States today. It was developed by Allensworth and Kolbe (Allensworth DD, Kolbe LJ. The comprehensive school health program: exploring an expanded concept. *J Sch Health.* 1987;57:409-411) and has been adopted by the Centers for Disease Control and Prevention as the preferred model for school health (see http://www.cdc.gov/nccdphp/dash/about/school_health.htm).

1) Health education: comprehensive, developmentally appropriate, sequential, preschool to 12th grade
2) Physical education: planned, developmentally appropriate physical education emphasizing lifetime physical health
3) Health services: health services range from prevention and screening to full-service school-based health centers
4) Nutrition services: nutrition education and healthy meals and snacks at school

5) Health promotion for staff: programs that encourage healthy staff and build support of staff for healthy students

6) Counseling, psychological, and social services: preventative and direct services for mental health and social needs of students

7) Healthy school environment: physical safety and psychosocial health

8) Parent and community involvement: wide range of programs to engage parents and community in student health

C) Nader Model: Nader proposed an expanded model in 1990 that included the 8-component model. This model added the important interactions of school, family, friends, media, and community. More information about the Nader model can be found at http://www.healthinschools.org/sh/pn2.asp.

D) Health Promoting Schools Model: This model has been adopted by the World Health Organization and has been extensively used in Europe and Australia. Although it includes all of the components of the 8-component model, it has a simpler framework developed around:

1) Curriculum

2) School organization, ethos, and environment

3) Partnerships and services

A full description of this model can be found at http://www.who.dk/eprise/main/WHO/Progs/ENHPS/Home.

E) School-Based Health Centers: Since the mid-1970s, school-based health centers (SBHCs) have evolved as a comprehensive model in the delivery of health services in schools. Currently, there are more than 1300 SBHCs in the United States. Please visit the National Assembly for School-based Health Care's Web site at http://www.nasbhc.org for more information about SBHCs.

Appendix B
School Health Online Resources

Academy for Educational Development
www.aed.org/health/health_projects7.html

Action for Healthy Kids, Inc
www.actionforhealthykids.org

Advocates for Youth
www.advocatesforyouth.org

American Academy of Child and Adolescent Psychiatry
www.aacap.org

American Academy of Family Physicians
www.aafp.org

American Academy of Pediatrics
www.aap.org
www.schoolhealth.org

American Alliance for Health, Physical Education, Recreation, and Dance
www.aahperd.org

American Association for Health Education
www.aahperd.org/aahe

American Association of School Administrators
www.aasa.org

American Bar Association, Center on Children and the Law
www.abanet.org/child

American Board of Pediatrics
www.abp.org

American Cancer Society
www.cancer.org

American Dental Association
www.ada.org

American Dietetic Association
www.eatright.org

American Heart Association
www.americanheart.org

American Lung Association
www.lungusa.org

American Medical Association
www.ama-assn.org

American Nurses Association
www.nursingworld.org

American Occupational Therapy Association
www.aota.org

American Psychiatric Association
www.psych.org

American Psychological Association
www.apa.org

American Public Health Association
www.apha.org

American Public Human Services Association
www.aphsa.org

American Red Cross
www.redcross.org

American School Counselor Association
www.schoolcounselor.org

American School Food Service Association
www.asfsa.org

American School Health Association
www.ashaweb.org

America's Promise – The Alliance for Youth
www.americaspromise.org

Association of Maternal and Child Health Programs
www.amchp1.org

Association of State and Territorial Health Officials
www.astho.org

Asthma and Allergy Foundation of America
www.aafa.org

Boys and Girls Clubs of America
www.bgca.org

Centers for School Mental Health Assistance
http://csmha.umaryland.edu/csmha2001/main.php3

The Center for Health and Health Care in Schools
www.healthinschools.org/home.asp

Centers for School, Family, and Community Partnerships
www.csos.jhu.edu/p2000/center.htm

Centers for Disease Control and Prevention, Division of Adolescent and School Health
www.cdc.gov/nccdphp/dash/index.htm

Child Abuse Prevention Services
www.kidsafe-caps.org

Children's Environmental Health Coalition
www.checnet.org

Children's Environmental Health Network
www.cehn.org

Children's Safety Network
www.childrenssafetynetwork.org

Comprehensive Health Education Foundation
www.chef.org

Council of Chief State School Officers
www.ccsso.org

Council of the Great City Schools
www.cgcs.org

Council for Exceptional Children
www.cec.sped.org

Education Development Center
http://main.edc.org/theme/schools.asp

Emergency Medical Services for Children
www.acep.org/policy/msemsc4.htm

Emergency Nurses Association
www.ena.org

ETR Associates
www.etr-associates.org

Family Support America
www.frca.org

Federal Emergency Management Agency
www.fema.gov

Healthy Mothers, Healthy Babies Coalition
www.hmhb.org

Institute for Family-Centered Care
www.familycenteredcare.org

Institute of Medicine
www.iom.edu

Maternal and Child Health Bureau
www.mchb.hrsa.gov/

National Assembly on School-Based Health Care
www.nasbhc.org

National Association for the Education of Young Children
www.naeyc.org

National Association for Sport and Physical Education
www.aahperd.org/naspe/template.csf

National Association of Community Health Centers
www.nachc.com

National Association of Elementary School Principals
www.naesp.org

National Association of Partners in Education
www.napehq.org

National Association of Pediatric Nurse Practitioners
www.napnap.org

National Association of School Nurses
www.nasn.org

National Association of School Psychologists
www.nasponline.org

National Association of Secondary School Principals
www.nassp.org

National Association of Social Workers
www.naswdc.org

National Association of State Alcohol/Drug Abuse Directors
www.nasadad.org

National Association of State Boards of Education
www.nasbe.org

National Association of State School Nurse Consultants
http://lserver.aea14.k12.ia.us/swp/tadkins/nassnc/nassnc.html

National Center for Health Education
www.nche.org

National Center for Injury Prevention and Control
www.cdc.gov/ncipc/ncipchm.htm

National Coalition for Parent Involvement in Education
www.ncpie.org

National Committee to Prevent Child Abuse
www.childabuse.org

National Conference of State Legislatures
www.ncsl.org

National Education Association
www.nea.org

National Environmental Health Association
www.neha.org

National Family Partnership
www.nfp.org

National Federation of State High School Associations
www.nfhs.org

National Head Start Association
www.nhsa.org

National Highway Traffic Safety Administration
www.nhtsa.dot.gov

National Institute of Mental Health
www.nimh.nih.gov

National Medical Association
www.nmanet.org

National Mental Health Association
www.nmha.org

National Middle School Association
www.nmsa.org

National Network for Youth
www.nn4youth.org

National Program for Playground Safety
www.uni.edu/playground

National PTA
www.pta.org

National Rural Health Association
www.nrharural.org

National Safety Council
www.nsc.org

National School Boards Association
www.nsba.org

National School Safety Center
www.nssc1.org

National School Transportation Association
www.schooltrans.com

National Wellness Institute
www.nationalwellness.org

National Youth Sports Safety Foundation
www.nyssf.org

Office of Juvenile Justice and Delinquency Prevention
www.ojjdp.ncjrs.org

President's Council on Physical Fitness and Sports
www.fitness.gov

Public Education Network
www.publiceducation.org

The Robert Wood Johnson Foundation
www.rwjf.org/main.html

Safe and Drug Free Schools
www.ed.gov/about/offices/list/osdfs/index.html?src=mr

Safe Schools Coalition, Inc
www.ed.mtu.edu/safe

Save a Life Foundation
www.salf.org

Society for Adolescent Medicine
www.adolescenthealth.org

Society for Public Health Education
www.sophe.org

US Consumer Product Safety Commission
www.cpsc.gov/index.html

US Department of Agriculture
Food, Nutrition, and Consumer Services
www.fns.usda.gov/fncs

YMCA of the United Stated of America
www.ymca.net

YWCA of the United States of America
www.ywca.org

Attempts have been made to include valuable school health online resources at the national level. If your organization is not listed, we apologize for the omission. Please contact Su Li, MPA, by e-mail at sli@aap.org.

Index

A

Abrasions as sign of physical abuse, 92

Abstinence-based sex education, 79, 227

Abuse
    physical, 91–92
    reporting, 94–95
    sexual, 93–94

Accommodation, need for, in physical education program, 174–175

Accountability
    in program evaluation, 257
    in school-based health center, 140

Achievement, connection between nutrition and, 146

Activity programming, 2

Adaptive physical education programs, 174–175
    role of physician in, 175–176

Administration in school-based health center, 140

Administrators, promoting physical activity programs to, 168–170

Adolescents. *See also* Pregnant and parenting adolescents
    after-school programs for, 110
    driving by, 204–205
    treatment of mental health problems in, 120–121

Adrenocorticotropic hormone, 187

Advisory Committee on Immunization Practices of the Centers for Disease Control and Prevention, 33

Advocacy, 7

AED, *See* automated external defibrillator

Aerobic activity, 172

After-school youth development programs, 110

Age-appropriate playground equipment, 198

Air pollution, 240–241
    indoor, 235–236

Air quality, 235–237

Alcohol, 3, 237

Aliphatic hydrocarbons, 237

Allergies, 17, 23–24
    food, 23, 155–158
    latex, 64

Alliance of Genetic Support Groups, 60

Alternative therapies, 18–19

Amebiasis, 99

Amenorrhea, 182

American Academy of Child and Adolescent Psychiatry, 115

American Academy of Family Physicians, 33

American Academy of Pediatrics (AAP), 5, 33
    Committee on Children With Disabilities, 58–59
    policy statement on medication administration, 16
    Section on School Health, 5

American Lung Association's Open Airways program, 27

American Nurses Association, 244

American School Health Association, 5–6